**family handyman**

# BEST
# TIPS
# & PROJECTS

# family handyman

# BEST TIPS & PROJECTS

by The Editors of *Family Handyman* magazine

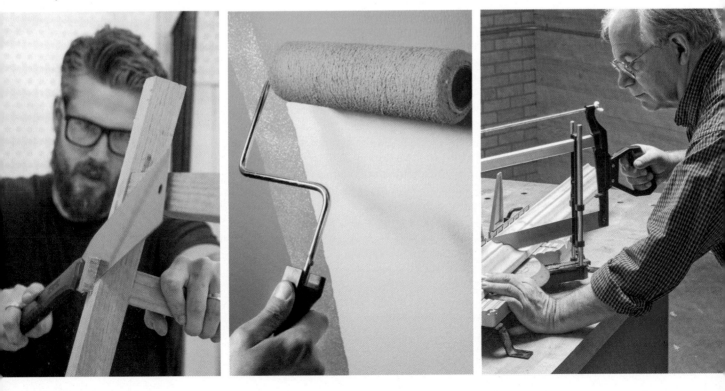

A *FAMILY HANDYMAN* BOOK

Copyright © 2022 Home Services Publications, a subsidiary of Trusted Media Brands, Inc.
2915 Commers Drive, Suite 700
Eagan, MN 55121

ISBN 978-1-62145-797-8 (dated), 978-1-62145-798-5 (undated)

Component number 118300108H (dated), 118300110H (undated)

We are committed to both the quality of our products and the service we provide to our customers. We value your comments, so please feel free to contact us at TMBBookTeam@TrustedMediaBrands.com.

For more *Family Handyman* products and information, visit our website: *www.familyhandyman.com*

Printed in U.S.A.
10 9 8 7 6 5 4 3 2 1

Text, photography and illustrations for *Family Handyman Best Tips & Projects 2022* are based on articles previously published in *Family Handyman* magazine (*familyhandyman.com*).

**WARNING**
All do-it-yourself activities involve a degree of risk. Skills, materials, tools, and site conditions vary widely. Although the editors have made every effort to ensure accuracy, the reader remains responsible for the selection and use of tools, materials and methods. Always obey local codes and laws, follow manufacturer's operating instructions, and observe safety precautions.

**Photo Credits**
p. 30–31, prints in frames: Aesthetic Apparatus; p. 37, framed artwork: Christina Keith Studios; p. 37, first two art prints: Aesthetic Apparatus; p. 37, second two art prints: original artwork by Adam Turman; p. 56, background: onurdongel/Getty Images; p. 68, patio: In-Lite Design Corporation; p. 69, walkway: cjmckendry/ Getty Images; p. 70, deck: Comstock/Getty Images; p. 72, patio: In-Lite Design Corporation; p. 73, robotic mower: Husqvarna UK; p. 74, alarm system: Konnected; p. 88, shower: deepblue4you/Getty Images; p. 91, shower, bottom: MosayMay/Getty Images; p. 92, faucet and faucet drawing: Pfister Faucets; p. 93, infographic, bottom: Kara Caldwell Courtesy Con-Air Industries - Filtration Group; p. 106–112, Curtis and project action photos: Josh Gicker; p. 108, High Valley: Corey Kelly; p. 113, top: Cody O'Loughlin; p. 113, bottom: Hugh Harriss; p. 151, Hikesterson/Getty Images; p. 163, label: Courtesy US EPA ENERGY STAR; p. 165, top: ozgurcoskun/Getty Images; p. 166, grill: Lauri Patterson/Getty Images; p. 167, vintage frame: Tolga Tezcan/Getty Images; p. 172, background: Aldra/Getty Images; p. 172, grills from left to right: Traeger, Kamado Joe, Masterbuilt; p. 173, top: Traeger; p. 175, top: Masterbuilt Manufacturing, LLC/ Kamado Joe®; p. 177, top: Masterbuilt Manufacturing, LLC/Kamado Joe®; p. 178, app: Masterbuilt Manufacturing, LLC/Kamado Joe®; p. 182, large deck: James Pintar/Getty Images; p. 187, bottom right: Tina Sargeant; p. 189, bottom: Westbury® Aluminum Railing by Diggers Specialties, Inc.; p. 191, bottom left: TimberTech; p. 194, deck, poolside, color, temperature: TimberTech; p. 196, illustration: Simpson Strong-Tie Co. Inc; p. 200, johnnygrieg/Getty Images; p. 202, gardening: Ariel Skelley/Getty Images; p. 203, illustration: Ken Clubb; p. 203, middle left: Ariel Skelley/Getty Images; p. 203, middle right: Bill Zuehlke; p. 204, top right: Bill Zuehlke; p. 204, bottom: Masterfile; p. 205, top right: Bill Zuehlke; p. 205, bottom right: Bill Zuehlke; p. 206, plants: Jill Ferry/Getty Images; p. 207, cjp/Getty Images; p. 233, vintage frames: Tolga Tezcan/Getty Images; p. 235, Kreg Jig: KREG; p. 241, Milwaukee photos: Courtesy of *Amazon.com*; p. 254, background: muratkoc/Getty Images; p. 260, background: andresr/Getty Images; p. 265, background: mesamong/Getty Images; all cartoon illustrations throughout book: Steve Björkman

# SAFETY FIRST—ALWAYS!

Tackling home improvement projects and repairs can be endlessly rewarding. But as most of us know, with the rewards come risks. DIYers use chain saws, climb ladders and tear into walls that can contain big and hazardous surprises.

The good news is that armed with the right knowledge, tools and procedures, homeowners can minimize risk. As you go about your projects and repairs, stay alert for these hazards:

## Aluminum wiring

Aluminum wiring, installed in about 7 million homes between 1965 and 1973, requires special techniques and materials to make safe connections. This wiring is dull gray, not the dull orange characteristic of copper. Hire a licensed electrician certified to work with it. For more information, go to *cpsc.gov* and search for "aluminum wiring."

## Spontaneous combustion

Rags saturated with oil finishes like Danish oil and linseed oil, and oil-based paints and stains can spontaneously combust if left bunched up. Always dry them outdoors, spread out loosely. When the oil has thoroughly dried, you can safely throw them in the trash.

## Vision and hearing protection

Safety glasses or goggles should be worn whenever you're working on DIY projects that involve chemicals, dust and anything that could shatter or chip off and hit your eye. Sounds louder than 80 decibels (dB) are considered potentially dangerous. Sound levels from a lawn mower can be 90 dB, and shop tools and chain saws can be 90 to 100 dB.

## Lead paint

If your home was built before 1979, it may contain lead paint, which is a serious health hazard, especially for children six and under. Take precautions when you scrape or remove it. Contact your public health department for detailed safety information or call (800) 424-LEAD (5323) to receive an information pamphlet. Or visit *epa.gov/lead*.

## Buried utilities

A few days before you dig in your yard, have your underground water, gas and electrical lines marked. Just call 811 or go to *call811.com*.

## Smoke and carbon monoxide (CO) alarms

The risk of dying in reported home structure fires is cut in half in homes with working smoke alarms. Test your smoke alarms every month, replace batteries as necessary and replace units that are more than 10 years old. As you make your home more energy-efficient and airtight, existing ducts and chimneys can't always successfully vent combustion gases, including potentially deadly carbon monoxide (CO). Install a UL-listed CO detector, and test your CO and smoke alarms at the same time.

## Five-gallon buckets and window covering cords

Anywhere from 10 to 40 children a year drown in 5-gallon buckets, according to the U.S. Consumer Products Safety Commission. Always store them upside down and store ones containing liquid with the covers securely snapped.

According to Parents for Window Blind Safety, hundreds of children in the United States are injured every year after becoming entangled in looped window treatment cords. For more information, visit *pfwbs.org* or *cpsc.gov*.

## Working up high

If you have to get up on your roof to do a repair or installation, always install roof brackets and wear a roof harness.

## Asbestos

Texture sprayed on ceilings before 1978, adhesives and tiles for vinyl and asphalt floors before 1980, and vermiculite insulation (with gray granules) all may contain asbestos. Other building materials, made between 1940 and 1980, could also contain asbestos. If you suspect that materials you're removing or working around contain asbestos, contact your health department or visit *epa.gov/asbestos* for information.

# Contents

## 1. INTERIOR PROJECTS, REPAIRS & REMODELING

## 2. ELECTRICAL & HIGH TECH

## 3. PLUMBING, HVAC & APPLIANCES

## 4. WOODWORKING & WORKSHOP PROJECTS & TIPS

# 5. EXTERIOR REPAIRS & IMPROVEMENTS

# 6. OUTDOOR STRUCTURES, LANDSCAPING & GARDENING

# 7. USING DIY TOOLS & MATERIALS

# 1 Interior Projects, Repairs & Remodeling

## WHAT IT TAKES

**TIME**
*A few days*

**COST**
*$600-$1,200*

**SKILL LEVEL**
*Intermediate*

**TOOLS**
*Brick set chisel, 3-lb. maul, 5-gallon buckets, chalk line, drill, 3/4-in. round-notch trowel, margin trowel, rail tile saw (rental), angle grinder, oscillating multitool*

# FIREPLACE FACE-LIFT

## From dull and dated to modern masterpiece in one weekend

BY MIKE BERNER

A fireplace is THE focal point of the room it's in. The typical update is to paint it, and though that's an easy improvement, I wanted something bolder and more modern—something that would transform the look and feel of the room. I decided to cover the old brick with oversize tiles. I also removed the hearth for a more streamlined look. I'd never done a project quite like this, but it all came together without major snags. And the results are even better than I'd imagined.

BEFORE

**family handyman *flashback***

. . . Several ways *to revamp*

*your old fireplace . . .*

*easy-to-handle materials*

*to help you make the fireplace*

*the decorative*

**70 YEARS OF FIREPLACE PROJECTS**

**1951** *Family Handyman's* very first cover story was "How to Repair a Brick Fireplace," and we've been serving up fireplace projects ever since. In fact, we showed how to cover brick with tile way back in 1953. Since then, better tools and materials have made it much easier for DIYers to tackle a project like this. Tile manufacturing has improved too, with more choices available, like the large tiles we used for our modern fireplace makeover.

**MEET THE BUILDER**
Mike Berner, an associate editor, is an accomplished woodworker, carpenter and teacher.

**Painter's tape on finished surfaces**

**Duct tape**

**Hardboard**

**Rosin paper**

**Brick set chisel**

**Mini maul**

**Corbel**

## 1 PROTECT THE FLOOR

This project calls for the ultimate floor protection: Start with a layer of rosin paper taped at the seams and edges. Then cut sheets of hardboard to fit around the fireplace and join them with duct tape. The rosin paper keeps granules that might get under the hardboard from scratching the wood floor, and the hardboard protects against dents.

## 2 CHIP OUT THE CORBELS

After removing the mantel (ours wasn't even fastened), chip out the corbels with a maul and a brick set chisel. These bricks were embedded, but I lightly chipped all the way around them and eventually they sheared right off.

### Materials List

| ITEM |
|------|
| Rosin paper |
| Hardboard |
| Painter's tape |
| Duct tape |
| 2x4 x 8' lumber |
| 1/2" cement board |
| Cement board screws |
| Modified thin-set |
| Porcelain tile |
| Metal edging |

# *A few things I learned*

### ■ LARGE TILE CARRIES AN EXTRA COST

I chose Sofia Charcoal porcelain tile for its texture and consistent color, which made the seams almost disappear. I needed to cover about 60 sq. ft., but with large tile there's a lot of waste. I had to buy 90 sq. ft. at $9.20 per sq. ft., or just over $60 a tile.

### ■ TILE COSTS VARY A LOT

The total materials bill for my project was about $1,200. Tile was by far the biggest cost ($900), but you can find good-looking tile for less than half that price.

### ■ RENT A TILE SAW

For the 31 x 31-in. tiles I chose, I had to rent a large-capacity saw ($75 per day).

### ■ DIVE INTO SOMETHING NEW

In removing the hearth, I wasn't exactly sure what I was getting into. I'm usually not a fan of exploratory demolition, but one of the best ways to learn how to build something is to first take it apart.

### ■ CHOOSE REINFORCED THIN-SET

I used a modified thin-set ($60 per bag) reinforced with fiber. It allowed the tile to stay put on the wall without sagging and provided an extended working time, so I didn't have to rush.

### ■ WIDE-NOTCH TROWEL

Larger tile tends to be slightly cupped. To make sure the tile adhered well, I had to fill it with thin-set to compensate. I used a 3/4-in. round-notch trowel to be sure there was enough thin-set to adhere the tile.

### ■ MIND THE EDGES

I opted to install the tiles tight together instead of leaving gaps for grout. To get these tiles to match up perfectly, I placed the factory edges of the tiles together and kept the cut edges on the outside.

### ■ BEWARE OF PAINTED BRICK

If you tile over a painted fireplace, you'll be rolling the dice. If the paint peels, so will the tile. The safe approach is to remove most of the paint before tiling.

Protect the
fireplace

Solid
brick
here

Packed sand and
broken bricks

Big prying
tools come
in handy

**3**

# 3 BUST UP
# THE HEARTH

With a brick set chisel and a maul,
start chipping away at the corner of
the hearth. After peeling away the
first layer, I thought that the hearth
was solid brick. But as I kept chipping, I found packed sand, broken
bricks and even an old soda can
holding the rest of the bricks up.

# 4 CHANGE
# OF PLANS!

Most DIY projects include some
surprises and require on-the-spot
problem solving. In this case, I
had intended to leave the brick
ledge underneath the firebox, but
as I finished cleaning up the area,
I noticed nothing was holding
these bricks up. I decided to knock
them down and rebuild the ledge.

# 5 FILL THE EMPTY
# HEARTH SPACE

To fill the void left by removing the
hearth, I built up the ledge in front
of the fireplace. I set the 2x4 ledge
1/2 in. inside the opening, screwed
it to the floor and anchored it into
the brick at the sides. Then I covered this space with 1/2-in. cement
backer board.

Build a
ledge

Set back
1/2"

Cement
board
screws

Cement
backer board

Cool the blade with water

Slow down at the end

Cut close to the notch, but don't go past

**6**

Metal edging

Thin-set

Factory edge

"Back butter" the tile with thin-set

**7**

Spacers

**8**

Tile sides first

Tile sides first

Factory edge

Factory edges

**9**

## 6 CUT THE TILE

There are a few things to know about using a tile saw: Keep the blade cool with water and cut slow, especially through the last inch of tile. For notches, start with the tile saw and use an angle grinder or tile nippers to finish the cut.

## 7 TILE THE FLOOR FIRST

Cut metal tile edging to fit around the perimeter of the floor tile. Apply thin-set to the floor with a 3/4-in. round-notch trowel and press the metal edging into the thin-set. Starting with a full-width tile, spread a layer of thin-set on the back of it (called "back buttering"). Make sure the tile is centered and set it onto the floor. After the center tile is in place, cut and set the end tiles.

## 8 CUT THE TRIM

Instead of cutting the tile to fit the profile of the trim, cut the trim back and slip the tile against the wall. It's much easier. To cut the trim, use a piece of tile and a piece of hardboard as spacers and a guide for your multitool.

## 9 THEN START ON THE SIDES

Tile sides first so those tile edges will be covered by the tiles on the face of the fireplace. Throughout this project, plan your cuts so that factory edges will meet other tiles and cut edges won't. For the sides, that means the factory edges will be the top and bottom and the cut edges will go against the wall and flush to the face of the brick.

Smooth out thin-set

Margin trowel

Metal edging

**10**

Perfectly plumb

2x2 supports

Perfectly level **11**

Align factory edges

Mark the edges

Place on the tile

**12**

Cut edges on the outside

Factory corners

**13**

## 10 EMBED THE EDGING

Install edging over the sides of the fireplace and surrounding the firebox. Cover the edge of the tiles with metal edging. Spread thin-set near the corner and press the edging into the thin-set. Use a margin trowel to embed the edging and smooth the thin-set.

## 11 BEGIN IN THE MIDDLE

I started with the middle tiles to make sure they were perfectly centered, level and plumb. After setting the lower tiles, I placed 2x2s within the fireplace box to prevent the next rows of tile from sliding downward. I finished tiling to the top and kept the supports in while the thin-set cured.

## 12 MAKE PRECISE MARKS

Cutting the tile around the fire-place is tricky. If the tiles don't line up, you'll notice, so precise cuts are important. Cut a tile to the proper width and dry-fit it into place. Mark precisely where it will meet the edges of the adjacent tiles and cut the notch away.

## 13 PLACE THE REST OF THE TILES

Once the sides and center column of tiles are attached, the last few pieces will go in pretty quickly. Wipe away any thin-set residue with a sponge and a 50/50 mix of vinegar and water. You'll be able to remove the supports and use the fireplace after 48 hours.

# UNDER-STAIR PULLOUTS

## Organized, easy-access storage—and lots of it!

BY BILL BERGMANN

**N**eed extra storage space? You might already have it right under your feet! Builders rarely utilize the space under a staircase—it's much easier to just wall it in than to make custom pullouts. But you can reclaim that wasted space in a couple of weekends.

I built three pullouts to store everything from shoes to coats and backpacks. You can customize this design to get just the type of storage space you need.

### WHAT IT TAKES

| TIME | COST | SKILL LEVEL |
|------|------|-------------|
| 4 days | $800 | Intermediate |

**TOOLS**

Table saw, miter saw, 18-gauge finish nailer, drill driver, circular saw, random orbit sander, framing square, combination square, caulk gun, 2-ft. level, putty knife

### A GREAT IDEA MADE BETTER

**1955** My design is very similar to one we featured 66 years ago. The building process was much the same, but I upgraded the plywood, used modern ball-bearing slides and chose concealed push latches for a clean look.

Hidden behind the paneled wall is a lot of accessible, organized storage space.

**MEET THE BUILDER**
Bill Bergmann is an associate editor at *Family Handyman*.

# Figure A
## Pullouts

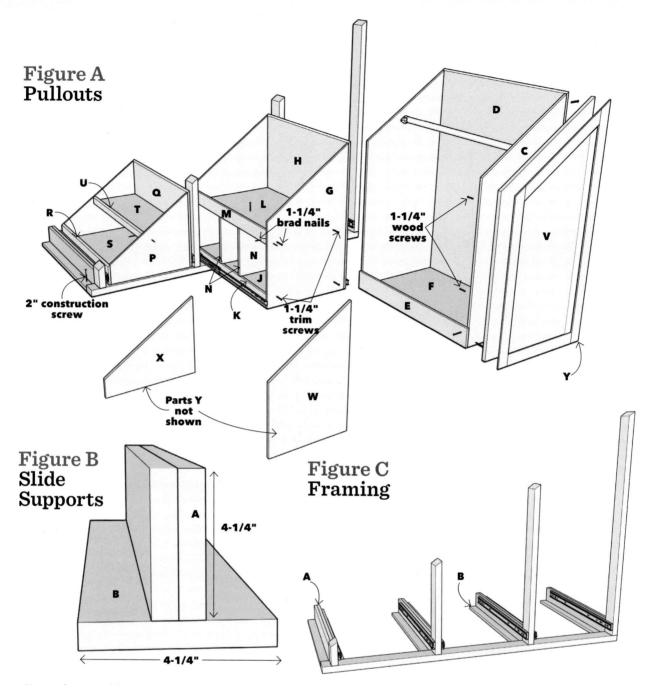

**2" construction screw**

**1-1/4" brad nails**

**1-1/4" wood screws**

**1-1/4" trim screws**

**Parts Y not shown**

# Figure B
## Slide Supports

4-1/4"

4-1/4"

# Figure C
## Framing

# Cutting List

| KEY | QTY. | PART | MATERIAL |
|-----|------|------|----------|
| A | 8 | Slide support verticals | 3/4" plywood |
| B | 4 | Slide support horizontals | 3/4" plywood |
| C | 2 | Large drawer front & back | 1/2" plywood |
| D | 1 | Large drawer tall side | 1/2" plywood |
| E | 1 | Large drawer short side | 1/2" plywood |
| F | 1 | Large drawer bottom | 3/4" plywood |
| G | 2 | Middle drawer front & back | 1/2" plywood |
| H | 1 | Middle drawer tall side | 1/2" plywood |
| J | 1 | Middle drawer bottom | 3/4" plywood |
| K | 1 | Middle drawer bottom lip | 3/4" solid poplar |
| L | 1 | Middle drawer shelf | 3/4" plywood |
| M | 1 | Middle drawer shelf lip | 3/4" solid poplar |
| N | 2 | Middle drawer verticals | 3/4" plywood |
| P | 2 | Small drawer front & back | 1/2" plywood |
| Q | 1 | Small drawer tall side | 1/2" plywood |
| R | 1 | Small drawer short side | 1/2" plywood |
| S | 1 | Small drawer bottom | 3/4" plywood |
| T | 1 | Small drawer shelf | 3/4" plywood |
| U | 1 | Small drawer shelf lip | 1/2" plywood |
| V | 1 | Large drawer front | 3/4" plywood |
| W | 1 | Middle drawer front | 3/4" plywood |
| X | 1 | Small drawer front | 3/4" plywood |
| Y | 12 | Drawer front framing | 1/4" solid poplar |

# Materials List

| ITEM | QTY. |
|------|------|
| 1/2" x 48" x 96" Baltic birch plywood | 2 |
| 3/4" x 48" x 96" veneer-core birch plywood | 1 |
| 1x6 x 8' poplar | 3 |
| 34" Extra Heavy Duty drawer slides (500 lb.) | 3 pr. |
| Primer | 1 qt. |
| Satin enamel paint | 1 qt. |
| Waterborne polyurethane | 2 qt. |
| Spackling compound or wood filler | |
| Fast-tack construction adhesive | |
| 18-gauge brad nails, 5/8", 1-1/4" and 2" | |
| 1-1/4" trim screws | |
| 1-1/4" wood screws | |
| 2" and 2-1/4" construction screws | |
| Shims | |

## 1 OPEN THE WALL

Pry off the baseboard, and then remove the drywall. I cut out a small section of drywall first, so I could see inside and verify that there were no wires or other obstructions in the cavity. If there is an existing outlet, you'll have to relocate it. I used a reciprocating saw to cut the drywall, taking care not to cut into the stair stringer.

## 2 REFRAME THE OPENING

Remove the studs, salvaging what you can for reframing. Attach a stud at each end of the opening, and divide the remaining space into three openings of equal width. Cut and attach the two inner studs, making sure they're plumb and accurately placed. To be sure that my pullout wouldn't hit the baseboard on the adjoining wall, I installed that tallest stud and trim 1-1/2 in. away from that corner.

## 3 BUILD THE DRAWER SLIDE SUPPORTS

Assemble the T-shaped drawer slide supports using glue and finish nails. Then add 1-1/4-in. wood screws for strength. The available depth under my stairs was 36 in., so I used 34-in. drawer slides. Subtracting 3-1/2 in. for the stud plate left 30-1/2 in. for the slide support length.

1-1/4" brad nail

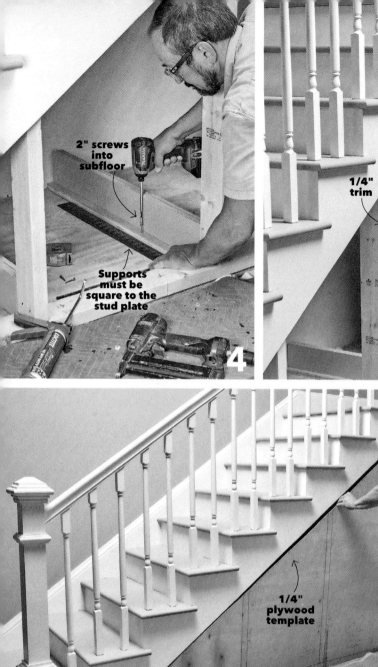

**2" screws into subfloor**

**Supports must be square to the stud plate**

**1/4" trim**

**1/2" furring strip**

**3/4" trim**

**1/4" plywood template**

**1-1/4" brad nails**

## 4 INSTALL SLIDE SUPPORTS

Attach the slide supports directly behind the studs using construction adhesive and 2-in. screws. Use a framing square to make sure the supports are square to the bottom plate so the drawer slides won't bind.

## 5 ADD FURRING STRIPS AND TRIM

I chose inset drawer faces, but I wanted the faces and trim flush with the skirt board. This meant adding 1/2-in. furring strips to the adjoining wall stud and floor stud plate before attaching the trim. The drawer faces cover the other three studs, so they didn't need furring strips—just 1/4-in.-thick trim. I primed and painted the trim pieces before applying them.

## 6 MAKE A TEMPLATE

Building for this angled opening was tricky. A full-size plywood template of the opening proved very helpful for calculating drawer and drawer front sizes.

## 7 ASSEMBLE DRAWER BOXES

To calculate the drawer width, measure the opening and then subtract the thickness of two drawer slides. Make the drawers as deep as the drawer slide length. Make each drawer box height 3/4 in. less than the height of the opening, for 3/8-in. clearance top and bottom. Glue and nail the boxes together, adding trim screws later for strength.

# 8 RESAW FRAME STOCK

Applying a hardwood frame to the face of 3/4-in. plywood is an easy way to simulate a frame-and-panel drawer front. Rip the frame stock to width, then resaw it into 1/4-in.-thick stock. Set your saw's fence to 1/4 in., then raise the blade to cut just over halfway through the board. Make the first pass, flip the board—keeping the same side against the fence—and finish the cut. Use a push stick as you get close to the blade. You can skip this step if you can find 1/4-in.-thick lumber at your local home center.

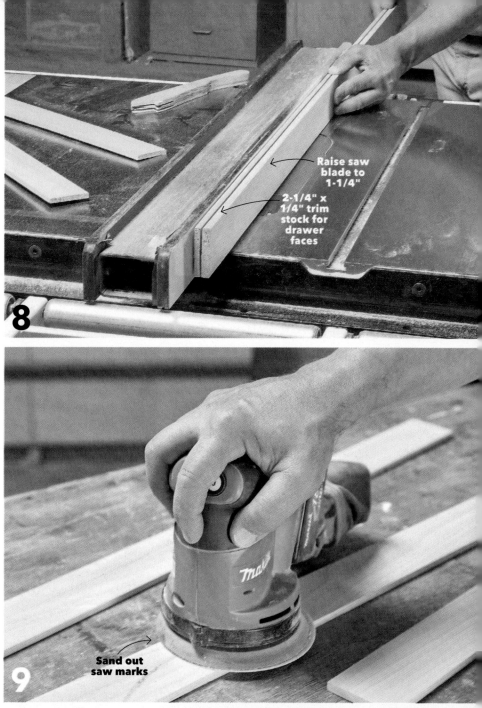

Raise saw blade to 1-1/4"

2-1/4" x 1/4" trim stock for drawer faces

8

# 9 SAND OUT ANY SAW MARKS

Sand out any saw marks with a random orbit sander. A new or newly sharpened saw blade all but eliminates marks. Tag the sanded surfaces for gluing so the factory sides face out on the drawer fronts.

Sand out saw marks

9

# 10 APPLY FRAMES

Cut the drawer fronts to size, and the frame parts to rough length. Mark, cut and attach the frame pieces, using glue and 5/8-in. brad nails. For accuracy, instead of taking measurements, hold each piece in place, and then mark and cut them to length. Run the two vertical sides, or "stiles," long to hide the end grain of the horizontal rails.

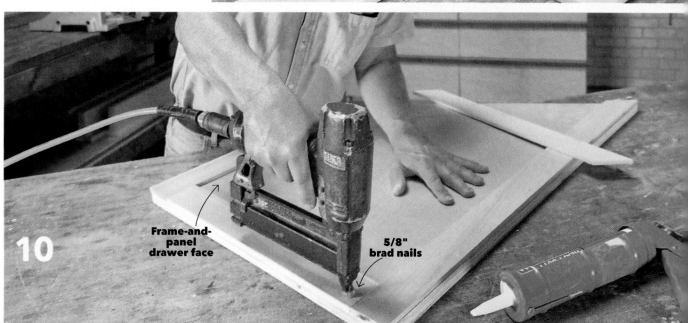

Frame-and-panel drawer face

5/8" brad nails

10

**Fill edges of drawer faces**

**11** **12**

**Sanding block**

**13**

**Scrap of 2-by lumber**

**14**

## 11 FILL THE EDGES

Fill any voids and gaps on the drawer front edges with putty or spackling compound. Fill the nail holes on the faces as well.

## 12 SAND THE DRAWER FRONTS

Once the filler has dried, sand the drawer fronts. I used 120-grit sandpaper on a block for the edges and a random orbit sander for the large surfaces. Soften any sharp edges.

## 13 PAINT THE DRAWER FRONTS

Prime the frames, and then apply two coats of paint. Because I used prefinished plywood for the drawer fronts, I didn't need to prime them. I just reduced the gloss with 120-grit sandpaper before painting. The backs of the drawer fronts need paint only around the perimeter, about 3 in. from the edge, as they're mostly covered by the drawer boxes.

## 14 INSTALL THE DRAWERS

Set the slides 3/16 in. back from the face of the finished furring strips and attach them to the supports, making sure they're level. These heavy-duty slides don't come apart, so the mounting procedure is a bit different. With the slides extended, set the back end of the drawer on a 3/8-in. shim in the opening. Then using a 2x4 and shims, level the drawer and attach the slides to it.

## 15 POSITION THE DRAWER FRONTS

Drive a couple of screws through each drawer from the inside, until the points poke through. Set each drawer front on two shims that create an equal gap, top and bottom, and lean the front into the opening. Adjust the gaps around the drawer front by sliding it right or left and raising or lowering it with shims. I usually eyeball the gap, but you can mark the gap on a shim and use it as a gauge for all the fronts. Once the gap is set, push the drawer front against the protruding screws, leaving two indents. Drill pilot holes at these points.

## 16 ATTACH THE DRAWER FRONTS

Drill and countersink holes where the marking screws were, and then attach the drawer fronts with 1-1/4-in. wood screws. Verify that the gap is still correct, then add more screws. I used eight on the large front, six on the middle one and four on the small one.

## 17 INSTALL THE PUSH LATCHES

Attach the push latch in its approximate location using the two oblong holes. Stick the latch plate magnetically to the end of the fully extended latch. Push the drawer front in until it contacts the plate. Hold the plate while pulling the drawer front and plate free of the latch. Mark the plate location and attach the plate. Test the latch, adjust it as needed and then install the final two screws.

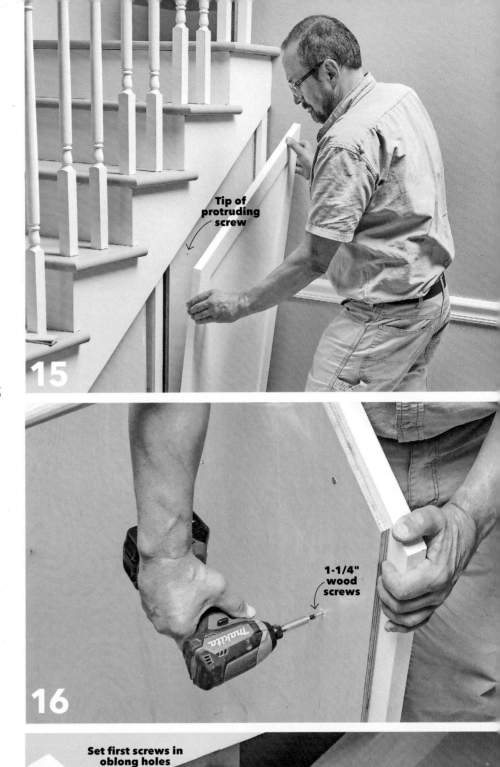

Tip of protruding screw

1-1/4" wood screws

Set first screws in oblong holes

Push latch

Latch plate

# DYNAMIC
# ACCENT WALL

**Turn a blank wall into a showpiece that will transform the entire room!**

BY BRAD HOLDEN

This might be the easiest way to totally change the look of a room. Once you've created your design, using this simple glue-and-stick application, you can finish it up in a weekend.

**family handyman** *flashback*

**1960** **THREE DIMENSIONS ON A WALL** In June 1960, we applied a three-dimensional design to a wall by cutting and painting Styrofoam. Inexpensive and easy to work with, it was a good choice then. But now we have medium-density fiberboard (MDF). It's inexpensive and easy to work with, plus it takes paint well and is much more durable than Styrofoam.

## WHAT IT TAKES

| TIME | COST | SKILL LEVEL |
|------|------|-------------|
| 2 days | $100 | Beginner |

**TOOLS**
*Table saw, miter box or miter saw, finish nailer, putty knife, laser level, Speed square*

## 1 SKETCH OUT YOUR DESIGN

Make a scale drawing of your wall and draw different designs until you're satisfied. The internet is a good source of inspiration. A CAD program like SketchUp makes this process easy and accurate, but pencil and paper is fine.

## 2 PAINT THE WALL

Choose your paint color and paint the entire wall. It's easier to paint it before the strips are attached, and the results look better, too.

## 3 RIP THE STRIPS

Using your design plan, estimate how many linear feet of strips you'll need, and rip them to 1-1/4 in. wide on the table saw. We used 1/2-in. MDF because when ripped into thin strips, it's thick enough to create a shadow yet flexible enough to follow minor wall irregularities.

## 4 SAND THE STRIPS

A sharp corner doesn't hold paint well, so sand the sharp corners on the faces of each strip with a sanding block. It doesn't take much—just enough to turn the sharp corner into a tiny bevel.

# 5 PAINT THE STRIPS

Spread out the strips on your work table and roll on a coat of primer. This is an important step with MDF; paint causes it to get really rough. Shellac-based primer is a good choice because it dries fast and sands very smooth. When the primer has dried, sand the strips with a 220-grit sanding sponge. Wipe off the dust and paint the strips. They'll probably require two coats.

# 6 LOCATE THE STUDS

Find the studs and mark them with tape. We relied mainly on adhesive to hold the strips in place, but it's helpful to know where the studs are. If a strip needs a little more convincing to stay put, you can shoot a brad nail into a stud.

# 7 LAY OUT THE FIRST STRIP

Set up a laser level to get the long lines accurate. We used a self-leveling cross-line model from Skil (about $60 at home centers). It doesn't shoot a 45-degree line, but if you use a large Speed square and the level's locking mechanism, you can set it at 45.

## LIVING ROOM-FRIENDLY MITER SAW

Running a miter saw in the house is a bad idea—it blows dust all over. But running to the shop for each cut doesn't make sense either. So, we made this simple "miter box" for a pull saw. First, make accurate 45- and 90-degree cuts on a 2x4 using a miter saw. Then, glue and nail these pieces to a scrap of plywood, using the saw's blade as a spacer. Now just clamp the miter box to a sawhorse right in the room where your accent wall is and make your cuts. No airborne dust, and no running back and forth to the shop!

## 8 GLUE THE FIRST STRIP

Cut the 45-degree angle on one end of the first strip, and then glue the back. Apply glue sparingly so the glue doesn't keep the strip from seating fully on the wall. We used a fast-grabbing construction adhesive (Loctite Power Grab) for this project. It has a fast initial tack, so it stays put as soon as you press it into place. But if necessary, you can still shift it until it cures.

## 9 PRESS THE FIRST STRIP INTO PLACE

Line up the strip with the laser line, and then press it against the wall. Since this first one is so long, tacking it on with a brad nail every 2 ft. will help keep it straight.

## 10 ADD THE SECOND STRIP

The first line in our design requires two pieces, butt jointed together. Make the 45-degree cut on the second piece, hold it in place and then mark the butt joint. Cut the strip to length and glue it to the wall.

## 11 OUTLINE THE BIG SHAPES

Continue marking, cutting and attaching strips to outline the large shapes, as you did for the first piece. Use the laser level and adhesive, nailing where needed.

## 12 FILL IN THE SHAPES

Add the rest of the strips, working from longest to shortest, filling in the large shapes.

## 13 FINISH UP

Fill any gaps or nail holes with spackling compound. When the spackling compound has dried, sand it smooth and touch it up with paint.

## Materials

| ITEM |
| --- |
| 1/2" x 48" x 96" sheet of MDF |
| 1 gallon of paint |
| Spackling compound |
| Fast-tack construction adhesive |
| Brad nails |

**11**

**12**

**13**

### *Pro Tip*

If you need to tack a strip where there's no stud, shoot two brad nails at opposing angles—so they cross each other in the drywall—to hold the strip flat while the adhesive dries.

# THE ART OF *HIDING* *A TV*

## BY MIKE BERNER

**WHAT IT TAKES**

| TIME | COST | SKILL LEVEL |
|------|------|-------------|
| *A few days* | *$400* | *Intermediate* |

**TOOLS**
*Table saw, drill, level, miter saw, wire stripper, 18-gauge nailer, screwdriver*

## Sliding doors can make the TV room a family room again

I'm willing to bet that a TV is the focal point of at least one room in your home. That's great for movie nights and sporting events, but when you're focusing on friends or family, you likely want the TV to disappear. Unlike a phone or a tablet, a TV can't just be put away, so I developed this system that lets you hide it with artwork instead!

**AUTOMATE IT!**
This double sliding door belt system is slick: When you slide one door, the other slides, too. To make it happen, all you need are a belt and pulleys (about $20). Even better, I added a motor and remote control ($50). It took a lot of experimenting, but now that I've figured out a system, you can replicate it in an hour or two. The automation is optional—if you like, keep it simple and slide the doors by hand.

Shelf end supports

Cleat

Wall stud

**MEET THE BUILDER**
Mike Berner is an editor at *Family Handyman*—and a former science teacher who loves a good problem to solve.

# 1 MOUNT THE CLEAT

Determine the heights of the floating shelves, making sure to leave 3 in. between the top cleat and top of TV. Locate the wall studs. Before attaching the cleats to the wall, fasten the shelf end supports (G) to the ends of each cleat.

# 2 BUILD UP THE SUPPORT ARMS

Fasten the center spacer (B) to top cleat with glue and brad nails, then glue and nail track support arms (C) to each side of the spacer. Add narrow spacers (D) and arms the full length of the pocket door track. I used a two-door pocket door kit, and I cut the tracks to 60-3/4 in.

## Figure A
## Shelves

**OVERALL DIMENSIONS:**
**50-3/4" x 140-1/2" x 8-1/4"**
***FOR A 65" TV**

## Cutting List

| KEY | QTY. | DIMENSIONS | PART |
|-----|------|-----------|------|
| A | 2 | 3/4" x 3-1/2" x 139" | Cleats |
| B | 1 | 3/4" x 2-1/2" x 2-1/2" | Center spacer |
| C | 12 | 3/4" x 2-1/2" x 6-3/4" | Track support arms |
| D | 10 | 3/4" x 2-1/2" x 11-1/4" * | Narrow spacer |
| E | 14 | 3/4" x 3-1/2" x 11-1/4" * | Wide spacer |
| F | 16 | 3/4" x 3-1/2" x 6-3/4" | Shelf arms |
| G | 4 | 3/4" x 3-1/2" x 7-1/2" | Shelf end supports |
| H | 1 | 3/4" x 1" x 124" | Nailer |
| J | 2 | 3/4" x 30" x 40-1/4" | Doors |
| K | 2 | 3/4" x 1-1/2" x 37-1/4" | Picture frame stiles |
| L | 2 | 3/4" x 1-1/2" x 31" | Picture frame rails |
| M | 2 | 1/2" x 7-1/2" x 140-1/2" | Shelf top |
| N | 2 | 1/2" x 7-1/2" x 140-1/2" | Shelf bottom |
| P | 1 | 3/4" x 4-1/2" x 140-1/2" | Shelf fascia |
| Q | 2 | 60-3/4" | Pocket door tracks |

*Cut end pieces to fit

## Materials List

| ITEM |
|------|
| 18/2 thermostat wire (25' roll) |
| 3/4" plywood |
| 1/2" hardwood plywood |
| Two-door 72" pocket door kit |
| 24V 85RPM DC motor |
| Motor bracket |
| GT2 5mm wide belt |
| GT2 drive wheel w/6mm bore |
| Two-channel RF transmitter |
| 24V power adapter |
| Limit switches |
| GT2 idler pulleys w/5mm bore |
| Extra-strong hook-and-loop tape |

The track support arms are 1 in. narrower than the cleat to hide the track inside the finished shelf.

## 3 MOUNT THE TRACK

Drill holes in the track to line up with the track support arms. Hold the track in place, flush to the front of the arms, and drill pilot holes into the arms. Fasten the track to the arms with wood screws. Then fasten a nailer (H) behind the tracks and cap the outside ends with full-height shelf arms (F) to contain the wheels.

## 4 HANG THE DOORS

Predrill and screw two door brackets to the top of each door, about 4 in. from the door's edges. Slide the door hangers into the tracks and connect the door brackets to the door hangers.

**2** Track support arm — Spacer — Center spacer

**3** Aluminum pocket door track

**4** Pocket door hanger — Pocket door bracket

M

Motor

A

D C F

E G

Pulleys

N

Q

A

E

F

G

At this point, you could finish the shelves, add picture frames to the doors and call it a day. But for about $70, you can add a pulley system made using 3D printer replacement parts and a DC motor so you can open the doors from your favorite seat!

## 5

**DC motor**

**Motor bracket**

**Mounting block**

**Drive wheel**

### 5 INSTALL THE MOTOR

Fasten the motor bracket to a mounting block, then bolt the motor to the bracket. Secure the mounting block to a support arm near the end of the track, then slide the drive wheel over the shaft. Make sure the wheel is level and just below the track, then tighten the drive-wheel setscrews.

**3" from motor**

**Pulley**

### 6 PLACE THE PULLEYS

At each end of the track, screw a pulley to the shelf arm, centered on the track. I attached two more pulleys to add tension to the belt, screwing them to the nailer on each side of the drive wheel, 3 in. from the motor.

### 7 ROUTE THE BELT

Glue and clamp one end of each belt around the door hanger posts. I used polyurethane glue and a binder clip. Center the doors on the track in their closed position, then route the belts around the pulleys and clamp the other end around the post on the opposite door. Don't glue these ends of the belts yet. Just clamp them until the motor is hooked up in case you need to adjust the belt tension.

**Glue and clamp one end only**

**Nailer**

## Figure B
## Belt Diagram

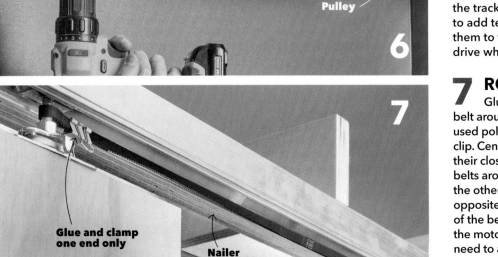

**The right door pulls the left door open**

**Pocket door hardware**

**The motor rotates counter-clockwise to open**

**Motor**

**Door**

**The motor pulls the right door open**

***When closing, the motor spins clockwise and the belt travels in the reverse direction.**

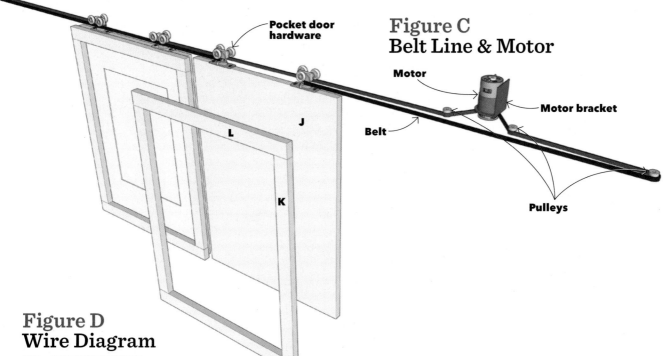

Pocket door hardware

## Figure C
## Belt Line & Motor

Motor

Motor bracket

Belt

Pulleys

J

L

K

## Figure D
## Wire Diagram

**NO = NORMALLY OPEN**
**NC = NORMALLY CLOSED**
**C = COMMON**

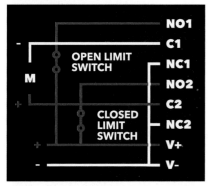

NO1
C1
NC1
NO2
C2
NC2
V+
V-

OPEN LIMIT SWITCH

CLOSED LIMIT SWITCH

M

## 8 WIRE THE TRANSMITTER

This transmitter uses two channels: one to make the motor spin clockwise, one for counterclockwise. I used the included wiring diagram to make the connections but added limit switches between the (+) lead and each "NO" terminal.

## 9 POSITION THE LIMIT SWITCHES

You'll need limit switches at each end of one track. When the wheels contact them, they tell the motor to stop. Connect lengths of wire to the "common" and "normally closed" terminals on the limit switches, then feed the wires through a hole in the top of the track. I secured the switches with strong hook-and-loop tape so I could adjust their positions.

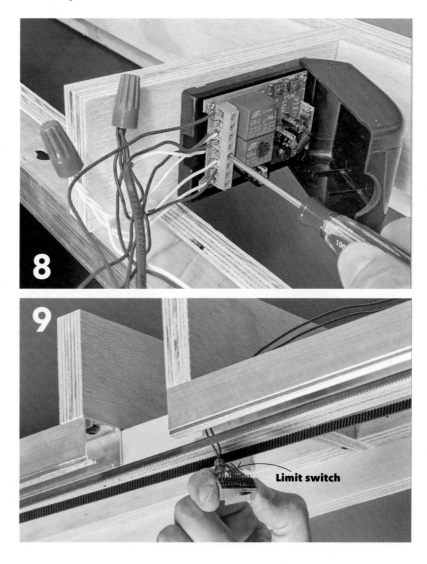

Limit switch

**Blocks hold fascia in place for nailing**

## 10 SKIN THE SHELVES

Nail the shelf top to the arms. Then trace and cut a large notch out of the underside to fit the pulleys and the track. Nail the shelf bottom to the nailer, the cleat and the arms at the ends of the shelf. Finish it off with a hardwood fascia to cover the plywood edges. I tacked scraps to the top of the fascia to hold it while I nailed it on.

## 11 ASSEMBLE THE PICTURE FRAMES

Put the picture frames together using glue and pocket hole joinery. To keep the frame pieces flush, clamp the joints to your work surface while you drive in the screws.

## 12 RABBET THE FRAMES

Rout a 1/2 x 3/8-in. rabbet around the inside of each frame's back. The frame screws are close to the action here. It's a good idea to remove them and reinstall them after routing. Don't make my mistake and nick the router bit!

## 13 SQUARE THE CORNERS

The router leaves a rounded corner in the rabbet. Mark the corner square and chisel it out to fit the matting and glass. Your chisel work won't be seen, so don't worry if it's a tad sloppy.

## 14 INSTALL THE HARDWARE

Drill a recess for the turn buttons. Use a 5/8-in. Forstner bit to ensure the screw heads are flush with the frame's back surface. You'll need to do the same with the keyhole hangers. Trace the hangers, then line up the Forstner bit and drill out just enough material for the hanger to sit flush with the surface. Drill a little deeper in the center to allow room for the screw head, then clean up the recess with a chisel.

## 15 ADD YOUR ARTWORK

I had custom matting and glass cut at the local frame shop to fit the frame and the artwork perfectly. I carefully placed a screw in the door to accept the keyhole hanger and then hung my artwork.

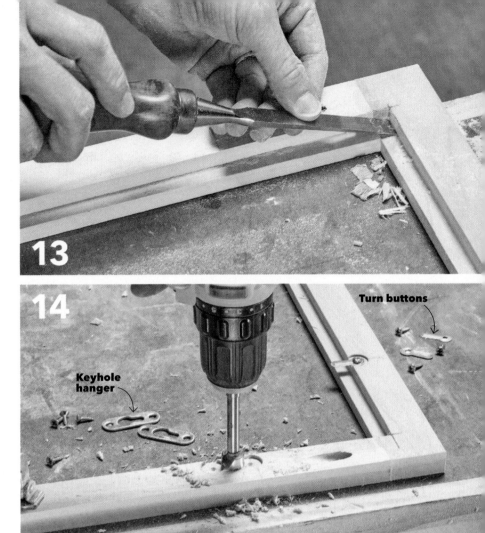

**13**

**14**

Turn buttons

Keyhole hanger

**15**

Screw for keyhole hanger

**ROTATE YOUR ART COLLECTION** You can easily change up your decor by replacing the artwork in the frames. Just take the frames down to switch out the current artwork with a new set.

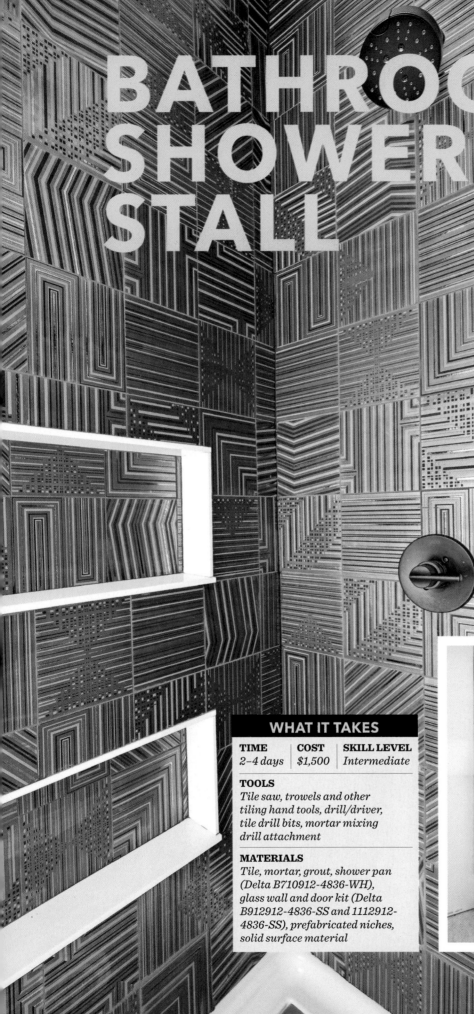

# BATHROOM SHOWER STALL

## Easy install makes an attractive addition

BY BRAD HOLDEN

**W**hen installing a tile shower, the most difficult part is building the sloped base for the floor. By using a prefabricated pan, you can skip that challenge. All you need to do is set the pan and tile the walls.

Built-in wall niches are a snap; they're prefabricated as well. And to let the beautiful tile shine and make the small space seem roomier, install a glass door and enclosure. Here's how:

### WHAT IT TAKES

| TIME | COST | SKILL LEVEL |
|------|------|-------------|
| 2–4 days | $1,500 | Intermediate |

**TOOLS**
*Tile saw, trowels and other tiling hand tools, drill/driver, tile drill bits, mortar mixing drill attachment*

**MATERIALS**
*Tile, mortar, grout, shower pan (Delta B710912-4836-WH), glass wall and door kit (Delta B912912-4836-SS and 1112912-4836-SS), prefabricated niches, solid surface material*

**Prefab shower pan**

**Niche framing**

**Prefab shower niche**

**Solid surface niche ledge**

# 1 SET THE SHOWER PAN

Set the pan in place and level it with plastic shims if needed. Lift the pan and staple the shims to the subfloor. Apply construction adhesive to the subfloor and press the pan down onto the shims. Recheck for level. Let the adhesive set for at least 24 hours before you stand in the pan. Some pans require mortar. Our pan from Delta requires only adhesive.

# 2 INSTALL THE NICHES

I installed two niches: one high and one low. The lower one—16 in. off the floor—is both an accessible shelf for small kids and a footrest for leg shaving. Notch studs to accommodate the prefab niches, and add nailers and blocking where necessary. Attach the niches with backer board screws. Apply the rest of the backer board, and then tape and mortar the seams and cover the screw heads. Allow the wall installation to dry overnight.

# 3 SET THE NICHE LEDGES

Set the niche ledges in place—angled toward the shower—using thin-set. The ledges run the niches' full width. Cut them wide enough to stand proud of the finished tile surface by about 1/2 in. Solid surface material is easy to cut with standard carbide blades.

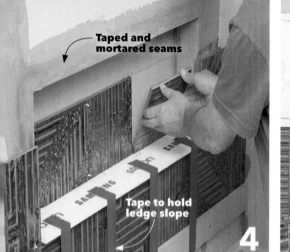

Taped and mortared seams

Tape to hold ledge slope

4

Waterproof backer board

Prop stick

5

## 4 TILE AND FINISH OFF THE NICHES

Mix a batch of mortar and install tile on the backs of the niches. Cut the top solid surface material full length and wide enough to stand proud of the finished tile surface by about 1/4 in. Cut the sides to fit between the top and bottom. That way, when you install the sides, they'll support the ends of the top. Use a prop stick to support the center. Angle the bottom ends of the side pieces to match the slope of the ledges.

## 5 TILE THE WALLS

Mix your mortar, and apply your tile to the walls. Allow the mortar to set at least 24 hours, then grout your tile.

## 6 ADD THE GLASS WALLS

The installation of glass wall and door kits varies. Our kit from Delta uses jambs on the wall. Use a masonry bit to predrill into the tile to install the jambs. Install each jamb with stainless steel screws, usually included with the kit. Slip the glass panel flange over the jamb.

## 7 HANG THE DOOR

Install the roller track on the panels, making sure it's level, and then fasten the rollers to the door. Hang the door. The rollers will likely have adjustment cams to ensure the door hangs level on the track. Once the installation is plumb and level, screw the panel flanges to the wall jambs and caulk all the seams where the hardware attaches to the walls and pan.

Glass panel

Glass panel wall jamb

### Pro Tip

Before applying backer board, figure out where the jambs will go and make sure there are studs to anchor them.

6

Roller

Door track

7

# KITCHEN ISLAND

## Build your own with ready-to-assemble cabinets

BY JOE CRUZ

The kitchen island is the central gathering point in any home that has one. It's where meals are prepped, homework is sweated over and birthday candles are blown out. Building a kitchen island using ready-to-assemble cabinets is an inexpensive DIY project that will add more counter space to any kitchen.

## DESIGN & PLANNING

Consider both form and function when you design your kitchen island. Having a kitchen sink in the island is handy for prepping food, especially for families who cook together. A cooktop or range in a kitchen island, however, isn't recommended because of the possibility of splattering grease on bystanders.

Free online kitchen planners can help you choose styles and colors of doors, drawers and countertops. You'll get a printable itemized list with the costs of all the materials you need. Before you start, check the accessibility of the plumbing and electrical needed for your island. If you're not doing the utility work yourself, get at least two estimates from plumbers and electricians. Check with your city inspector regarding any permits needed.

# 1 CABINET ASSEMBLY

RTA cabinet parts are shipped in a flat box; we got ours from the RTA Store (*thertastore.com*). You assemble them with dowels, glue and screws. Follow the manufacturer's steps to build each box.

# 2 CABINET PLACEMENT & LEVELING

Place the center cabinet first. Level the cabinet left to right and front to back by turning the adjustable legs. Set and level your next cabinet. Clamp this cabinet to the center one while you connect them with 1-1/4-in. screws. Continue setting, leveling and securing cabinets to one another. Once all are connected, use a 4- or 6-ft. level to verify the whole run is level.

# 3 SECURING CABINETS TO THE FLOOR

Measure the distance between the floor and the bottom of the cabinets and cut 2x4s to that length to create mounting blocks under the cabinets. We secured our two end cabinets this way. Secure the blocks to the floor with L-brackets and screws. Drive 2-in. screws through the bottoms of the cabinets and into the mounting blocks.

# 4 CUT PANELS & WRAP THE ISLAND

To create a custom look, cover the ends and backs of the assembled cabinets with overlay panels. These panels can be the full height from cabinet top to floor, or you can stop the panels at the bottom of the cabinet to allow toe-kick space. For a more enclosed look with an overhanging top, extend the end panels past the back of the island; this will also support the overhanging countertop. Measure the distance from the floor to the top of the cabinet. Cut both end panels to that height and the desired width using a track saw or table saw. If you're cutting the end panels from a large 4 x 8-ft. panel, you may need to edge-band the exposed edges.

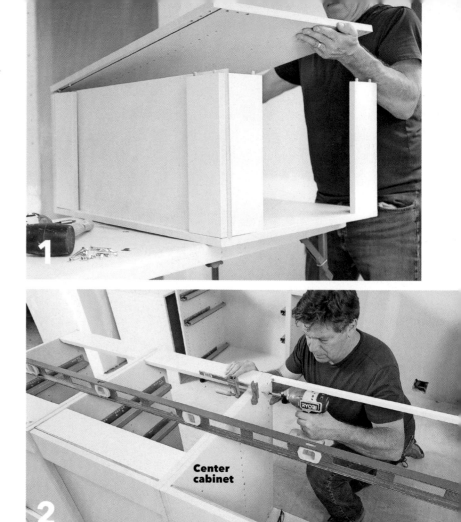

**1**

**2** Center cabinet

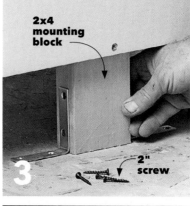

**3** 2x4 mounting block

2" screw

**4** Overlay end panel

## WHAT IT TAKES

| TIME | COST | SKILL LEVEL |
|---|---|---|
| 1–2 days | $1,000 | Intermediate |

**TOOLS**
*Drill/driver, drill bits, circular saw, straightedge, 4-ft. level, clamps*

**MATERIALS**
*Ready-to-assemble (RTA) cabinets, panel material, 2x4s, screws (countertop not included)*

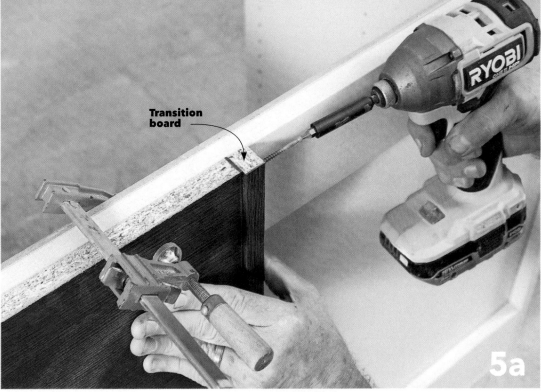

Transition
board

5a

## 5 ATTACH BACK PANELS

If your cabinet island is less than 8 ft. wide, you can use a one-piece back cover panel. If your island—like ours—is longer than 8 ft., you'll need to splice two panels together to make one long back panel.

The two back panels will meet in the middle, with a transition board between them. To make your transition board, rip a 7/8-in. piece of panel material the same height as the back panel. Be sure the piece is edge-banded along one long edge.

To find the overall length of each panel, measure the distance between the two end panels, divide that number in half and subtract 3/8 in. from each half panel. Cut the back panels to height and length using a circular saw or table saw.

Attach the transition board (**Photo 5a**) to the end of one of the two back panels using 1-1/4-in. finish screws. (Predrill the screw holes.) Clamp the back panel tight to the back of the cabinets and tight to the end panel.

Secure the back panel (**Photo 5b**) by driving 1-1/4-in. screws from the inside of each corner of the cabinet into the panel. Attach the second panel the same way, and be sure it's tight to the transition board and the other end panel.

5b

### Pro Tip
If the second back panel is too tight, instead of cutting it, loosen the screws on the end panel.

# SINK & COUNTERTOPS

## DIY laminate counter with an undermount sink

Composite rim of undermount sink

**P**lastic laminate is durable, affordable and easy to maintain. And the bonus? It offers patterns, colors and DIY edge profiles you can't get with other countertop materials. Plus, you can install an undermount sink and do it all yourself.

We built our kitchen island countertop and installed the 33-in. Karran E-540 sink with just basic tools and know-how. Follow the details here and you won't have to worry about water damaging your laminate countertop material.

FROM OUR GETAWAY

BY BILL BERGMANN

# 1 PLACE AND CUT OUT SINK

After you size the substrate and apply the laminate to the edges, mark the location of the sink. Place the sink 2-1/2 in. back from the front edge of the countertop and center it on the cabinet. When you're tracing the sink shape onto the substrate, keep your pencil vertical so the cutting line is offset about 1/8 in. Drill a 1/2-in. starter hole and cut out the sink opening with a jigsaw.

# 2 LAYING OUT LAMINATE

Rough-cut the sheet of laminate to fit the substrate, leaving an extra 1 in. all around. Place the laminate on the substrate and mark the sink cutout on the bottom.

# 3 SECURE THE SINK

For a rectangular sink, glue and staple four strips of 3/4-in.-thick particleboard to hold the sink in position by its rim. Use several short blocks to hold a round sink.

# 4 MAKE SURE IT'S FLUSH

The sink must be perfectly flush with the top of the substrate. Use a carpenter's square to check. You can make small adjustments from below using screws through the support strips. Take your time with this step; the slightest variation can show when you install the laminate.

# 5 FILL THE GAP

Using a 6-in. putty knife, fill the gap between the sink rim and the substrate with Bondo auto body filler. To extend the setting time and workability, go easy on the hardener. If necessary, mix a second batch to fill any voids, then feather the edges out as far as possible. Once the filler is dry, sand it flush with a belt sander and 120-grit paper. Go light, slow and steady to avoid digging into the substrate.

# 6 APPLY CONTACT ADHESIVE

Using a short-nap roller, apply contact adhesive to both the substrate and the laminate. Don't apply adhesive to the sink edges or the sink outline on the laminate.

1-1/2" x 3/4" support strips

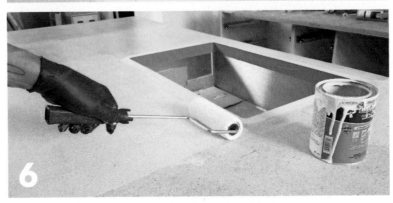

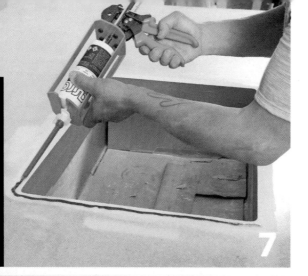

## 7 APPLY SINK SEAM SEALER

Once the contact adhesive is ready to bond, wipe the sink top with denatured alcohol. Apply the seam adhesive to the perimeter of the sink. Mask the top of the sink bowl with painter's tape to protect it. This sealer sets in less than 30 minutes, so work quickly through the next step.

## 8 PLACING THE LAMINATE

Contact adhesive sticks immediately; there are no second chances. For precise placement, set 1/2 x 1/2-in. standoff sticks on the substrate, and lay the glued laminate on the sticks, making sure it has an equal overhang all around. Starting at the center, remove the sticks one at a time, pressing the laminate down as you go. When it is positioned properly, roll it with a J-roller for a sure bond.

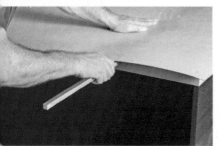

## 9 ROUT THE SINK OPENING

Cut a pilot hole to rout over to the sink bowl edge. Trim the laminate using a 10° bevel bit with an oversize bearing (available from Karran). Make a single, slow pass.

## 10 FINISH EDGES

File the laminate flush with the sink wall using a laminate file. Use a round file for corners. For the final finish sanding, use 80- or 60-micron paper, focusing on the upper 1/4 in. of the bowl wall and the laminate.

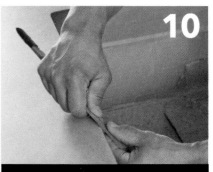

**Trace the edge of the counter**

**1**

**Score the line**

**2**

**Dig out the drywall**

**3**

**4**

# A better way to make countertops fit the wall

If you've ever tried to fit a counter-top or cabinet to a wall, you know how frustrating it is when walls aren't flat and corners aren't square. It's equally frustrating to scribe, cut and sand a countertop to perfectly fit the wall, particularly with an integral backsplash, as shown in the photos. So, in most cases, whether it's a cabinet or countertop, I just don't bother. I cut out the wall instead. Here's how to do it.

Take note of where the gap is widest and roughly how wide the gap is. You'll only need to cut where the counter touches or is very close to the wall. Trace the outline of your countertop onto the wall where it makes contact **(Photo 1)**. Next, cut on the line with a utility knife **(Photo 2)**, making sure to cut through the paper. A little deeper is good. Chisel out enough drywall inside the cut to make a recess roughly as deep as the widest gap **(Photo 3)**. Slide the countertop into position **(Photo 4)**; repeat the process if necessary. If you find that you're digging close to the full depth of the drywall, take extra care in case there are pipes or wires inside the wall.

Don't worry about making it perfect. Most countertops get a finishing bead of caulk, so as long as you stay within a 1/8-in. margin of error, you'll get a clean installation.

**MEET THE EXPERT**
**Seth Prince owns PrinceWorks, a Minneapolis remodeling company specializing in transforming kitchens, baths and other interior spaces.**

# READY FOR RELAXATION

## Our getaway is complete! C'mon inside & check it out.

BY GLENN HANSEN

**FROM OUR GETAWAY**

**W**elcome to the *Family Handyman* Getaway. From the DIY kitchen island to the large windows and roll-up door to the inviting wraparound deck, the styled interior reveals the simple beauty of the finished build.

One Kichler pendant light above our DIY kitchen island provides plenty of light and minimizes clutter overhead.

We love the Wayne Dalton insulated glass panel door that keeps us connected with the outdoors.

This is where it happens, all of it—at the kitchen island. We made ours a functional and stylish centerpiece of the room.

This Delta faucet has the clean look we wanted, as well as modern features.

This Bellawood Artisan flooring from LL Flooring was easy to install and looks as natural as our surroundings.

# THE GETAWAY

These triple bunks turn the small bedroom into a sleepover zone.

We made our own trim in a minimalist style and saved hundreds of dollars.

The Getaway's two bedrooms and three-quarter bath are small but well designed with high ceilings and ample windows for lighting and views. The spaces are functional and still offer design opportunities with plenty of wall space and minimal trim carpentry.

We chose pendant lights in the main bedroom because we like the wood style and the extra space on the nightstands.

A pair of Kichler pendant lights illuminate the bathroom sink and countertop, as well as the ready-to-assemble cabinet beneath.

The shower, tiled in Daltile's Geometric Fusion porcelain, features a pair of built-in wall niches.

The angular Delta plumbing fixtures work well with the Getaway's modern, minimalist style.

The composite decking from Deckorators adds woodsy appeal with little maintenance needed. The surrounding cable rail is nearly invisible.

Our Getaway gives us space to keep working, too. We can always come up with another project.

# Great Goofs®

**Laughs and lessons from our readers**

## THE EYE OF THE BEHOLDER

I was remodeling my daughter's second-floor bedroom and had finished all the demo work. I was ready to start the next phase when I saw daylight coming up through a hole in a floorboard. But that didn't make any sense. How could there be light between the ceiling downstairs and the floor upstairs? So I got down on my hands and knees and peered through the little hole—only to see an eyeball looking right back at me! I almost had a heart attack. When I gained enough courage to take a second look, I realized that a piece of broken mirror had lodged itself in a knot-hole. I'd nearly frightened myself to death by staring at my own eyeball!

**ROBERT ARNOLD**

## A BIT OF A PROBLEM

I was on the couch knitting while my husband was downstairs working on our basement. He was using a 6-ft. flexible drill bit to drill holes through the floor joists in the finished ceiling so he could fish wire through them and install new recessed lights. All of a sudden, I felt the couch vibrate. This went on for about 10 seconds and then stopped. I was totally confused until my husband ran into the room, looked at the couch and in a very quiet voice said, "Oooops, there's the problem." I peeked over the side of the couch and saw that the drill bit had come up through the floor, through the wall-to-wall carpeting and through the bottom corner of our leather couch. It was now sticking out the side. Apparently the drill bit had hit a vent and was driven off course. My husband finished the job and the new lights look great. So does our new couch.

**CHARLA SCHAFER**

# 2 Electrical & High Tech

# INSTALL A SMART SWITCH

## Advice you won't find in the instructions

BY BRAD HOLDEN

**Installing a smart light switch is as simple as installing a regular switch, aside from connecting the light switch to your Wi-Fi. Smart light switches are considerably more expensive than standard switches ($40 vs. $3 at home centers), but they can do much more. Here, we are replacing our existing standard switches with Leviton Decora Smart switches, but the tips apply to any brand.**

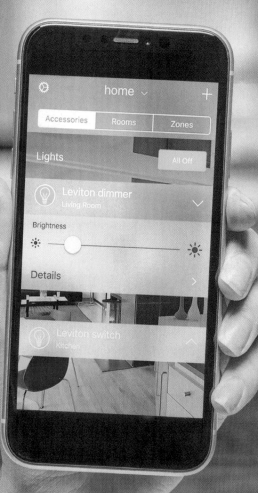

## WHAT CAN A SMART SWITCH DO FOR YOU?

With a smart switch, you can program lights to turn on and off to suit your schedule. You can also operate your lights by using an app on your phone or via voice command through a home assistant. And, yes, you can also operate them manually.

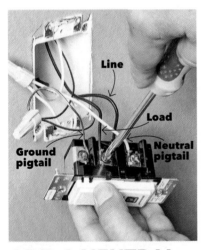

## ADD A NEUTRAL

Unlike with a standard switch, you'll need to splice the neutral wires in the box and add a pigtail to connect to the neutral terminal on the smart switch.

## MAKE SURE YOU HAVE A NEUTRAL

If your home is more than 15 years old, a junction box might have two hot wires and no neutral. So, before you shop for a smart switch, check to see if you have a neutral. If you don't, choose a smart switch that doesn't require a neutral.

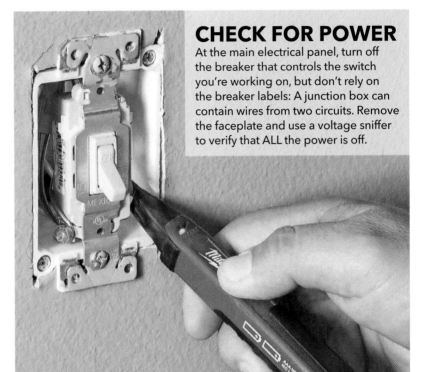

## CHECK FOR POWER

At the main electrical panel, turn off the breaker that controls the switch you're working on, but don't rely on the breaker labels: A junction box can contain wires from two circuits. Remove the faceplate and use a voltage sniffer to verify that ALL the power is off.

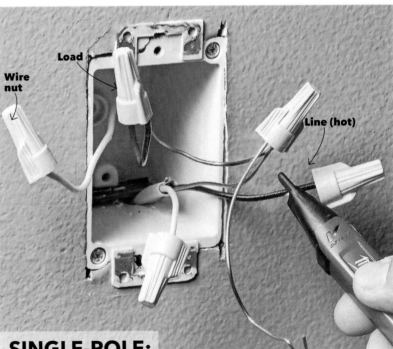

## SINGLE-POLE: IDENTIFY THE LINE AND THE LOAD

A single-pole switch controls a light or receptacle from a single location. Look at the cables entering the box. In newer houses, you'll typically see a power supply cable (the "line") coming in from the bottom of the junction box, with black (hot), white (neutral) and bare copper (ground) wires. Another cable (the "load") with the same color wires, goes out the top of the junction box to the light fixture. If it's unclear which is which, put a wire nut on each wire, turn the power back on and test to see which black wire still has power (that's the line), then turn the breaker off again.

## TAPE THE TERMINALS

Wrap the wired switch with electrical tape to avoid arcing from bare terminals to ground wires or a metal box. When you're done, carefully fold the wires into the box and reinstall the switch.

## CHECK MANUAL OPERATION

Before you go through the Wi-Fi/app setup, turn the power back on and check your installation by operating the switch manually. If it's not working because you haven't connected it properly, you can correct the problem without having to do the setup twice.

# *Tips for Three-Way Smart Switches*

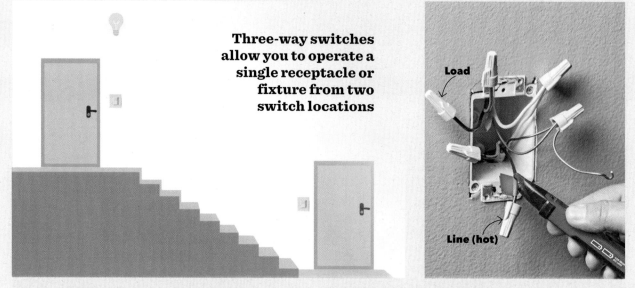

**Three-way switches allow you to operate a single receptacle or fixture from two switch locations**

Load

Line (hot)

## ■ THREE-WAY: IDENTIFY THE LINE AND THE LOAD

The procedure is the same as it is for a single-pole switch, except only one of the two boxes contains the line. With the power off, disconnect all the wires and twist a wire nut on each individual wire. Turn the breaker back on and test the taped (common) wires in each box using a noncontact voltage detector. The one that still has power is your line feed. The taped wire that doesn't have power (in the other box) is the load connection, which goes to the light fixture. Once the line is located, turn off the power again.

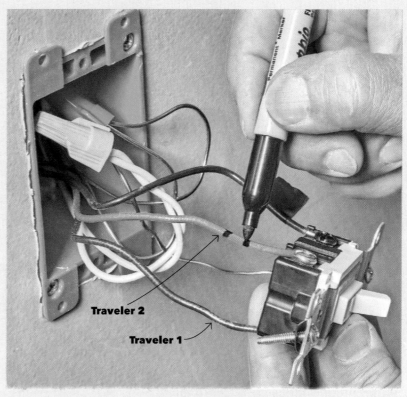

## ■ FLAG THE COMMON WIRE

Leaving the wires attached, pull both switches out of their boxes. Locate the black terminal (marked "common") on both switches. Use electrical tape to mark the wires attached to these terminals on both switches.

**Black terminal**

**Traveler 2**

**Traveler 1**

## ■ IDENTIFY THE TRAVELERS

Each switch has two wires connected to opposite terminals. These terminals are usually brass colored, and the wires connected to them are typically black and red, but not always. These are the traveler wires, which enable three-way switches to work together by creating two potential pathways to complete the circuit and send power to the light fixture. Mark these wires as Traveler 1 and Traveler 2.

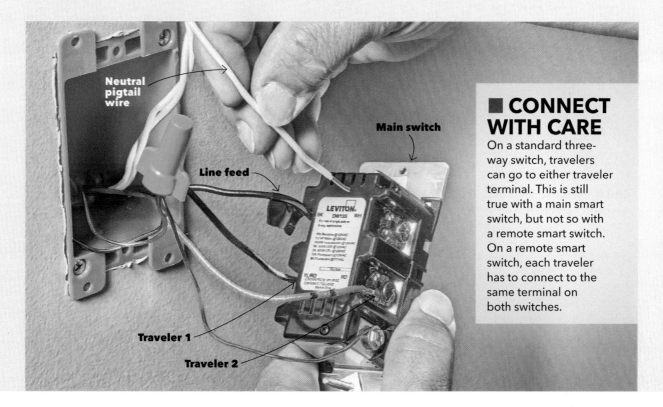

**Neutral pigtail wire**

**Line feed**

**Main switch**

**Traveler 1**

**Traveler 2**

## ■ CONNECT WITH CARE

On a standard three-way switch, travelers can go to either traveler terminal. This is still true with a main smart switch, but not so with a remote smart switch. On a remote smart switch, each traveler has to connect to the same terminal on both switches.

**No C-wire**

# Get Wired for a Smart Thermostat

If you're replacing an old dial thermostat with a smart thermostat, you may find that you're missing a wire. Don't worry. Usually all you need is an adapter kit to add a "C-wire." An adapter is often included with a smart thermostat, and it's easy to install.

## 1 CHECK FOR A C-WIRE

Cut power to your furnace. Remove the old thermostat and label the wires according to the terminal they're attached to. If there is a wire in the "C" terminal, you're good. If not, you'll connect the adapter to your furnace's control board.

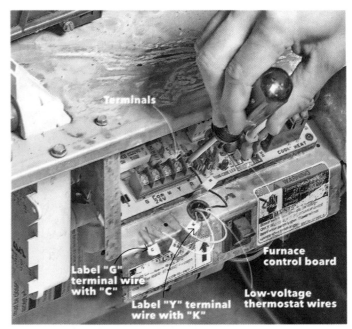

Terminals

Label "G" terminal wire with "C"

Label "Y" terminal wire with "K"

Furnace control board

Low-voltage thermostat wires

## 2 LABEL AND REMOVE THE WIRES AT THE FURNACE

Find the furnace control board and take a photo of the wire arrangement. Label the wires according to which terminals they're in, except for the "G" and "Y" terminal wires. Label the "G" terminal wire with a "C" and the "Y" terminal wire with a "K." Unscrew the terminals and remove the wires. If there are wires that aren't connected to anything, leave them alone.

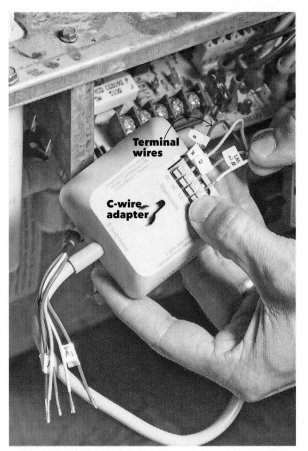

Terminal wires

C-wire adapter

## 3 WIRE THE ADAPTER

Connect the wires to their corresponding terminals on the C-wire adapter.

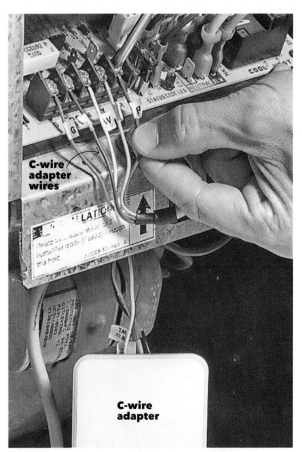

C-wire adapter wires

C-wire adapter

## 4 CONNECT THE ADAPTER TO THE FURNACE

Connect the wires from the adapter to their corresponding terminals on the furnace control board. Mount the adapter inside the furnace and close the furnace cover.

## 5 CONNECT THE NEW THERMOSTAT

With the new wall plate fastened to the wall, connect the wires to the corresponding terminals.

# PULL WIRES
## ANYWHERE YOU WANT THEM

**"Fishing" wire is easier with these tips and tools**

BY MIKE BERNER

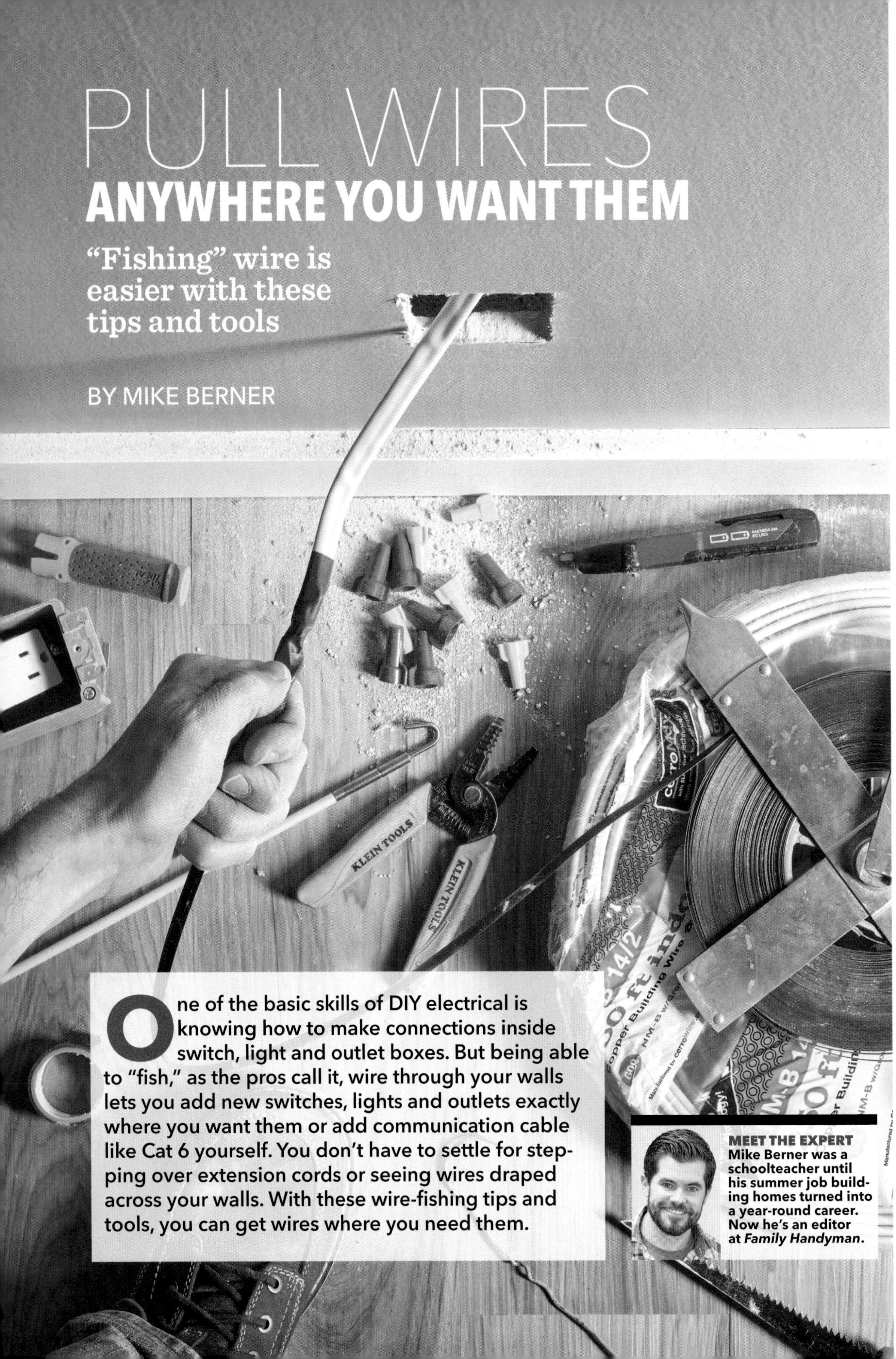

One of the basic skills of DIY electrical is knowing how to make connections inside switch, light and outlet boxes. But being able to "fish," as the pros call it, wire through your walls lets you add new switches, lights and outlets exactly where you want them or add communication cable like Cat 6 yourself. You don't have to settle for stepping over extension cords or seeing wires draped across your walls. With these wire-fishing tips and tools, you can get wires where you need them.

**MEET THE EXPERT**
Mike Berner was a schoolteacher until his summer job building homes turned into a year-round career. Now he's an editor at *Family Handyman*.

## DON'T FISH POWER CORDS

Cords that power appliances, TVs and power strips cannot be placed inside a wall. The National Electrical Code says these cords cannot replace permanent wiring. To avoid seeing these power cords, you can fish cable to add a new outlet nearby.

## ▲ MAKE A BEVEL CUT

If you have to cut an access hole, make the cut at an angle. Then when it's time to patch it, spread joint compound around the hole and press the cutout back in. The mud will hold the plug in place—there's no need for screws or backing and the plug won't fall through the hole.

## ▲ MAKE A CHASE WITH TRIM

Run conduit or BX cable (armored cable) along the top corner of a wall and cover the cable with crown molding. You can cut small holes in the wall or ceiling where the wiring needs to exit the room.

## ▲ ROUTE CABLE BEHIND BASEBOARD

If you are like me and would rather install miles of trim than patch drywall, this is the way to go. Remove the baseboard and cut a long, narrow hole in its place. Then drill holes in the studs for your wire to pass through. This works best with wide base trim but can be done with narrow base trim as well. Be sure to keep the holes in the studs at least 1-1/4 in. away from the stud edges to avoid the need for protective metal plates.

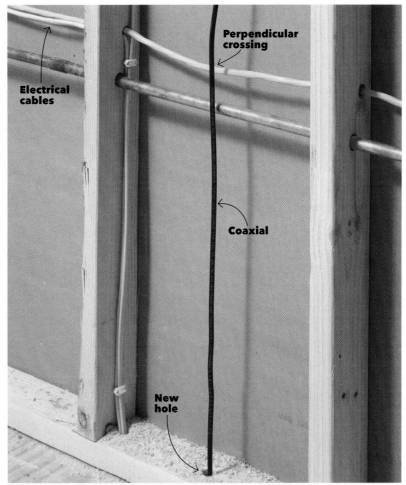

## ▲ GIVE COMMUNICATION CABLE ENOUGH SPACE

Communication cable like coax or Cat 6 should be kept away from cables that carry high voltage to outlets and lights. Pros recommend keeping them 12 to 16 in. away. If you must cross these cables, do so at a 90-degree angle.

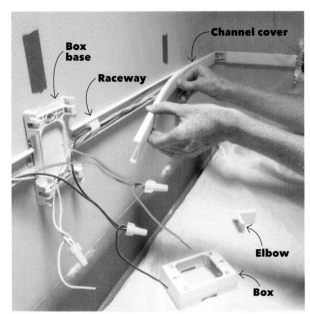

## ▲ HIDE WIRES WITH RACEWAY

Running wires on a wall surface with raceway is a great way to get power right where you want it without fishing wires through walls. You can hide the raceway behind furniture and paint it to match the wall. Build the raceway from an existing electrical box with snap-together components and hide the wire inside the channel.

## ▲ FIND THE EASIEST ROUTE

The easiest route is not always the most direct. Take advantage of unfinished spaces like basements and attics to run wire from one end of the house to the other. You might use an extra 50 ft. of wire, but it will save you lots of time.

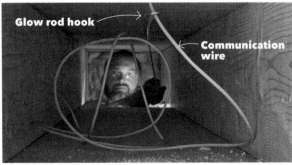

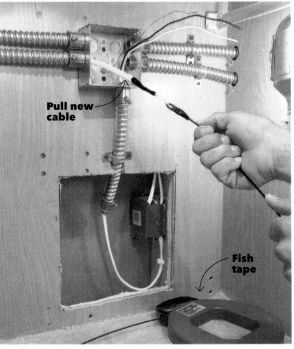

## ▲ USE A LOT OF CABLE

Pushing far more cable than you need into the walls or ceilings is helpful for a few reasons. First, it makes the job of hooking the cable you're fishing much easier. It also eliminates lots of tugging, which can damage fragile Cat 6 cables.

## ▲ RUN CONDUIT IN CLOSETS OR CABINETS

Conduit or armored cable is another terrific option for surface wiring, and it's about half the cost of raceway. You wouldn't want to run it over your walls as you would raceway, but it won't be visible in a dark closet or along the backs of cabinets.

**Electrical cable**

**Coat hanger**

**Electrical tape**

## ▲ SPLICE LIKE A PRO

Sometimes you have to pull hard to get a cable through a wall, so make sure the cable is securely tied to your pulling tool, whether it's a fish tape or a coat hanger. This is my favorite method: Put the wire through the eyelet or around the hook, then wrap it around your fishing tool. Tape them together with electrical tape, making sure to taper the wrapped section so it will slide through holes.

## ▲ WIRE ALONG THE PLUMBING STACK

Adding power in an upper level can mean running wires from the basement to the attic. In a two-story home, you'd have three ceilings to go through. But in older homes, sometimes this is as easy as lowering a plumb bob along the plumbing vent stack and pulling up the cable. Newer homes might not have enough space around the stack, but it's worth checking first.

**Plumb bob**

## DON'T RUN CABLE IN DUCTWORK

Running cable inside ductwork, as convenient as it may be, is not allowed by code. You can run cable in plenum spaces like stud and joist bays for return air, but you'll need a plenum-rated cable. These cables have special jackets that are nontoxic and rated for fire. You can find plenum-rated Cat 6 and security cable at electrical supply stores. It will cost about twice as much as standard versions.

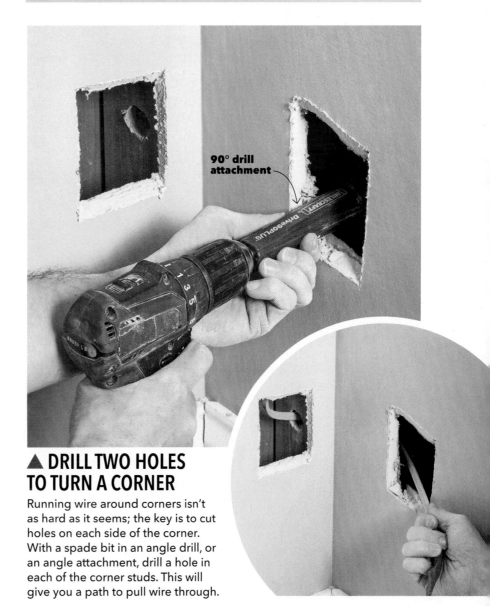

**90° drill attachment**

## ▲ DRILL TWO HOLES TO TURN A CORNER

Running wire around corners isn't as hard as it seems; the key is to cut holes on each side of the corner. With a spade bit in an angle drill, or an angle attachment, drill a hole in each of the corner studs. This will give you a path to pull wire through.

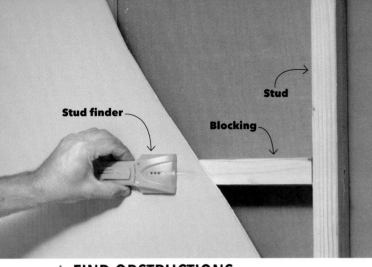

## ▲ FIND OBSTRUCTIONS

Before cutting any holes in walls, map out the route you want your wire to take. Scan the wall with a stud finder to locate any blocking that might obstruct that route. If there's blocking in one stud bay, the next one over might make a better path. You don't want to find out the hard way.

## ▲ DOUBLE-DUTY ACCESS HOLES

Instead of cutting new holes in your walls or ceilings, you can use holes that are already there. Remove light fixtures, switches or outlets to use existing holes, or plan ahead to use the access hole of a new fixture.

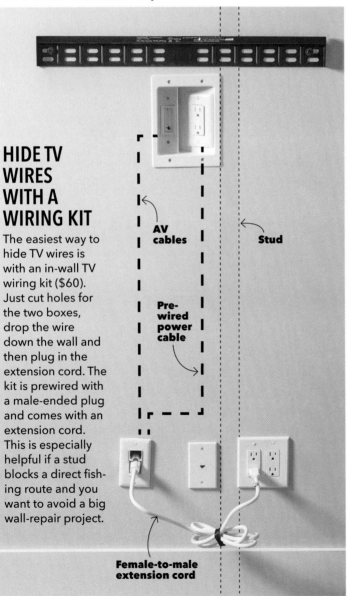

## HIDE TV WIRES WITH A WIRING KIT

The easiest way to hide TV wires is with an in-wall TV wiring kit ($60). Just cut holes for the two boxes, drop the wire down the wall and then plug in the extension cord. The kit is prewired with a male-ended plug and comes with an extension cord. This is especially helpful if a stud blocks a direct fishing route and you want to avoid a big wall-repair project.

## ▲ TUCK LOW-VOLTAGE WIRES

Low-voltage cable doesn't have the same installation requirements as household power cables. Speaker wire, cables that provide power to doorbells and thermostats, and communication lines like Cat 6 don't need to be run inside your walls. You can just tuck them under your baseboard, but not under carpet or rugs.

# Wire-fishing gear

Glow rods

Flex bit

Homemade hooks

### GLOW RODS

Glow rods are a staple for wire fishing. Just like steel tape, they can be pushed up walls and along ceilings, can usually be purchased in several lengths and can be screwed together for longer spans. Most come with a swivel eyelet tip and a hook tip. The luminescent rods glow in the dark, illuminating dark joist and stud bays. You can find them for $40 at home centers.

### FLEX BIT

If you need to run wire across a few joists or studs, reach for a flex bit. These bits come in long lengths, and extensions are available so you can drill holes through several joists. Each flex bit has an eyelet at the tip, so once you've made your holes, you can pull the wire back through with the same bit. One thing to note: Don't drill through insulation with these bits. Expect to pay about $50 for a 54-in. flex bit at a home center.

### HOMEMADE HOOKS

Some of my favorite fishing tools are ones you can make yourself. Small hooks made from cable or coat hangers let you grab cable just out of reach. Best of all, they're economical.

### 90-DEGREE DRILL ATTACHMENT

This is the perfect tool for drilling holes between stud bays. About $18 at most home centers, it's a lot cheaper than a dedicated angle drill and serves the same purpose. It can be a little tricky to use with larger bits, so hold on tight.

### WIRE-PULLING MAGNETS

With a few options at different prices, magnets are cool tools for pulling wire along an insulated stud bay. This Magnepull ($125) consists of a steel leader and a roller magnet. You can even use it to retrieve lost bits and other tools from inside walls. Wire-pulling magnets, which range from $40 to $125, can be found at electrical supply stores.

Roller magnet

Steel leader

90° drill attachment

Mud ring

### LOW-VOLTAGE MUD RING

I use mud rings to prevent marring drywall as I pull cable. They also have markers in the corners to outline the perfect hole size and shape for single-gang boxes. When you're done fishing, leave the mud ring in the wall and cover it with a blank faceplate to avoid patching (especially useful for hard-to-patch textured walls). These mud rings are available for less than $2 each at home centers.

### STEEL FISH TAPE

This long roll of stiff steel is great for pushing wire through insulated walls, up wall cavities and down long lengths of joists. A roll starts at $15 at home centers.

# BEAUTIFUL BACKYARD
# LIGHTING

**12 pointers for creating a safe and inviting outdoor space**

### BY JAY CORK

**D**on't let nightfall drive you indoors. Instead, create an inviting outdoor space with lights. Most outdoor lighting is low voltage, so it's safe and easy enough for any DIYer to install. I talked with Scott Pesta from Kichler Lighting to get his advice on creating a beautifully lit yard.

**MEET THE EXPERT**
Scott Pesta has been a landscape lighting technician with Kichler Lighting for 13 years.

**Surface-mounted lights**

**Staked bullet lights**

## Stick with a simple design

The first phase of any lighting project for the deck or yard is design. Scott says most DIYers start with too many lights. A simple installation of just a few lights makes a huge impact, he says. Start small and add more as needed.

**EXPERIMENT WITH CLAMP-ON LIGHTS** ·········································
Once you have a design in mind, use clamp-on lights to see if your design creates the look you want. Also, try out bulbs of different brightnesses and colors to determine what suits your installation best.

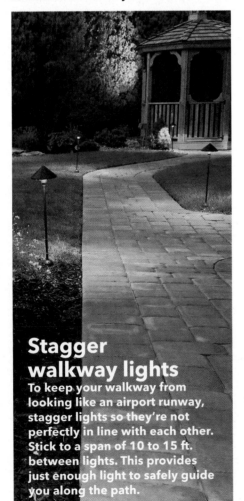

## Stagger walkway lights

To keep your walkway from looking like an airport runway, stagger lights so they're not perfectly in line with each other. Stick to a span of 10 to 15 ft. between lights. This provides just enough light to safely guide you along the path.

## Don't overlap light

Deck lighting is intended more for ambience than visibility. Scott recommends mounting lights far enough apart to avoid overlapping pools of light. For decks, choose fixtures that cast a 4- to 5-ft. pool of light. Position them 30 in. up off the deck floor and space them no more than 10 ft. apart.

**OVERLAPPED**

**CORRECT WAY**

## Illuminate stairways

Adding subtle lights to your deck stairs is not only aesthetically pleasing but also a safety feature for your deck at night.

## Solar is easy, but...

Options for solar landscape and deck lights have exploded at home centers. And there are good reasons to love them: instant installation, no wiring and no increase in your electric bill. But solar lights aren't as bright as those on a wired system. In some areas, that might be OK. But for a system that truly illuminates, choose low-voltage lighting.

**Solar panel**

**Solar panel**

**Solar deck post light**

**Solar stake light**

## Pick your transformer

A transformer's job is to convert 120-volt household current to 12-volt before sending it to power your fixtures. Until recently, you would have needed a 600- to 1,200-watt transformer to light an entire yard with halogen lamps. But because LEDs use fewer watts than halogen lamps, smaller transformers—45 to 300 watts—are usually all you need.

To determine the size transformer you need, add up the wattage for all the light fixtures you're planning to install, add 25% and then round up. In the example below, the installation calls for a 200-watt transformer.

**45 watts**

**200 watts**

| | |
|---|---|
| 4 STEP LIGHTS x 12 WATTS | **48 WATTS** |
| 3 POST LIGHTS x 20 WATTS | **60 WATTS** |
| 8 LANDSCAPE LIGHTS x 6 WATTS | **48 WATTS** |
| **SUBTOTAL** | **156 WATTS** |
| *ADD 25% EXCESS* | **40 WATTS** |
| **TRANSFORMER SIZE (ROUND UP)** | **200 WATTS** |

**Outdoor GFCI with cover**

## Use an outdoor GFCI outlet

No matter the size of your transformer, it needs to be plugged into an outdoor GFCI outlet on a dedicated circuit. If you're unsure about doing electrical work yourself, hire a licensed electrician.

## Use the right wire

Scott warns against using cheap, thin cable; it won't carry power far and isn't durable enough to withstand the elements. For most installations, 14-gauge cable is fine, but if your design calls for some long runs, plan to use heavier cable such as 12- or 10-gauge.

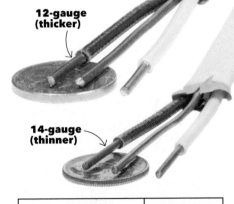

**12-gauge (thicker)**

**14-gauge (thinner)**

| CABLE LENGTH | WIRE SIZE |
|---|---|
| UP TO 100 FEET | **14-GAUGE** |
| 100 TO 250 FEET | **12-GAUGE** |
| 250-PLUS FEET | **10-GAUGE** |

### USE CONDUIT OR UF CABLE
**All outdoor wiring must be in conduit or be rated for direct burial.**

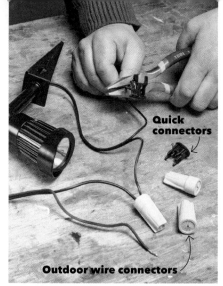

**Quick connectors**

**Outdoor wire connectors**

## Run wire under walkways
If you need to run wiring under an existing walkway, try this trick: Dig a small trench on both sides. Next, flatten one end of a piece of rigid metal conduit and use a sledgehammer to drive the conduit, flattened end first, horizontally under the walkway. Then cut off both ends of the conduit with a hacksaw. Finally, file off the sharp edges and feed your wire through the conduit. A 10-ft. stick of rigid steel conduit (the thick, heavy-duty stuff) is inexpensive and available at home centers.

**Sledgehammer**

**Rigid metal conduit with flattened end**

**File**

**Hacksaw**

## Use waterproof wire nuts
Some landscape lighting kits contain preinstalled quick connectors. Scott says these connectors work for a while but can corrode and fail over time if buried underground. Cut off the factory-installed connectors and splice the connections using gel-filled wire nuts made for outdoor use. They offer excellent protection for years of service, but they can't be reused.

## Indirect light for patios
Instead of focusing lights directly onto a patio, try lighting nearby objects, like landscaping elements and trees. This provides illumination without glare and creates attractive shadow effects.

# ROBOTIC MOWERS: WHAT TO KNOW

BY BILL BERGMANN

If you're intrigued by the idea of having a robot mow your lawn, you're not alone. We couldn't resist trying out this Husqvarna 450X Automower. Here are five things we learned:

## Boundary Setup

Robotic mowers require a boundary wire around the perimeter of your yard and any obstacles like trees or garden beds. Some also need a wire to guide them back to their charging dock. The setup for a typical city lot can be done in an afternoon.

## Phone App Control

Newer robotic mowers operate via a phone app. The Husqvarna uses GPS to map out your yard, and its Smart Connect app creates no-go zones where the mower might get stuck. The app also sets the cutting height and mowing schedules, accesses performance monitors, and connects with Alexa or Google Assistant.

## Noise Level and Safety

Robotic mowers are much quieter than gas mowers. The 450X runs at about 59 dB, compared to a gas mower's 95 dB. For safety, an auto-stop feature cuts power if the mower tips over. Also, there's ample space between the deck rim of the 450X and the blade, preventing hands or feet from reaching the blades accidentally. Regardless, it's best to turn it off when kids are playing in the yard.

## Continual Operation

Robotic mowers cut off only a fraction of an inch at a time, going back to the charger and starting up again to complete the job if necessary. Instead of a weekly job, mowing is done continually to keep your lawn well kept all the time. The Husqvarna varies its cut pattern and its route to the charger for optimal lawn health and appearance.

## Cost

The Husqvarna 450X costs $3,500 online. A Robomow RS630 runs about $2,300. Both cut up to 3/4 acre and have similar features. Both the 450X and the Robomow have antitheft features to protect your investment. The initial cost is high, but considering time saved, the cost of gas or the price of a lawn care service, it might be worth it.

# SMART UPGRADES

**Remote**

## PROGRAMMABLE SHADES

**BY BILL BERGMANN**

Given the cost of window coverings, one might not even consider paying extra for shades with luxury features, and those with remote control certainly fit in that category. However, now that mechanized shades are becoming "smart," the benefits might outweigh the pain of the luxury price tag.

Smart shades allow you to set up daily schedules for automatically opening and closing the shades, maximizing passive solar for warmth in the winter and minimizing it in the summer. The Hunter Douglas PowerView Hub uses light and temperature sensors to raise and lower your shades. You can also customize settings for specific rooms.

Like programmable lights, your shades will operate even when you are away, for a measure of security.

The Hunter Douglas Duette smart shades in our homeLAB offer energy savings. As with all honeycomb shades, multiple layers of fabric form cells to provide thermal insulation. They also insulate against sound and improve a room's acoustics.

## CONNECTED ALARM SYSTEM

**BY BILL BERGMANN**

If you'd like to upgrade your old wired security system to the world of smart technology, try one of these options that use your existing system. This Konnected interface installs in your alarm panel and integrates your existing sensors into several home automation platforms, including Samsung SmartThings, Home Assistant, Hubitat and OpenHAB.

These systems enable automation functions like lights turning on if a sensor is tripped or, in combination with a voice assistant like Alexa, announcing that a specific door or window is open.

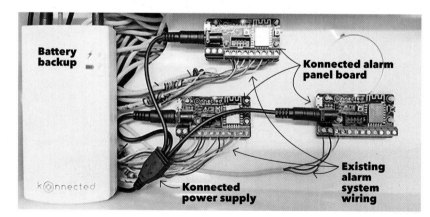

Battery backup

Konnected alarm panel board

Konnected power supply

Existing alarm system wiring

You can also monitor your system from your smartphone. Most of these kits still offer the assurance of an automated 911 call when alarms are triggered.

Some old systems aren't compatible with smart upgrades, so check with the smart system manufacturer before you buy. A six-zone Konnected kit costs $100. Twelve-, 18- and 24-zone kits are also available. Adding a battery backup ($38) lets you monitor your home during a power outage. If you're tech smart and DIY savvy, you'll find the installation straightforward.

Install it on the wall

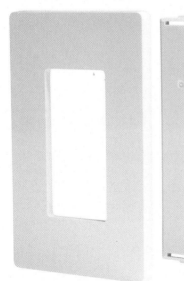

Or use it as a remote

Smart Plug adapter

**SWITCH VS. REMOTE**
I prefer using the wireless wall switch as a remote control, but it can also be mounted on the wall with included screws or removable tape. You can install the switch under a standard wall plate, too.

**Wall plate cover**

**Wall plate bracket**

**Wire-free switch**

# WIRE-FREE SWITCH
## BY GLENN HANSEN

Lighting hasn't been this cool and this fun since the lava lamp. Add in the convenience of light-switch-anywhere technology and this GE product mash-up sends that lava lamp straight to your garage-sale pile.

I tested a few items in the C by GE product line, starting with the Smart Switch. This wire-free switch mounts anywhere, is battery-powered and can control GE's Smart Bulbs and items plugged into GE's Smart Plug. Plus, it handles dimming and color control for bulbs that are so equipped.

It took me some time to grasp the wireless functionality. Powered by a common button battery, this switch attaches to any wall with screws or removable tape. The included wall plate cover hides the fasteners for a clean look. You can also mount it in a standard box and use a wall plate matching others in your house. I use it like a remote control; it sits on my bedside table. I love that I can easily change the light color or dim the bulb for late-night reading when my wife is asleep.

Of course, the switch needs a GE Smart family member to communicate with. Easiest and most versatile is the Smart Plug, which makes anything plugged in a smart thing. Control a lamp, turn a radio on or off, fire up a fan—the smart plug can handle any regular plugged appliance.

Now add a Smart Bulb to any lamp or light fixture and turn up the fun. I tried both the Full Color Smart Bulb and the Tunable White Smart Bulb. Both bulbs use Bluetooth technology to connect with the Smart Switch for easy-to-control lighting. I can also control the bulbs from the C by GE app installed on my phone, and that's free to use. If you use Alexa or Google Home in a smart home setting, you get even more connectivity options.

I had big fun with the color array of the Full Color bulb. My Smart Switch turns the light on and off, dims it to my desire and controls color settings. I haven't yet created any "scenes," but I can do so with the Smart Bulb and save settings using the app. And with the Tunable White bulb, I get to select cool daylight tones for early morning and warmer tones for nighttime. I can also set schedules for on and off, and I can control the bulbs from anywhere, with or without my remote Smart Switch.

# ELIMINATE WI-FI DEAD SPOTS

## Get strong Wi-Fi everywhere in your home—no expertise required!

BY JAY CORK

***It*** seems like almost everything is Wi-Fi enabled now. Computers, printers, home security systems, digital home assistants, even lightbulbs! While this can make life convenient, it's incredibly frustrating when things go wrong. I've discovered the solution usually isn't complicated or expensive. Here's a number of easy, low-tech tips for eliminating Wi-Fi dead spots and improving your home network.

**MEET THE EXPERT**
Jay Cork is an associate editor at *Family Handyman*. One of his many past professions was installing home telecommunication, network and audio systems.

**Netgear Nighthawk AC1900 router ($160)**

# TEST WI-FI STRENGTH WITH YOUR PHONE

With the help of a Wi-Fi analyzer app on your phone, you can determine the strength of the Wi-Fi signal throughout your house. I use a free one from *olgor.com*, and it's a really great tool. To use it, simply walk around your house and watch how the Wi-Fi signal changes. The higher the negative number, the better. For example, negative 40 is better than negative 70. Make some corrective changes, then walk around the house again to see if the signal has improved.

**Fine-tune your Wi-Fi signal by switching to a less congested channel**

# UPGRADE YOUR ROUTER ANTENNA

If your router has an external antenna, you should be able to swap it out for a more powerful one. They're available online for about $25 and are very easy to change—simply unscrew the old one and attach the new one. For best results, choose an antenna that provides at least 9 dB of boost.

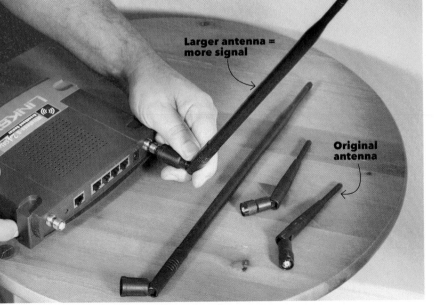

**Larger antenna = more signal**

**Original antenna**

## MOVE THE ROUTER

One of the simplest fixes to improve Wi-Fi coverage is to simply move the router to a new location in your home. I know it doesn't seem logical, but a router placed in an upper floor broadcasts to the lower floors better than a router in the basement broadcasting upward. You might have to experiment, but start with a central location and go from there. Avoid locations with obvious barriers, like under a stairway or in a closet.

## PLUG IN WHEN POSSIBLE

A router can handle only so many wireless devices competing for the available bandwidth. Whenever possible, plug into your router with an ethernet cable. This frees up more bandwidth for other Wi-Fi devices.

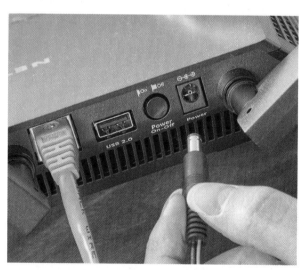

Linksys AC750 WiFi extender ($70)

## ADD A WI-FI RANGE EXTENDER

If some areas of your house are getting weak coverage, like the basement workshop or the garage, a Wi-Fi range extender may be a good solution. They're relatively inexpensive ($50 to $150) and very easy to set up; all you need to do is plug it into an open outlet.

## UNPLUG YOUR ROUTER

If you're having problems with devices connecting to the internet at home, the first thing you should do is unplug the power cable from your router, wait about a minute and plug it back in. Often this simple step, called rebooting, will get things back up and running just like magic. Even if you're not having problems, reboot once a week to keep your router operating smoothly. In fact, some routers are programmable to automatically reboot at a scheduled time.

# Change your router settings and boost your Wi-Fi

Changing some of your router settings can greatly improve Wi-Fi performance. You have to log in to the "admin console," which is easier than it sounds. You can access the admin console by typing a series of numbers, called an IP address, into your internet browser. The default IP address of most routers is usually 192.168.1.1. It's typically printed on a label on the router or found in the user manual along with the default user-name and password.

## 1. Avoid congested Wi-Fi channels

Cordless phones, baby monitors, smart devices and even microwave ovens all operate on the 2.4-GHz frequency band. Even your neighbor's wireless network can add to the confusion. But the way to improve perfor-mance is to log in to your router and change the channel. Each frequency band has multiple channels to choose from, and the Wi-Fi analyzer app has a function that helps determine what channels are congested.

## 2. Set priorities

Most modern routers have Quality of Service (QoS) tools to limit the amount of bandwidth that apps use. After logging in to your router's admin console, you can prioritize which apps and devices get the highest speed. This can free up bandwidth.

## 3. Don't skimp on security

Don't let anyone piggyback on your Wi-Fi or, worse yet, gain access to your computers! If your firewall is turned off or you are not using encryption, anybody within range can access your Wi-Fi network. Log in to your router's admin console and make sure the firewall is turned on. Also, double-check that your router's encryption mode is set to WPA2-AES. Older encryption modes like WEP can be easily hacked.

## 4. Upgrade your router firmware

Log in to your router's admin console and look for a software update button. Just like the operating system on your home computer or smartphones, a router's firmware needs to be updated occasionally to fix bugs or provide security updates.

TP-Link Deco M3 mesh router ($120)

Google Nest Wifi ($300)

Netgear EX6400 WiFi extender ($150)

## UPGRADE TO A MESH NETWORK

Mesh networks are great solutions for large houses and those with multiple levels. Instead of purchasing individual extenders, you buy them as a complete system with a dedicated router and multiple satellite extenders, which means they can't be used with your current wireless router. Mesh networks typically cost a little more, so expect to pay at least $300 for a system.

This router has no room to breathe!

## DON'T CROWD YOUR ROUTER

If your router is tucked into a crowded bookshelf or behind a piece of furniture, the airflow may not be adequate to keep it cool. This is bad. When a router overheats, it will start to perform poorly; eventually it will just shut down. Put the router in a place that allows sufficient airflow.

## *Smart devices use the 2.4-GHz frequency*

Smart locks, smart switches and hubs need a router that operates on the 2.4-GHz frequency band. Most modern routers can be set up to broadcast on either 2.4 GHz or 5 GHz. If you're having problems connecting your smart tech, make sure your router is set to broadcast on 2.4 GHz.

# 3 Plumbing, HVAC & Appliances

# TROUBLE-FREE
# PEX

## Advice for leak-free plumbing

BY JAY CORK

**P**EX plumbing is inexpensive and reliable, not to mention fast and almost goof-proof to install. Almost. Some mistakes can lead to leaks right after installation—or years down the road. To learn how to avoid these mistakes, I talked with a 21-year veteran plumber who has seen them all.

**MEET THE EXPERT**
Master plumber Bret Hepola owns and operates All City Plumbing.

# Bret uses PEX-A

Home centers commonly carry two types of PEX piping: PEX-A and PEX-B. PEX-A has several advantages over PEX-B: It installs faster, it's more flexible and it's less likely to burst when frozen. For these reasons, PEX-A makes sense for Bret. But for most DIYers doing a small job, PEX-B might be a less expensive option—taking into account both the price per foot and the required tools.

# Bret's favorite tools

### PEX CUTTER
The bottom jaw of this cutter is flat and cradles the pipe, making quick work of cutting PEX perfectly straight. Find it at your home center for about $20.

### GREASE PENCIL
Regular pencils and markers don't work well for marking PEX. Use a grease pencil to make highly visible marks that won't rub off.

### MILWAUKEE PROPEX EXPANDER
The full kit is pricey ($450), but you'll actually enjoy installing PEX-A piping with this tool. (PEX-B tubing requires a different tool.) If the job you're doing is small, consider renting one for about $40 a day.

# Go with the branch method

PEX lines can be run in two ways: With the manifold method, individual lines run from a manifold directly to every fixture, and with the branch method, lines branch off to the kitchen and bathrooms, then branch off again to each fixture. While manifolds allow greater control over individual fixtures, they use up to three times the material and waste a lot of hot water. That's why Bret believes the branch method is the way to go.

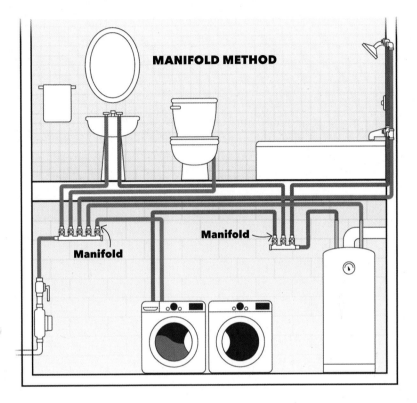

MANIFOLD METHOD

Manifold

Manifold

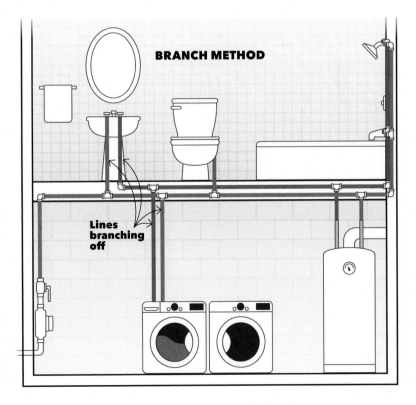

BRANCH METHOD

Lines branching off

## Give the hot lines extra support

PEX lines sag over time, especially the hot ones. PEX is supposed to be supported by straps every 32 in. However, because the hot lines have a greater tendency to sag, Bret always places their hangers closer together.

16"

32"

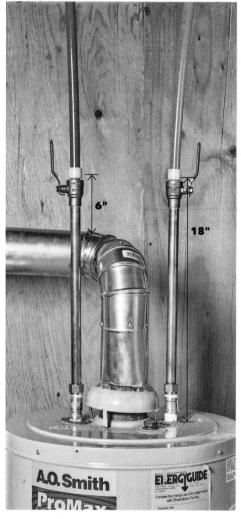

6"

18"

A.O. Smith
ENERGYGUIDE
ProMax

Move the heat around the fitting

## Keep PEX away from hot spots

PEX is plastic and can melt. If you're running PEX to your water heater, there must be an 18-in. extension up from the tank. Also, keep PEX at least 6 in. away from any exhaust flue.

## Heat a leaky fitting

If your PEX-A fitting has a small leak, try warming it with a heat gun. This momentarily softens the plastic, which then again contracts around the fitting. This is a big time-saver for Bret; instead of removing and replacing a fitting, he'll first try heating it.

## Repair kinks in PEX-A with heat

PEX-A tubing is stronger and more flexible than PEX-B, and kinks in PEX-A can be repaired by applying a little heat. If PEX-B gets kinked, the damaged section must be cut out and repaired with a coupling.

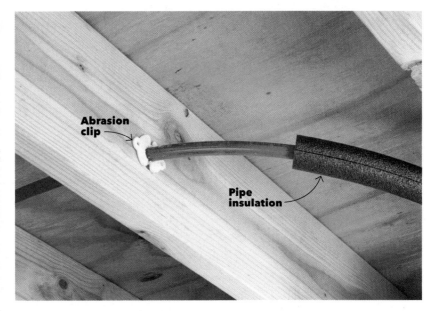

## Protect your PEX

If PEX needs to be run through a joist space where it can't be fastened, Bret suggests that you first wrap it in pipe insulation. This protects it from nails or other protrusions during installation and guards against abrasion from water hammering. He also uses an abrasion clip to protect the PEX when it passes through the joist adjacent to a bend.

## Colors are optional

PEX tubing comes in three colors: red, blue and white. But there's no difference in the material. Bret uses only the white PEX because having only one spool in one color makes his job simpler. For most DIYers, the red and blue colors help keep everything clear and quickly identifiable.

**STICKS OR COILS?**
For the large jobs Bret usually takes on, he uses large coils of PEX. However, the average homeowner may find it easier to purchase sticks of PEX rather than coils. Because PEX has "memory," a coil wants to stay coiled, making installation difficult in tight places.

Red for hot

Blue for cold

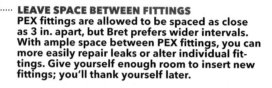

### LEAVE SPACE BETWEEN FITTINGS

PEX fittings are allowed to be spaced as close as 3 in. apart, but Bret prefers wider intervals. With ample space between PEX fittings, you can more easily repair leaks or alter individual fittings. Give yourself enough room to insert new fittings; you'll thank yourself later.

## Use copper stub-outs

You can connect shutoff valves directly to PEX, but Bret prefers to use copper stub-outs for sink and toilet connections because they provide a more solid connection to the shutoff valves.

**Expansion/ contraction loop**

## Give PEX room to move

Long runs of PEX expand and contract a lot. This stresses the fittings. For runs longer than 40 ft., create an expansion loop along the way.

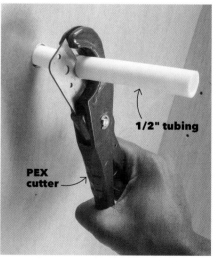

**1/2" tubing**

**PEX cutter**

## Cut it straight

Angled cuts can lead to leaks. To ensure a proper marriage between the PEX and the fittings, you need a cutter specifically designed for plastic tubing. A cutter costs only $20 or so and is designed to make this job simple. With a little care, you can easily cut PEX perfectly square.

# MECHANICALS

## HVAC & Plumbing Plans

**American Standard ERV air exchanger**

**American Standard Gold humidifier**

**American Standard Platinum 95 furnace**

**American Standard Accuclean whole-home air cleaner**

**Hookup not complete as shown**

BY JAY CORK

**W**hen sized correctly for your home, your furnace and water heater will each provide a long life of efficient service. We estimated the Btu requirements for our furnace by multiplying our square footage by the heating factor for Climate Zone 6 (50 to 60 Btu per square foot). Working with our technician from American Standard Heating & Air Conditioning, we sized our furnace perfectly for our needs at the *Family Handyman* Getaway.

## Save on propane with dual fuel

We chose a dual-fuel air conditioner that supplements our furnace until the outside air temperature drops to around 20 degrees. Below that temperature, the variable-speed furnace will take over to efficiently heat the home. This reduces our annual propane usage.

## No big tank to heat!

We chose a high-efficiency, on-demand tankless water heater, eliminating the big water tank so we don't need to heat 50 gallons of water while we are away from the Getaway. It was also easier and less expensive to install the necessary venting.

## Breathe easy

Our system makes the most of the fresh air around us. The air exchanger enhances the efficiency of the system by removing stale air and replacing it with outdoor air. The American Standard Accuclean whole-home air cleaner removes allergens and dust to maximize the quality of the air inside.

## Balance size with demand

Sizing a tankless water heater involved a tricky balance. We looked at maximum demand (in gallons per minute), the incoming water temperature and the desired hot water temperature. Joel Myers of My Plumbers, LLC, helped us determine that 6 gpm is our maximum possible hot water demand. Groundwater in this zone is about 45 degrees, and we want our hot water to be 115 degrees. To accommodate a 70-degree rise at 6 gpm, we chose the gas-powered Navien NPE-240S2.

## Well water challenges

Yes, you can use a tankless water heater with well water, but it will require some maintenance. Sediment and lime scale buildup can be a problem. We will drain and flush our system once a year at least. We can add a sediment filter later on if we determine that annual draining and flushing aren't doing the job.

# A SHOWER WITH POWER

## Get a better flow with these tips from a pro

BY BILL BERGMANN

**E**ver come home from a fancy hotel stay and find yourself disappointed by your own shower? If your showerhead is weak, you may think it's caused by low water pressure—and it could be—but it's more likely that faulty plumbing or fixtures are reducing the flow or volume of water at your showerhead. I sat down with Master Plumber Suzanne Boyer to sleuth out this situation, discuss common causes and offer solutions.

**MEET THE EXPERT**

**Suzanne Boyer** *is among the 4.3% of master plumbers nationally who are women. In her 20-plus years of experience, her M.O. has become simple: "My purpose is to help people. Plumbing allows me to do that. I make people smile. That's what it's all about."*

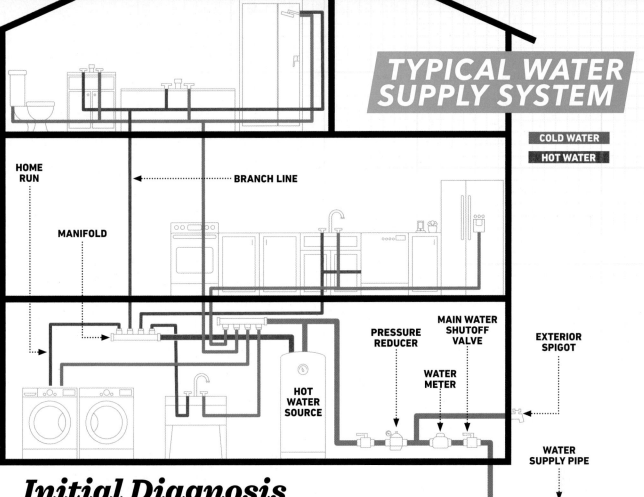

HOME RUN

BRANCH LINE

MANIFOLD

PRESSURE REDUCER

MAIN WATER SHUTOFF VALVE

EXTERIOR SPIGOT

WATER METER

HOT WATER SOURCE

WATER SUPPLY PIPE

# Initial Diagnosis

## MAIN WATER PRESSURE

If your plumbing fixtures don't provide an adequate stream of water, the water pressure entering your home could be low. However, Boyer says the water pressure from the street is usually too high instead of too low. Optimal pressure is about 40 to 60 pounds per square inch (psi). Boyer has seen it as high as 150 to 200 psi. And that's why many homes have a water pressure regulator or pressure reducing valve (PRV) installed near where the water main enters the house. Low water flow in your house could be caused by a faulty PRV, or the main water valve could be clogged or stuck partially open.

You can check the water pressure coming into your house using a water pressure gauge that costs about $10. Attach the gauge to an outdoor spigot near your water main and open the spigot valve. If it reads well above 60 psi, you need a new PRV. If it's below 40 psi (and it's probably not), check with neighbors to see what they're experiencing. The next step is to call a plumber;

you may have a leak somewhere. In the meantime, keep reading, because we might have a fix for you and your inadequate showerhead.

## BRANCH LINE OR HOME RUN?

If you experience low water flow with just a few fixtures in your home, like in your shower, you may have a clogged branch line or a line that's plumbed incorrectly or has too many fixtures on it. It's common in older homes to have more than one fixture on the same supply pipe.

The new homes that Boyer plumbs have direct supply pipes, or "home runs," serving each fixture. She says it's best to have one dedicated branch supply line for each bathroom. She often gets calls to correct this issue for clients and then ends up upgrading most of the plumbing in these older homes.

"Today's PEX piping installs so much faster and cheaper than copper, so redoing the supply piping in a whole house is an affordable upgrade, especially if you get them all taken care of in one fell swoop."

## HOT OR COLD?

If the amount of hot and cold are unbalanced, the first things to check, Boyer says, are any shutoff valves that are integral to the supply piping. They could be faulty or just not open completely. If it's only hot that's lacking, you could

have a water heater issue, but more likely it's calcium buildup in the fixture itself. Boyer says most municipal water has a disinfecting additive called chloramine that will cause calcification, especially in the hot side of a fixture.

Chloramine is also known to break down rubber seals. A whole-house carbon filter can remove the chlorine and contaminants, including particulate matter, but it won't remove any of the ammonia that is found in chloramine.

# The Simple Fixes

**SHOWERHEAD:** It could be all in your head—your showerhead, that is. Calcium or iron deposits can affect water flow through the showerhead. A good soaking in a 1:1 solution of vinegar and water will break down particle buildup that you can then scrub off with an old toothbrush. Either remove the showerhead or tie on a plastic bag full of the solution. Check the manufacturer's guidance for cleaning. Vinegar can damage the finish of some showerheads.

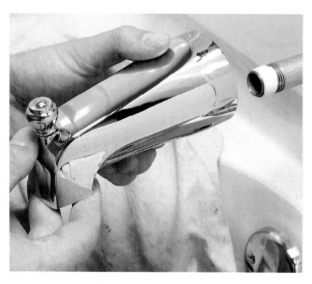

**TUB SPOUT DIVERTER:** For a shower in the bathtub, the tub/shower diverter in the spout may be cheating your shower of adequate flow. Grab a pipe wrench or wide-mouth pliers and, after wrapping the spout with a rag to protect the finish, remove the spout and examine the diverter gate to see if it's stuck or clogged. Boyer says you can fix the diverter mechanism with a rebuild kit, or go buy a new diverter spout for less than $50.

**VALVE CARTRIDGE:** If your showerhead isn't the problem, check the valve cartridge. Remove the handle and faceplate to access the cartridge. Cartridges vary. For many, you remove a retainer clip to get the cartridge out (you may need a specific puller tool). Examine the plastic and rubber seals. You can clean it all with vinegar and water, but if it looks worse for wear, it's best to get a new cartridge. "Most manufacturers stand behind their warranties," says Boyer, "and will provide a replacement for free."

## THE NOT-SO-SIMPLE FIX

**FAULTY SUPPLY PIPES:** Steel pipes are the most common cause of low water flow in older homes. They don't last forever, even though they're galvanized. The steel pipes will eventually rust from the inside, creating sediment and buildup that restrict flow and clog fixtures.

If your water runs rusty after periods of no use or if you see rusty deposits in your showerhead, your home's old pipes may need to be replaced. With the advent of PEX piping, "these pipes are much easier to replace than back in the copper piping days," Boyer says. If you're upgrading, replace all the piping, not just the easily accessible pipes. Some home sellers will do a partial plumbing upgrade, replacing just the most visible steel pipes with copper or PEX, leaving the steel pipes where they're not visible and where they're more expensive to replace.

## DIY PLUMBING IS NOW EASIER THAN EVER

New materials and technologies have simplified the work of copper plumbing, but that doesn't mean plumbers are charging any less. You might want to do this upgrade yourself. Plumbing has always been an intimidating task for DIYers, but now with PEX piping and more push-to-connect fittings, it's far less daunting. Push-to-connect fittings are now code approved in most states, and PEX piping is affordable and available even at the corner hardware store. It's now more feasible than ever to consider replumbing the water supply in your home.

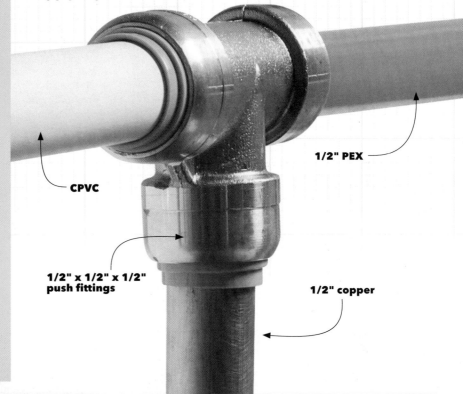

CPVC

1/2" PEX

1/2" x 1/2" x 1/2" push fittings

1/2" copper

## LOW-FLOW SHOWERHEADS— IT'S THE LAW

The average family uses nearly 40 gallons of water each day just by showering. That's a lot of water— nearly one-fifth of all residential indoor water use (according to the EPA). And it's why, beginning in the early 1990s, Congress set a 2.5 gallon-per-minute maximum flow rate for showerheads. Now showerhead design has become key. You can enjoy the shower you want even with a low-flow showerhead that puts out 2.0 gpm.

Do your homework, and shop wisely. "Do not go cheap," says Boyer. "You rely on efficient water flowing in your house every day. You can feel the weight difference in a quality fixture made of brass and ceramic, not plastic and thin steel. It's just one of those things you'll appreciate every day."

# HOME CARE

A gallon or two should do the trick

## DRAIN YOUR WATER HEATER

### BY JAY CORK

**P**eriodically draining your water heater will extend its life and lower your energy bills. Over time, sediment collects at the bottom of the tank. On gas-powered heaters, this creates hot spots that can damage the tank and cause leaks. On an electric water heater, sediment buildup can cause the lower heating element to fail prematurely. Curtis recommends clearing sediment from your water heater at least once a year.

**MEET THE EXPERT**
Curtis Petersen lives in St. Paul, Minnesota, and keeps two luxury apartment buildings in perfect condition. The tenants love him!

## TIGHTEN-FROM-THE-TOP FAUCET INSTALL

### BY GLENN HANSEN

**W**oodworking jobs are great; we get to cut and drill on the *top side* of the workbench. For many plumbing projects, however, we're often straining below a kitchen cabinet. Down there, it's cramped, dark and crowded, and special tools may be required.

Pfister is changing that with its Top Pfit faucets. The design allows "above-the-deck" installation so you won't need to borrow or buy a basin wrench. Instead, you secure this faucet from the top side of the kitchen sink using a simple tool included with the purchase.

We installed the Ladera model faucet. This one-handle model has a pull-down spray head and other nice features, but its installation method is why we gave it a standing ovation. To install it (with or without a deck plate), hold the body of the faucet and feed the supply lines and attached bracket through the hole in the countertop. Then insert the special install tool into the head of the spout and begin tightening. You can do this by hand, with a screwdriver or with a drill/driver—it's all clearly outlined in Pfister's instructions. The install tool pivots and tightens the bracket to secure the faucet spout to the counter and sink.

It's that easy—installed completely from the top of the sink. Save your back and your knuckles, and have no fear of banging your head inside the cabinet. Of course, you'll have to go below deck to remove the old faucet, but that will be the last time!

## GAS OVEN WON'T LIGHT? THERE'S AN EASY FIX

If your oven won't light, first verify that it's plugged in and getting power and that the gas valve is open. If your oven still won't light, you probably need a new igniter. Even if you see the igniter glowing, it can be faulty.

First, turn off the gas valve and power for the oven. We removed the burner to the igniter **(Photo 1)**, but on some ovens this isn't necessary. To take out the igniter, remove the screws that secure it to the burner. Then remove the wires. Some igniters simply unplug. Others, like ours, require you to cut and strip the wires and connect the new igniter using the special ceramic wire connectors included with the igniter **(Photo 2)**.

Remove 1/2 in. of insulation from the wires with a wire-stripping tool. Connect the new igniter by aligning the ends of the stripped wires and twisting on the ceramic wire connectors. Reassemble the igniter and burner in the reverse order.

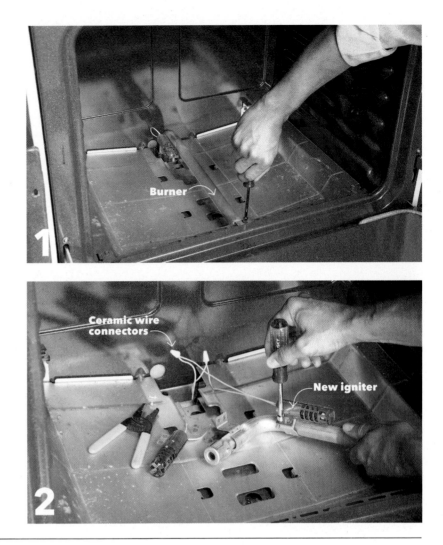

Burner

Ceramic wire connectors

New igniter

---

# FURNACE FILTER RATINGS DECODED

**MERV 6**
Home Basic

COMPARABLE TO MPR 300 & FPR N/A

**MERV 8**
Home Select

COMPARABLE TO MPR 600 & FPR 5

**MERV 11**
Home Plus

COMPARABLE TO MPR 1000-1200 & FPR 7

**MERV 13**
Home Ultimate

COMPARABLE TO MPR 1500-1900 & FPR 10

For optimum performance, comfort and system longevity, you need the right filter for your equipment. The industry standard for rating HVAC filter performance is MERV (minimum efficiency reporting value), but it's not the only rating system in use.

The other two are MPR (microparticle performance rating) and FPR (filter performance rating), used by 3M and Home Depot, respectively. The chart shows the standard MERV filter ratings plus their equivalents in the other rating systems.

**Kara Caldwell is the digital marketing manager at Air Filters Direct.**

# THE DIRT ON SEPTIC SYSTEMS

## What you need to know before & after installation

BY BRAD HOLDEN

### DO

- Keep grass or other vegetation growing on the drain field to prevent erosion and promote evaporation.
- Keep a sketch of your system handy, so you know where to access all of its components.
- Watch for settling soil that might direct water onto the drain field.
- Keep on top of system maintenance.
- Fix leaky faucets and toilets.
- Keep records of repairs, maintenance and your pumping schedule.
- Make sure the tank cover is accessible.
- A septic system can last 25 years or more. Your property will have a second area earmarked for a subsequent septic system. Protect this reserve area from soil compaction.

### DON'T

- Plant trees or shrubs near the system. Roots can damage pipes.
- Drive or park on the drain field.
- Build over the drain field or cover it with a hard surface.
- Let faucets run unnecessarily.
- Install automatic sprinklers that water over the system.
- Excessively water the grass on the drain field.
- Put anything but waste and wastewater into the tank.
- Use caustic drain cleaners.

### MEET THE EXPERT

Sara Heger is an instructor and researcher in the onsite sewage treatment program at the University of Minnesota.

## WHAT TYPE OF SYSTEM DO YOU NEED?

The soil test determines whether you can install a septic system or just a holding tank. What's the difference?

**HOLDING TANK:** A holding tank stores waste until it needs to be pumped out. It has an alarm to let you know when it's time. Don't ignore the alarm.

**SEPTIC SYSTEM:** A typical in-ground gravity septic system consists of a septic tank with lines running to a drain field. The septic tank may have a filter, which removes particles down to 1/8 in., and directs the effluent to the drain field, where the waste is treated and absorbed into the soil.

**ADVANCED TREATMENT SYSTEM:** A small percentage of homes may need more than a septic tank prior to discharge of the wastewater to the soil.

Common options for advanced pretreatment are aerobic treatment units and media filters. Mound systems can also work if your property has a high water table, very rocky soil or soil that is either too permeable or not permeable enough. This type of system treats and purifies wastewater in an above-ground mound before it enters the soil.

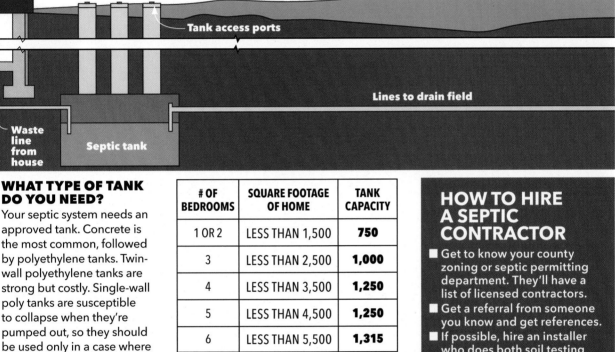

Tank access ports

Lines to drain field

Waste line from house

Septic tank

## WHAT TYPE OF TANK DO YOU NEED?

Your septic system needs an approved tank. Concrete is the most common, followed by polyethylene tanks. Twin-wall polyethylene tanks are strong but costly. Single-wall poly tanks are susceptible to collapse when they're pumped out, so they should be used only in a case where lot-line restrictions are so tight that the new tank can reach its destination only by collapsing.

| # OF BEDROOMS | SQUARE FOOTAGE OF HOME | TANK CAPACITY |
|---|---|---|
| 1 OR 2 | LESS THAN 1,500 | **750** |
| 3 | LESS THAN 2,500 | **1,000** |
| 4 | LESS THAN 3,500 | **1,250** |
| 5 | LESS THAN 4,500 | **1,250** |
| 6 | LESS THAN 5,500 | **1,315** |

### WHAT SIZE TANK DO YOU NEED?

The graph above is a general guideline. Regulations vary by state.

### HOUSEHOLD SIZE (# OF PEOPLE)

| TANK SIZE (GALLONS) | 1 | 2 | 3 | 4 | 5 | 6 | 7 | 8 | 9 | 10 |
|---|---|---|---|---|---|---|---|---|---|---|
| **500** | 5.8 | 2.6 | 1.5 | 1.0 | 0.07 | 0.04 | 0.03 | 0.01 | | |
| **750** | 9.1 | 4.2 | 2.6 | 1.8 | 1.3 | 1.0 | 0.07 | 0.06 | 0.04 | 0.03 |
| **1,000** | 12.4 | 5.9 | 3.7 | 2.6 | 2.0 | 1.5 | 1.2 | 1.0 | 0.8 | 0.7 |
| **1,250** | | 7.5 | 4.8 | 3.4 | 2.6 | 2.0 | 1.7 | 1.4 | 1.2 | 1.0 |
| **1,500** | | 9.1 | 5.9 | 4.2 | 3.3 | 2.6 | 2.1 | 1.8 | 1.5 | 1.3 |
| **1,750** | | | 6.5 | 5.0 | 3.9 | 3.1 | 2.6 | 2.0 | 1.9 | 1.6 |

## WHAT ABOUT MAINTENANCE?

Your drain field and system need monitoring and inspecting. Filters may need cleaning as often as every year, and the tank needs to be pumped out periodically. The chart above shows how often (in years) each tank size needs to be pumped depending on the number of occupants. Again, this is just an example, and regulations vary by state. A typical modern septic tank has three manhole covers: one to access the pump, one to access the filter and one to pump out the tank.

## HOW TO HIRE A SEPTIC CONTRACTOR

■ Get to know your county zoning or septic permitting department. They'll have a list of licensed contractors.

■ Get a referral from someone you know and get references.

■ If possible, hire an installer who does both soil testing and septic installation. That shortens the timeline for septic installation, as the contractor already knows the specifics and doesn't need to do any homework or talk with the soil tester. A case could also be made to get a design and then have several installers bid on the design. In some areas, the permitting authority or an engineer is required to do the design.

■ While percolation tests, or "perc tests," are still in use, the trend is moving toward a detailed soil description. A soil description gives a more accurate picture of the absorption rate of your soil, helping the installer design a system optimized for your location.

Septic alarm system

### IF SOMETHING DOES GO WRONG

If something goes wrong with a system that includes a pump, an alarm will alert you to the problem. If the alarm sounds, don't just call any septic company for repair; call the installer or whoever has been regularly servicing the system. They know your system and may be able to diagnose the problem before they arrive, saving you time and money.

Your installer should provide you and the permitting authority a packet of information that details system maintenance, tank specifics, soil treatment specifics and an as-built map of the system. This detail will be vital in case the system installer/designer isn't available for repair or maintenance.

# IN COLD CLIMATES, PROTECT YOUR SEPTIC SYSTEM FROM FREEZING

Like water pipes, your septic system can freeze. Here are some tips to prevent your septic system from freezing.

- Use it. Without hot water going through the system, it's susceptible to freezing, which can damage the tank, the piping, and the filter and its housing, causing waste to back up into the house—all costly and undesirable.

- When you have good snow cover over your system, don't shovel it off. The undisturbed snow is good insulation.

- If you don't have adequate snow cover before the temperature drops below freezing, insulate the system using straw bales or purpose-made insulating blankets.

- Stop mowing the grass over the system a few weeks before the end of the growing season. Extra vegetation provides another layer of insulation.

- Don't leave a trickle of water running—as people do to prevent pipes from freezing—since that can be just enough cold water added to your septic system to cause an ice clog.

- If you won't be using the home in the winter, keeping it heated at 56 to 58 degrees F is one option for freeze prevention.

- If you're rarely there during the winter and will be draining your water/winterizing your home, be sure to have the tank pumped out before freezing temperatures set in.

- Bury your septic tank as deep as possible. Septic tanks are buried to help prevent freezing. The maximum depth for a concrete tank is 8 ft. to the top of the tank. Plastic tanks can't be buried as deep as concrete (only a maximum of 24 in.). Burying a tank deep does make maintenance more difficult, as it's hard to see into the corners where sludge can build up.

- After installation, septic tanks "settle" for up to a year. The area over the tank and drain field should be "crowned" to minimize the effect of settling. This is important because water pooling around the tank freezes. If you do have to add more fill as a result of settling, don't use pea gravel around manhole covers. That doesn't redirect the flow away from your system's parts but allows water to flow toward the tank. Then the ground can freeze and lift the manhole covers, letting groundwater flow into the tank, shortening the system's life.

# Great Goofs®

**Laughs and lessons from our readers**

## CAN YOU HEAR ME NOW?

I was going to install a faucet in our upstairs bathroom and had brought home some new quarter-turn ball valves to replace the old shutoffs under the sink. My wife went shopping for the new faucet while I got started on the valves. When it was time to turn the main water line back on, I had my 15-year-old son stand in the bathroom with his cell phone to watch for leaks.

Out at the street I called him on my cell phone and said, "OK, here we go," as I turned on the water. Then my phone went dead. What a time for a dropped call! I quickly redialed, but the call rolled to my son's voice mail. I hung up and my phone rang immediately. "Dad, shut the water off!" I did and raced inside and up the stairs, only to find the entire bathroom and hallway carpet completely soaked. Turns out I'd left my slick new ball valves in the open position when I installed them.

**VAUGHN WILLIAMS**

## NO WAY OUT

I was relocating the shower in a bathroom that was built above a crawl space. To gain access, I cut a hole in the subfloor and slithered down between the joists with all my materials and tools. The floor would be an easy patch since I was retiling anyway. After I spent a few hours down there soldering copper pipes and gluing ABS drain lines, the new plumbing setup was perfect. Then it dawned on me that my beautiful new plumbing job blocked my way out through the opening. I was trapped! I didn't have the heart to rip it all out, so I used my cell phone to call my son. I cooled my heels down there for an hour until he showed up and cut another hole in the floor to let me out.

**JIM BIANCHINI**

# 4 Woodworking & Workshop Projects & Tips

# HI-LO TABLE

## A coffee table that becomes a dining table or a desk—in seconds!

### BY MIKE BERNER

I've got a large family, and when we all gather, it's become tradition to haul a card table up from the basement and evict the coffee table to make more space for dining. Our next big get-together will be different; instead of shifting furniture around, I'll just flip up the coffee table legs and round up the kids!

### WHAT IT TAKES

| TIME | COST | SKILL LEVEL |
|------|------|-------------|
| A few days | $200-$400 | Intermediate |

**TOOLS**

Miter saw, table saw, drill, tape measure, random orbital sander, flush-cut saw, jigsaw, 23-gauge pin nailer

### A VINTAGE PROJECT THAT STILL HAS LEGS TODAY

**1956** The inspiration for this project came from an article *Family Handyman* published way back in 1956. I thought the idea of a 2-in-1 table was brilliant, even for today. I used the same hinged-leg concept but updated a few key things:

■ The original article suggested using a door or solid wood for the tabletop. Plywood was available back then but in a limited range of options. Luckily for me (and you), we can now make projects faster, easier and often better with plywood.

■ In coffee table mode, this project looked awkward with its large overhangs and inward-tilted legs. I tweaked the design and found that placing all eight legs on the floor gave the coffee table a more balanced and unique look.

■ Since the legs will be swung in and out, I decided to build a half-lap joint instead of a miter, which would have to be reinforced. This also made assembling the legs much easier.

**3" border**

**Underside of tabletop**

**6" strips for mounting legs**

**1**

**3/4"**

**1/4"**

**2"**

**13° from 90°**

**2**

**Edging flush with the plywood**

**Flush ends at the top**

**Overhang the bevel**

**3**

**Painter's tape to protect the wood**

**Trim the bevel cut**

**Flush-cut saw**

**4**

## 1 BUILD UP THE TOP
I started with a piece of walnut plywood cut to size. On the underside I glued 3-in.-wide strips of the same plywood on the edges and pinned them into place. I put one more 3-in. strip in the middle, and added two 6-in.-wide strips to provide mounting surfaces for the legs. Doubling the top like this adds stiffness without too much additional weight.

## 2 BEVEL THE EDGING
The top is wrapped with edging to hide the plywood edges. Square edging would be fine, but I cut a 13-degree bevel on the edging stock. This bevel matches the angle of the legs and gives the table a more refined look.

## 3 ADD THE EDGING
Fasten the edging to the ends of the table first. When I added the side edging, I let it protrude beyond the bevels of the end edging. Instead of fumbling with long clamps, I used a pin nailer to hold the edging in place while the glue dried.

## 4 TRIM THE EDGING
Trim the overhanging ends of the edging to match the bevel. Protect the wood from the saw teeth with a layer or two of painter's tape. Then sand the cuts smooth and flush.

## Materials List

| ITEM | QTY. |
|---|---|
| 3/4" x 4' x 8' walnut plywood | 1 |
| 3/4" x 3-1/2" x 8' walnut board | 5 |
| 3/4" x 2" x 8' walnut board | 2 |
| 1-1/2" x 4' piano hinge | 1 |
| Trim screws | |
| Glue | |
| Pin nails | |
| Toggle clamps | 2 |
| Knob set | 2 |

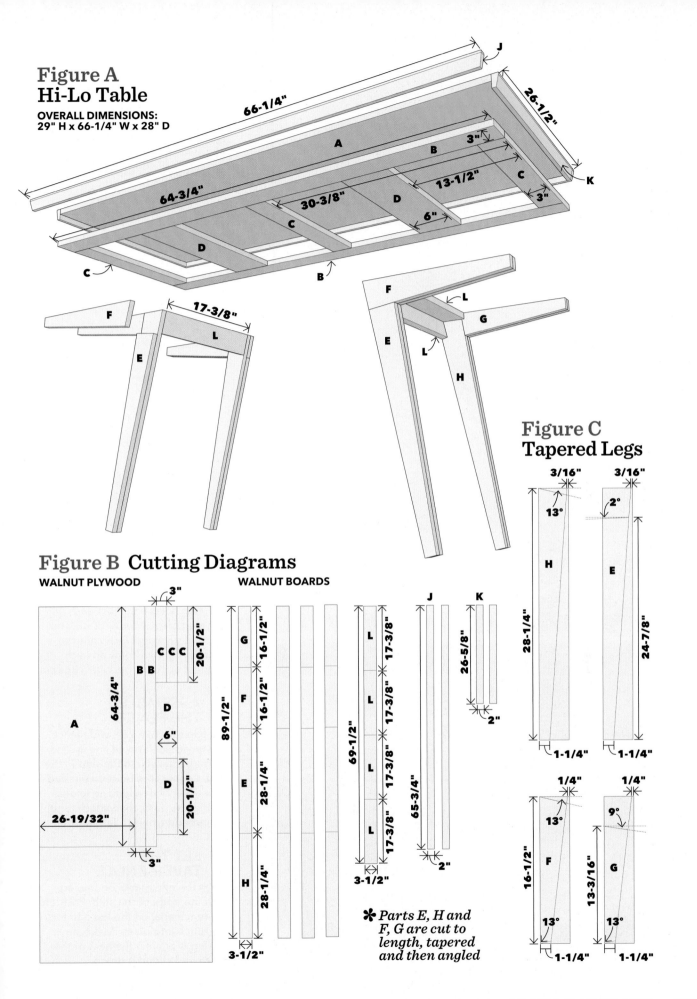

# Figure A
## Hi-Lo Table
**OVERALL DIMENSIONS:**
**29" H x 66-1/4" W x 28" D**

66-1/4"

26-1/2"

J

A

B

3"

C

13-1/2"

D

3"

64-3/4"

30-3/8"

C

6"

D

B

C

K

F

L

17-3/8"

L

G

F

E

L

E

H

# Figure C
## Tapered Legs

3/16"    3/16"

13°    2°

H    E

28-1/4"    24-7/8"

1-1/4"    1-1/4"

1/4"    1/4"

13°    9°

16-1/2"    13-3/16"

F    G

13°    13°

1-1/4"    1-1/4"

# Figure B  Cutting Diagrams

**WALNUT PLYWOOD**

3"

20-1/2"

C C C

B B

64-3/4"

D

6"

D

20-1/2"

A

26-19/32"

3"

**WALNUT BOARDS**

G

16-1/2"

F    16-1/2"

89-1/2"

E

28-1/4"

H

28-1/4"

3-1/2"

L    17-3/8"

L    17-3/8"

L    17-3/8"

69-1/2"

L    17-3/8"

L    17-3/8"

3-1/2"

J

65-3/4"

2"

K

26-5/8"

2"

✱ *Parts E, H and*
*F, G are cut to*
*length, tapered*
*and then angled*

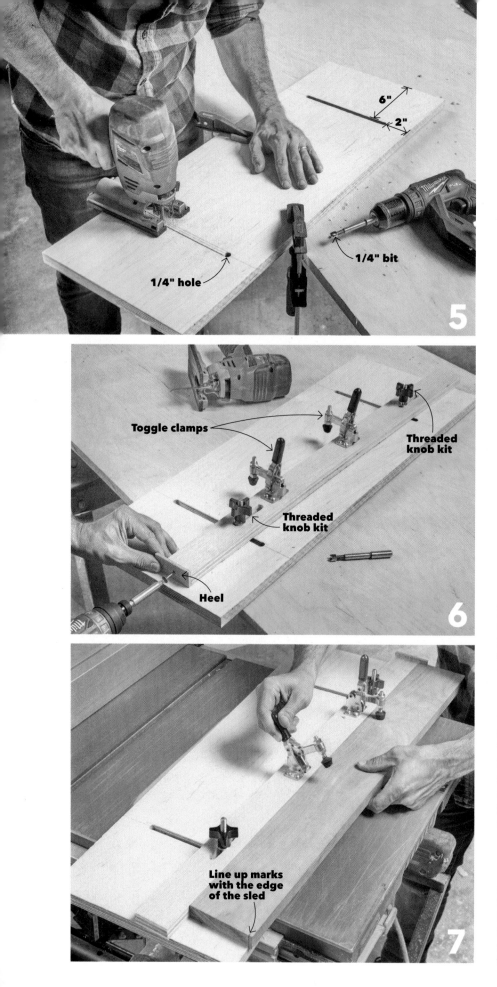

6"

2"

1/4" hole

1/4" bit

**5**

Toggle clamps

Threaded knob kit

Threaded knob kit

Heel

**6**

Line up marks with the edge of the sled

**7**

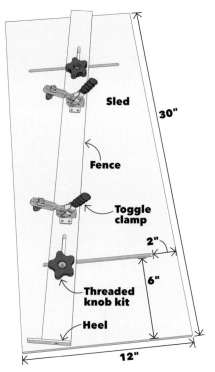

### A JIG MAKES TAPERED LEGS EASY

To safely cut the tapered legs, you'll need a jig for the table saw. There are simpler jig designs, but this one is my favorite. You'll need just a few scraps of plywood, a pair of toggle clamps and knobs. In 30 minutes you'll have a great jig for this and future projects.

Sled

30"

Fence

Toggle clamp

2"

6"

Threaded knob kit

Heel

12"

## 5 CUT SLOTS IN THE SLED

Drill two holes 6 in. from each end of a sled made from a 12 x 30-in. piece of plywood. Draw lines to connect the two holes on each end; cut out the slots with a jigsaw.

## 6 ASSEMBLE THE FENCE

Cut two slots in a 2-in.-wide fence. The fence slots should line up and be perpendicular to the slots in the sled. Connect the fence to the sled with a pair of threaded jig knobs and 1/4-in. bolts, then attach toggle clamps and a heel to finish the jig.

## 7 SET THE TAPER ANGLE

Align the end marks on the leg with the edge of the sled. Position the fence against the leg and lock the fence into place. Make sure the leg is against the heel of the fence and clamp it down.

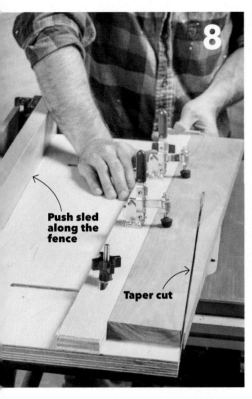

Push sled along the fence

Taper cut

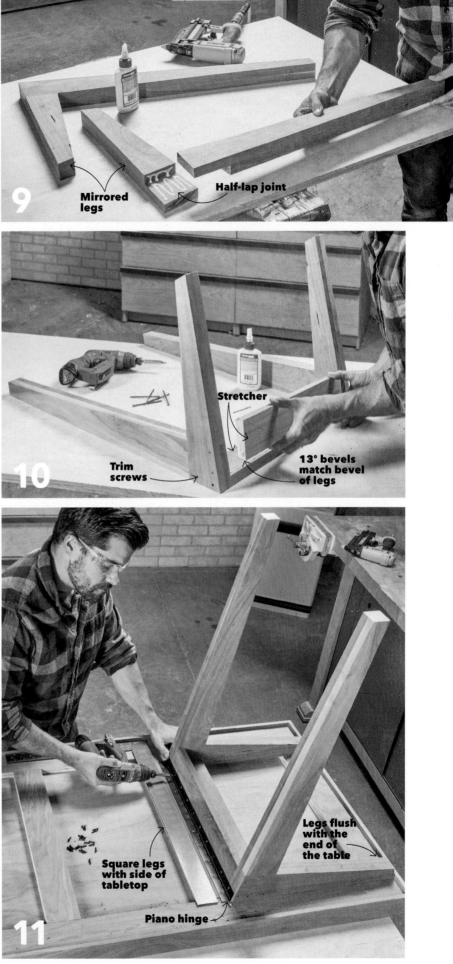

**Mirrored legs**

**Half-lap joint**

**Stretcher**

**Trim screws**

**13° bevels match bevel of legs**

**Square legs with side of tabletop**

**Piano hinge**

**Legs flush with the end of the table**

## 8 TAPER THE LEGS

Adjust the table saw fence to cut along the edge of the jig and then make the cut. Cut all the long legs with the same jig setup, then adjust the jig to cut the shorter legs.

## 9 ASSEMBLE THE LEGS

The half-lap joints for the legs are made by layering the leg parts. Fasten the parts with glue and a nailer or clamps. I built two leg sets at a time, laying them out on my workbench to make sure I got a "mirrored match."

## 10 CONNECT THE LEGS

I cut another 13-degree bevel in the stretcher, then glued and screwed it between a pair of legs. I fastened a second stretcher to make a strong corner where the legs will pivot on the hinge.

## 11 ATTACH THE PIANO HINGE

Align ends of the short legs to the inside of the edging. Position the legs with a framing square, then predrill and screw a length of piano hinge to the tabletop and the legs.

Curtis Rempel is a maker and a musician who was recently in the country music duo High Valley.

# SLING CHAIR SIMPLIFIED

## Timeless style, designed for the weekend woodworker

### BY CURTIS REMPEL

**W**hether it's names for my children or designs for furniture, I'm always on the lookout for something timeless. A piece's durability, look and feel need to transcend the ages and stay relevant for lifetimes to come. That's the goal with this chair. In addition, I designed this project for simplicity, so you can make one yourself without special skills or tools.

## Wood and leather, great together

The wood frame is assembled with glue only, no nails or screws. It includes two types of interlocking joints: bridle joints and half laps. Both require a tight fit to make a chair sturdy. You don't have to be a veteran woodworker to make this project, but it's not a good one for a first-timer. I used 1-1/2-in.-thick oak for this project. Alternatively, you could glue 3/4-in. boards together. I finished the wood with a couple coats of Watco Danish Oil (Natural).

Don't let the leather put you off this project. It's about as simple as leatherwork gets. If you have the skills to do the woodworking, you'll have no trouble with the leather. Or, if you prefer, you can use canvas or other fabrics, which cost much less. I bought my leather for $250 at *buckleguy.com*.

## WHAT IT TAKES

| TIME | COST | SKILL LEVEL |
|------|------|-------------|
| Weekend | $150-$400 | Intermediate |

**TOOLS**
Basic woodworking tools, circular saw, jigsaw, table saw, dado blade, leather punch

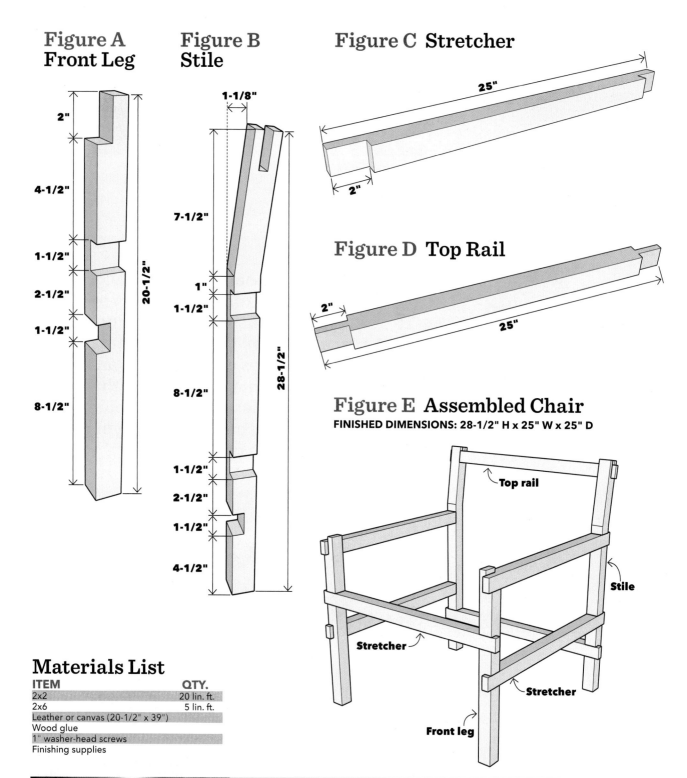

## Figure A
### Front Leg

2"
4-1/2"
1-1/2"
2-1/2"
1-1/2"
8-1/2"
20-1/2"

## Figure B
### Stile

1-1/8"
7-1/2"
1"
1-1/2"
8-1/2"
1-1/2"
2-1/2"
1-1/2"
4-1/2"
28-1/2"

## Figure C  Stretcher

25"
2"

## Figure D  Top Rail

2"
25"

## Figure E  Assembled Chair
**FINISHED DIMENSIONS: 28-1/2" H x 25" W x 25" D**

Top rail

Stile

Stretcher

Stretcher

Front leg

## Materials List

| ITEM | QTY. |
|---|---|
| 2x2 | 20 lin. ft. |
| 2x6 | 5 lin. ft. |
| Leather or canvas (20-1/2" x 39") | |
| Wood glue | |
| 1" washer-head screws | |
| Finishing supplies | |

## Meet the builder

If Curtis Rempel looks familiar, it may be because you've seen him in a music video. If you listen to country music, you've certainly heard his voice—Curtis and his brother, Brad, recently made up the duo High Valley. Next to music, Curtis's passion is working with his hands—with wood, leather or just fixing things around his place. You can check out the band at *highvalleymusic.com* or buy his handmade leather and wood creations at *curtandmyr.co*.

## 1 CUT THE PARTS
This chair is made mostly of straight, simple parts you can cut on a table saw, but the two back stiles are curved. I first cut the straight sections with a circular saw, stopping when I reached the curved segment. Then I cut the curves with a jigsaw.

## 2 SAND THE STILES
Smooth out the imperfections in the first stile and then use it as a template to mark the second. After you've cut and sanded the second stile, clamp them together and sand both until they're identical.

## 3 CUT THE SLOTS
I built a plywood box jig (8 x 14 in.) to hold the stiles upright while I cut the slots. The slots are too large to cut in a single pass with my benchtop table saw, so I set up my dado blade for 1/4-in.-wide cuts.

## 4 CUT THE TENONS
I cut the tenons the same way I cut the slots, taking 1/4-in. bites and adjusting the fence after each cut. This was time-consuming, but it gave me clean, tight-fitting joints.

**WARNING:** You have to remove your blade guard for upright cuts. Be extra careful!

Box jig

Stile

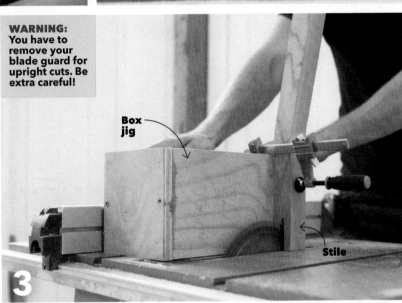

## Figure F Stile Cutting Diagram

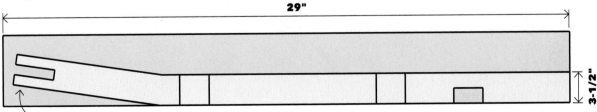

29"

3-1/2"

8° angle

Dado blade

Table saw sled

**5**

## 5 CUT THE HALF LAPS

I used a table saw sled to cut notches and tenons for the half lap joints. To build your own table saw sled, search for "table saw sled" at *familyhandyman.com*.

## 6 GLUE IT UP

Completely assemble the whole chair without glue. This "dry run" might feel like a waste of time, but it's better than discovering problems during the glue-up. After the dry run, go ahead and assemble the chair with glue.

## GETTING A CLOSE FIT

For tight-fitting joints, I cut slots and notches first. Later, as I cut tenons, I stopped and tested each fit before adjusting the table saw fence and making the final passes using the box jig. I aimed for a slightly too-tight fit. Then, when needed, I cut paper-thin shavings off the tenons with a sharp chisel.

**6**

**7**

**8**

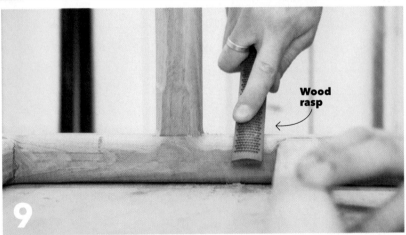

**9**

**10**

Wood rasp

**7 TRIM THE TENONS**
I cut off the excess length with a Japanese saw, but any flush-cutting saw will work.

**8 ROUT THE EDGES**
Sharp corners will damage the leather, so the top rail and front stretcher must be rounded. The other parts don't require it, but I rounded them all with a 1/2-in. round-over bit anyway.

**9 CLEAN UP THE ROUND-OVERS**
My router work was far from perfect, but smoothing out the flaws was easy with a rasp.

**10 SAND, SAND, SAND...**
Perfecting the round-overs and joints took me over an hour. I began with a random orbit sander and 100-grit discs, then used 150-grit. To remove the swirls left by the sander, I sanded by hand with 150-grit.

**11**

Leather punch

**12**

**13**

## 11 CUT THE LEATHER

To make the sling, cut leather to 20-1/2 x 39 in. Mark the leather by dragging a nail along a straightedge. That will leave a scratch line on the leather. Then put a fresh, sharp blade in your utility knife and cut along the scratch line.

## 12 PUNCH HOLES IN THE SLING

At both ends of the sling, punch screw holes 1/2 in. from the edges and about 4 in. apart. A leather punch costs about $15 online.

## 13 FASTEN THE SLING

Screw the sling to the undersides of the top rail and the front stretcher using washer-head screws. When you're driving screws with a drill, it's easy for the bit to slip and damage the leather, so I drove these screws by hand.

# How to choose leather

For this chair, I supplied Curtis with our Wickett & Craig Traditional Harness veg tanned leather in a 9-11 oz. weight. If you don't know leather jargon, that sounds pretty confusing. Understanding these five terms will help you make a smart choice:

**Thickness**, or "weight," is given in ounces, usually 2 oz. up to 16 oz. Thick leather is used for items like saddles, shoe soles and belts. Thin leather is used for wallets and handbags.

**Temper** refers to suppleness. Leather temper can be described as firm, medium, semi-soft and soft. Stiffer leathers are best for things that have to hold their shape, like tool pouches. Softer leather is best for items that need to move and bend, like handbags.

**Grain** refers to the composition and appearance of the hide. Generally, the highest quality leathers are "full grain," meaning the surface is left untouched. Others, such as top grain, genuine or bonded, are usually sanded or buffed, resulting in a smooth texture with less visible natural grain.

**Color** can be added in several ways: 100% aniline dyes are translucent, allowing the true texture to remain. Other treatments, like semi-aniline or pigment, give a more consistent surface and resist wear better but show less grain. Finally, there's paint, which completely hides the grain.

**Tannage** refers to how the leather was processed. One method is vegetable, or "veg," tanning, which uses organic materials such as tree bark and tends to yield stiffer leather. It's usually more expensive. Chrome tanning uses some nonorganic chemicals and often produces softer leather.

**MEET THE EXPERT**
**Hugh Harriss is a fourth-generation leather expert in a family business that got its start by supplying English leather to U.S. shoemakers. Today, he runs a brass hardware factory and an online leather craft store. If you need leather, hardware, tools or expert advice, you'll find it at *buckleguy.com*.**

# SUPER-SPACIOUS
# STORAGE BED

## Turn that wasted space under your bed into easy-access storage

BY MIKE BERNER

**M**y growing family is quickly outgrowing our small home. Toys are overtaking the living room, and closets are more than full. My wife and I needed a new place to put stuff without adding any more space. Our bed was the answer: It was already sitting there taking up room—why not take advantage of it for storage? So, I built a few simple boxes and drawers, then assembled them to make a cool platform bed frame. Here's how I did it.

**MEET THE BUILDER**
Mike Berner is a carpenter and associate editor at *Family Handyman*. With a family of five living in a small house, he's always looking for a better place to put his slippers.

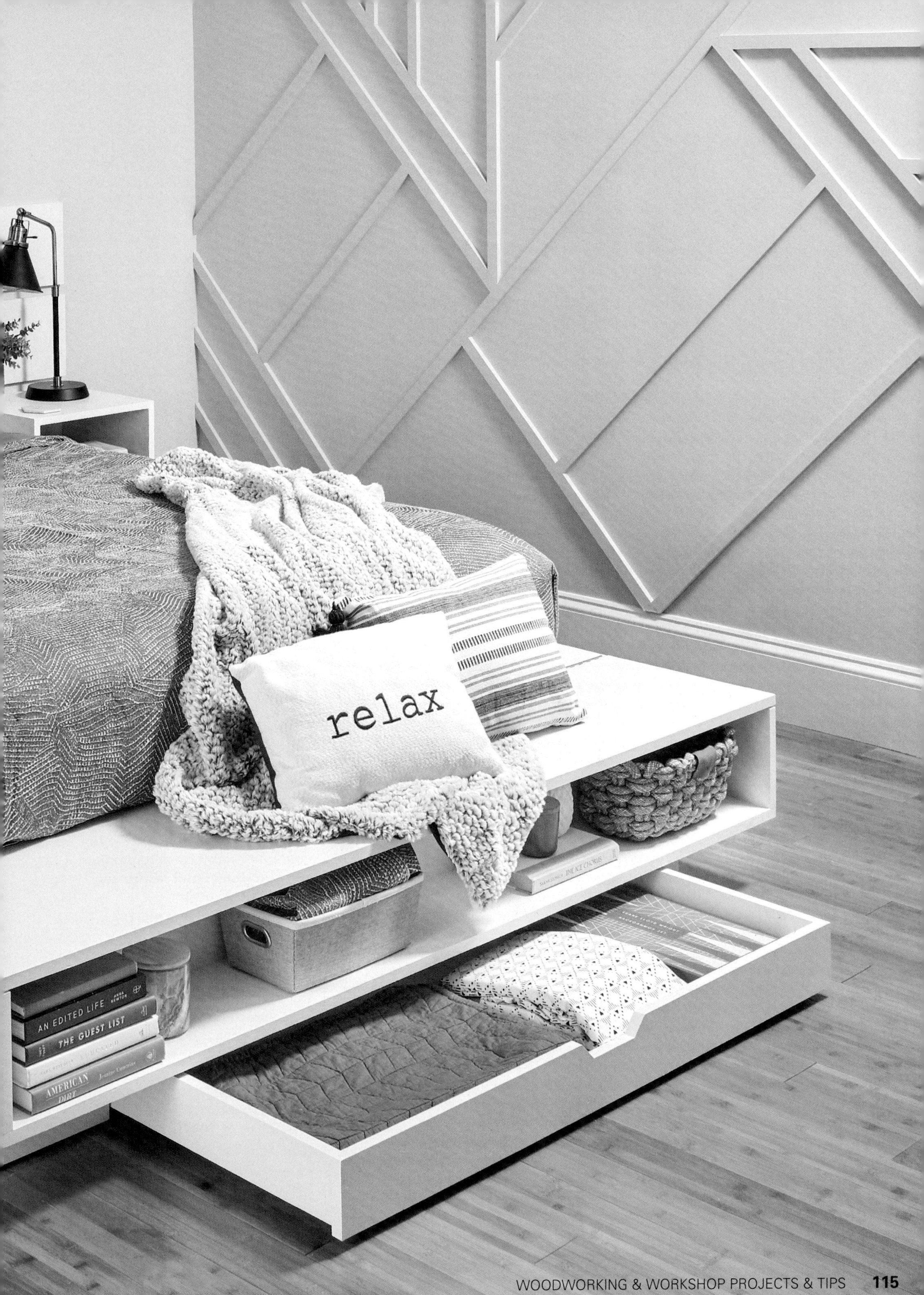

## IT'S LIKE ADDING MORE CLOSET SPACE!

A typical linen closet offers about 50 cu. ft. of storage. By enlarging the footprint of this queen-size bed by 6 in. on each side and 16 in. at the foot, I added the equivalent of almost half a linen closet in previously wasted space.

Saw guide

1-1/2" rigid foam

Storage bench divider

Storage bench side

Storage bench back

### 1 SLICE UP THE PLYWOOD

Large sheets of plywood are difficult to cut on a table saw, and making crosscuts is unsafe. To cut a sheet down into smaller pieces, I set it on a piece of rigid foam and made my cuts on the floor. The foam doesn't dull the blade, your parts won't crash to the floor and you won't need sawhorses.

### 2 ASSEMBLE THE BENCH AND BOXES

Glue and nail the sides to the bottom. Then fasten the back to the sides and bottom with glue and brad nails. Attach the extra divider in the storage bench the same way to support the lid. The tops will go on later.

### WHAT IT TAKES

| TIME | COST | SKILL LEVEL |
|------|------|-------------|
| A few days | $450 | Intermediate |

**TOOLS**
Basic hand tools, table saw, jigsaw, circular saw, drill, brad nailer

# Figure A
## Storage Bed

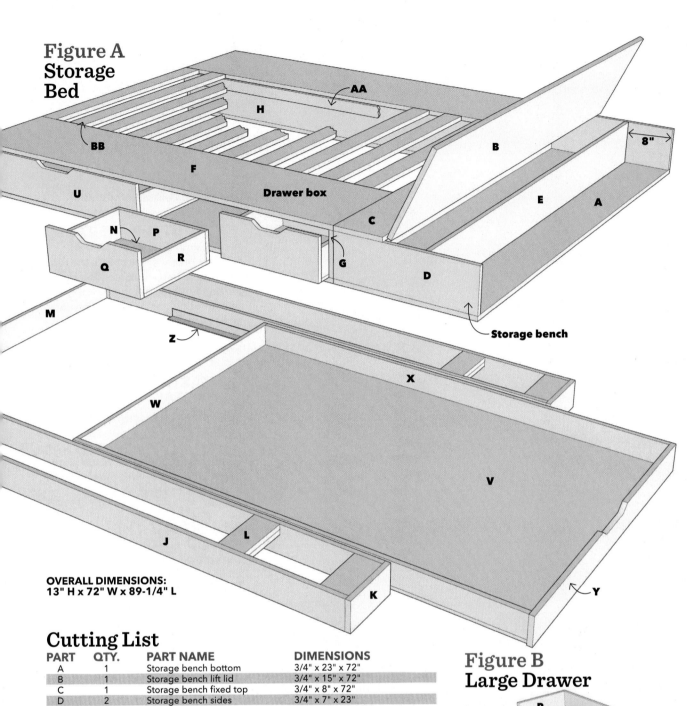

**OVERALL DIMENSIONS:**
**13" H x 72" W x 89-1/4" L**

## Cutting List

| PART | QTY. | PART NAME | DIMENSIONS |
|------|------|-----------|------------|
| A | 1 | Storage bench bottom | 3/4" x 23" x 72" |
| B | 1 | Storage bench lift lid | 3/4" x 15" x 72" |
| C | 1 | Storage bench fixed top | 3/4" x 8" x 72" |
| D | 2 | Storage bench sides | 3/4" x 7" x 23" |
| E | 1 | Storage bench divider | 3/4" x 7" x 70-1/2" |
| F | 4 | Drawer box tops/bottoms | 3/4" x 16" x 72" |
| G | 4 | Drawer box sides | 3/4" x 7" x 16" |
| H | 3 | Storage/drawer box backs | 1/2" x 7" x 70-1/2" |
| J | 4 | Toe-kick sides | 3/4" x 4-1/2" x 87" |
| K | 4 | Toe-kick ends | 3/4" x 4-1/2" x 9" |
| L | 12 | Toe-kick blocks | 3/4" x 4-1/2" x 7-1/2" |
| M | 1 | Toe-kick stretcher | 3/4" x 4-1/2" x 64-3/4" |
| N | 4 | Small drawer bottoms | 1/2" x 14-1/4" x 17-1/4" |
| P | 4 | Small drawer backs | 3/4" x 4-1/2" x 17-1/4" |
| Q | 4 | Small drawer fronts | 3/4" x 6-3/4" x 17-1/4" |
| R | 12 | Drawer sides | 3/4" x 4-1/2" x 13-3/4" |
| S | 2 | Large drawer bottoms | 3/4" x 14-1/4" x 34-1/2" |
| T | 2 | Large drawer backs | 3/4" x 4-1/2" x 34-1/2" |
| U | 2 | Large drawer fronts | 3/4" x 6-3/4" x 34-1/2" |
| V | 1 | Toe-kick drawer bottom | 1/2" x 45-7/8" x 72" |
| W | 1 | Toe-kick drawer back | 3/4" x 3-1/2" x 45-7/8" |
| X | 2 | Toe-kick drawer sides | 3/4" x 3-1/2" x 70-1/2" |
| Y | 1 | Toe-kick drawer front | 3/4" x 4-1/2" x 45-7/8" |
| Z | 2 | Aluminum drawer runners | 1-1/2" x 1-1/2" x 72" |
| AA | 2 | Slat cleats | 3/4" x 2" x 72" |
| BB | 11 | Mattress slats | 3/4" x 3-1/2" x 39-3/4" |

# Figure B
## Large Drawer

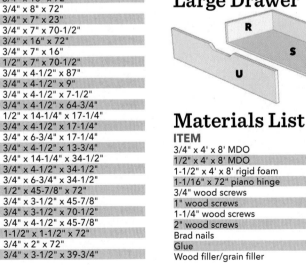

## Materials List

| ITEM | QTY. |
|------|------|
| 3/4" x 4' x 8' MDO | 4 |
| 1/2" x 4' x 8' MDO | 2 |
| 1-1/2" x 4' x 8' rigid foam | 1 |
| 1-1/16" x 72" piano hinge | 1 |
| 3/4" wood screws | |
| 1" wood screws | |
| 1-1/4" wood screws | |
| 2" wood screws | |
| Brad nails | |
| Glue | |
| Wood filler/grain filler | |

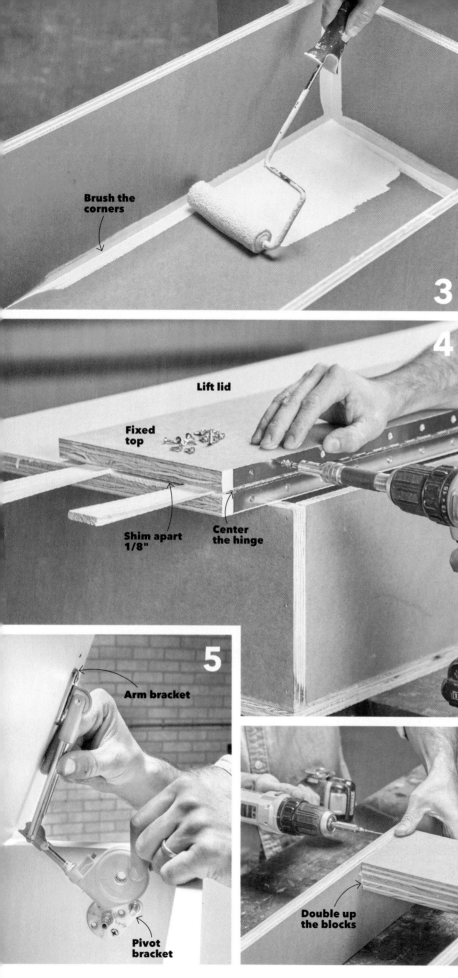

Brush the corners

## 3 PAINT THE INSIDE

Painting the inside of the boxes is much easier before the tops are added. Use a brush on the corners and roll the flat areas. Apply a coat of primer and one or two coats of latex paint. When the paint has dried, fasten the tops to the drawer boxes with glue and brad nails.

Lift lid

Fixed top

Shim apart 1/8"

Center the hinge

## 4 FASTEN THE HINGE, INSTALL THE LID

Stack the lift lid (part B) and the fixed top (part C), flush up one side of the long edges and shim the edges apart about 1/8 in. Center the piano hinge between the two parts, then predrill and screw it to both edges.

## 5 INSTALL THE LID STAY

The soft-close lid stays hold the lid up while you grab pillows and blankets from inside and keep it from slamming when you close it. Attach the pivot bracket to the side, then open the lid and extend the arm. Fasten the arm bracket where the arm lands on the lid. Do the same on the opposite side.

Arm bracket

Pivot bracket

Double up the blocks

17" to the center of the block

Toe-kick

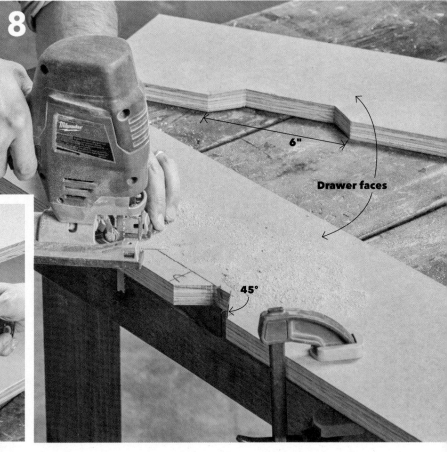

## 6 BUILD TOE-KICKS

The toe-kicks raise the boxes off the floor and keep you from stubbing your toes as you get into bed. Simply glue and screw the ends to the sides. Then attach three blocks flush to the top of the toe-kicks: one at each end and a third centered 17 in. from the front.

## 7 BUILD THE DRAWERS

Cut the bottoms of the drawers to size from 1/2-in. plywood and fasten the drawer backs through the bottoms with glue and brad nails. Then fasten the sides the same way.

## 8 CUT DRAWER PULLS

Instead of using knobs, I cut out a handle for each drawer. I found the center of each drawer and measured a 6-in. opening. I traced the shape and cut it out with a jigsaw. Then I attached the face to the drawer.

## 9 FILL THE EDGES

To prep the plywood edges for paint, apply a sandable filler with a putty knife. Let it dry, sand it down, then prime and paint all the parts.

**12"**

**Aluminum drawer runner**

**3/4" 1/2"**

**3/4" wood screws**

**Countersink bit**

**10**

**Drawer box**

**11**

**17"**

**Drawer box**

**Line up edges**

**Storage bench**

**Toe-kick**

**12**

**13**

**Slat cleat**

**Spacer slat**

**Toe-kick stretcher**

## 10 ATTACH THE RUNNERS

Drill pilot holes in the aluminum angle every 12 in. At each hole, bore a countersink so the screw heads won't protrude. Screw the angle to the inside of the toe-kick.

## 11 ATTACH THE TOE-KICKS

Flip the drawer boxes upside down and center the toe-kicks, which should overhang the front by 17 in. Screw the toe-kicks to the bottoms of the boxes with 2-in. screws through the blocks.

## 12 ASSEMBLE THE BED

Flip the boxes upright and space them apart. Place the storage bench on top of the overhanging toe-kicks, and then line up the sides of the bench with the drawer boxes. Screw them together from the inside with 1-in. screws and into the blocks in the toe-kicks with 2-in. screws. Then connect the backs of the toe-kicks with the stretcher (part M).

## 13 FASTEN SLATS

Position the cleats on the inside of the bed assembly 3/4 in. below the top of the boxes and use 1-1/4-in. screws to fasten them. Cut slats from standard 1x4 boards to fit between the side boxes, and fasten them to the cleats with two screws on each side. Use one of the slats as a spacer to position them evenly. You could use a sheet of plywood instead of slats, but I found the standard pine boards or furring strips to be much cheaper. Once the slats are on, the bed is ready for your mattress!

# SLEEK & SIMPLE HEADBOARD

I designed this headboard and nightstand combination to match my storage bed, but it would work well with other beds, too. All you need is one sheet of plywood and a few hours to put it together.

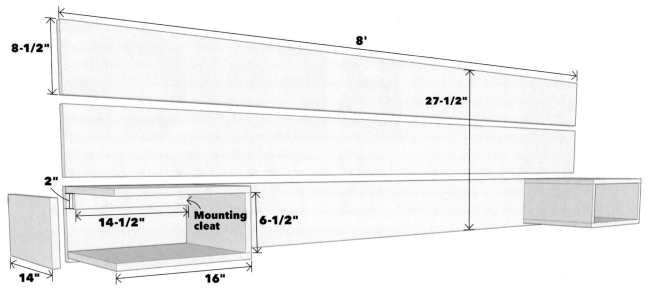

8-1/2"

8'

27-1/2"

2"

14-1/2"

**Mounting cleat**

6-1/2"

14"

16"

## 1 SCREW PLANKS TO THE WALL

Fill the edges and paint three 8-ft. lengths of plywood cut at 8-1/2 in. wide. Center the first strip 3 in. above the bed and attach it to studs with trim screws. Use a few 1-in. spacer blocks to evenly space the next two strips above the bed.

## 2 HANG THE NIGHTSTANDS

Screw the nightstands to a plank. I positioned them flush with the top of the lowest plank, but you could mount them at any height. Fill the screw holes, touch up the paint and you're done!

## Materials List

| ITEM | QTY. |
|---|---|
| 1-3/4" x 4' x 8' MDO | 1 |
| 1-1/2" x 4' x 8' rigid foam | 1 |
| 3" trim screws | |
| 2" wood screws | |
| Glue | |
| Brad nails | |

### WHAT IT TAKES

| TIME | COST | SKILL LEVEL |
|---|---|---|
| 2-3 hours | $60 | Beginner |

**TOOLS**
*Table saw, miter saw or circular saw, brad nailer, stud finder*

Magnetic stud finder

Headboard plank

1" spacer

3" gap

Fill and touch up nail holes

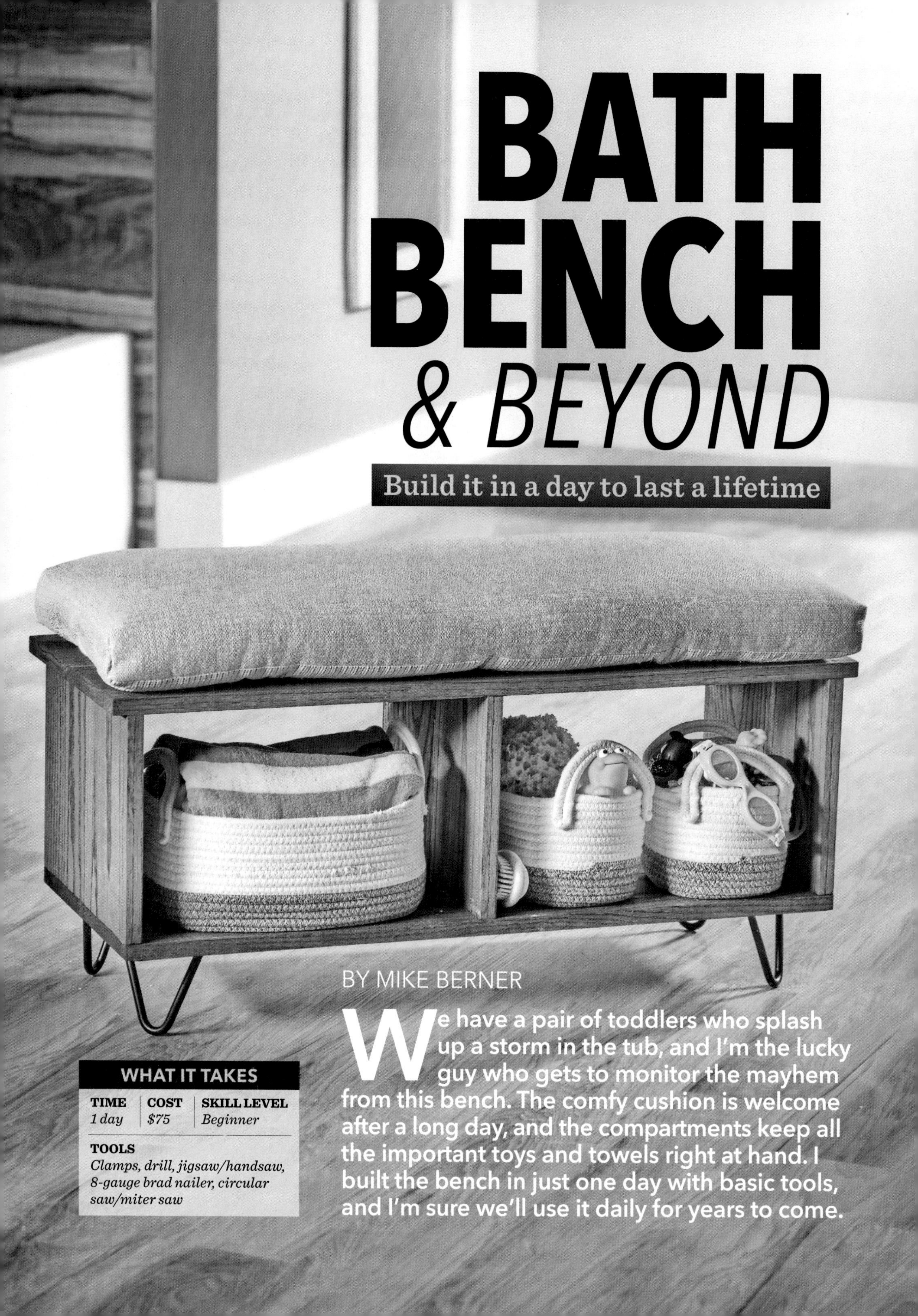

# BATH BENCH
## *& BEYOND*

**Build it in a day to last a lifetime**

BY MIKE BERNER

We have a pair of toddlers who splash up a storm in the tub, and I'm the lucky guy who gets to monitor the mayhem from this bench. The comfy cushion is welcome after a long day, and the compartments keep all the important toys and towels right at hand. I built the bench in just one day with basic tools, and I'm sure we'll use it daily for years to come.

## WHAT IT TAKES

| TIME | COST | SKILL LEVEL |
|------|------|-------------|
| 1 day | $75 | Beginner |

**TOOLS**
Clamps, drill, jigsaw/handsaw, 8-gauge brad nailer, circular saw/miter saw

# Figure A
## Bathroom Bench

**OVERALL DIMENSIONS:**
15-1/2" H x 36" W x 12-3/4" D

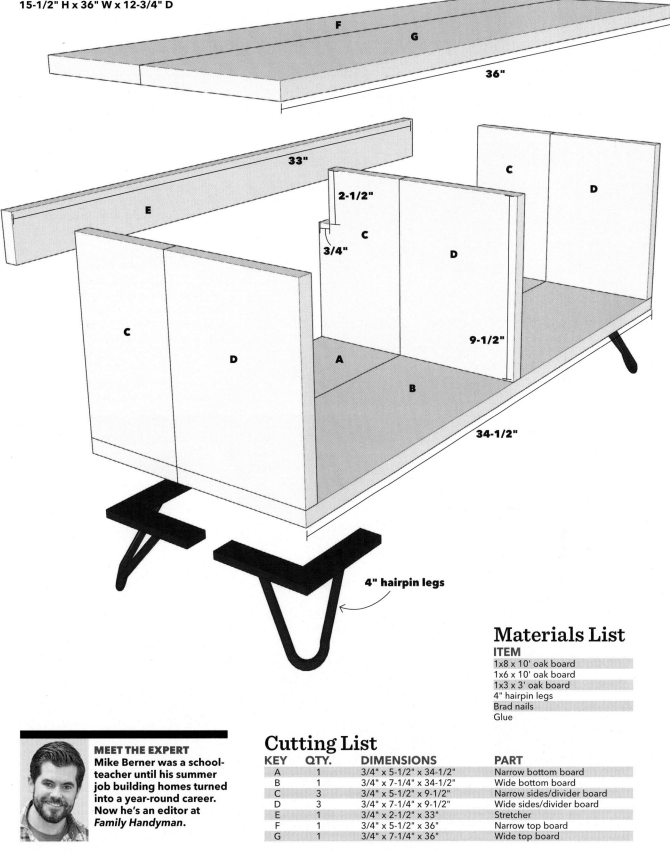

36"

33"

E

2-1/2"

3/4"

C

C

D

9-1/2"

A

B

34-1/2"

F

G

C

D

C

D

4" hairpin legs

**MEET THE EXPERT**
Mike Berner was a school-teacher until his summer job building homes turned into a year-round career. Now he's an editor at *Family Handyman.*

## Materials List

| ITEM |
| --- |
| 1x8 x 10' oak board |
| 1x6 x 10' oak board |
| 1x3 x 3' oak board |
| 4" hairpin legs |
| Brad nails |
| Glue |

## Cutting List

| KEY | QTY. | DIMENSIONS | PART |
| --- | --- | --- | --- |
| A | 1 | 3/4" x 5-1/2" x 34-1/2" | Narrow bottom board |
| B | 1 | 3/4" x 7-1/4" x 34-1/2" | Wide bottom board |
| C | 3 | 3/4" x 5-1/2" x 9-1/2" | Narrow sides/divider board |
| D | 3 | 3/4" x 7-1/4" x 9-1/2" | Wide sides/divider board |
| E | 1 | 3/4" x 2-1/2" x 33" | Stretcher |
| F | 1 | 3/4" x 5-1/2" x 36" | Narrow top board |
| G | 1 | 3/4" x 7-1/4" x 36" | Wide top board |

## 1 MAKE WIDE PANELS

Cut all the individual boards 1/2 in. longer than their final length. Then edge-glue the boards to make the top, bottom, sides and divider panel. Wipe away any excess glue and allow the panels to dry.

## 2 TRIM THE PANELS TO LENGTH

Trim one end of the panels, then cut the other end to final length. A 12-in. sliding miter saw like the one shown can cut the full 12-3/4-in. width. With a smaller saw, you have to flip each panel to finish the cuts. You could also make these cuts with a circular saw, using a large framing square as a guide.

## 3 ATTACH THE SIDES

Sand the parts smooth before assembling them. Start with 100-grit sandpaper and work up to 180. Then position the sides flush to the ends of the bottom board; fasten them with glue and brad nails. If you don't have a brad nailer, drive trim-head screws, sinking them below the surface and then covering them with wood putty.

## 4 NOTCH THE CENTER DIVIDER

Clamp the center divider to your work surface and cut a 3/4 x 2-1/2-in. notch on the top back corner. I used a jigsaw, but a handsaw would work just as well. Attach the center divider with glue and brad nails.

**2-1/2" from top of divider**

**3/4"**

## 5 INSTALL THE STRETCHER

Spread glue on the ends of the stretcher and in the notch of the center divider. Before you nail the parts, check that they're all in proper alignment using a Speed Square or framing square. Nail the stretcher in place through the sides and into the center divider.

## 6 SECURE THE TOP

Position the top so it over-hangs each side by 3/4 in. and is flush with the front and the back of the bench. Fasten the top with glue and finish nails, again checking with a square before driving the nails.

## 7 ADD THE LEGS

Flip the bench upside-down and set the legs in the corners. Keep them 1/2 in. away from the edges, then drill pilot holes and screw the legs to the bottom. Apply stain and polyurethane to ensure the bench will last through years of bath time. Top off the bench with a cushion that has a nonslip bottom, or leave it as is to show off the oak grain.

# A WORKBENCH
# YOU CAN BUILD ON!

## Start with a simple design and add features as you need them

BY BRAD HOLDEN

**A**fter countless hours standing at a workbench, I've found some features I really like. But there are three properties I can't do without: rigidity, flatness and mass. I hate working at a bench that wiggles or that slides around because it's not heavy enough. A workbench built with construction lumber like 2x4s will be solid, heavy and durable, but it won't be flat. If you ever plan to build cabinets or furniture pieces, which require accuracy, a flat bench gives you a leg up.

**INSTALL A VISE**
The heart of a good workbench

**ADD A TOOL PLATFORM**
Swing it up into place when you need it

**MAKE IT MOBILE**
Side-mount casters, so it moves only when you want it to

This bench is constructed from plywood (Baltic birch) and MDF (medium-density fiberboard). Both are inexpensive, flat and stable. The design is simple, with rigidity in mind, and the double-layer top adds necessary mass. Build the basic bench and call it good, or add all the extras.

| WHAT IT TAKES | | |
|---|---|---|
| **TIME** | **COST** | **SKILL LEVEL** |
| 1–3 days | $100 for basic bench; $250 as shown | Beginner |
| **TOOLS** | | |
| Table saw, miter saw, drill/driver, finish nailer | | |

**GET SUPPORT FROM A "DEAD MAN"**
Quick, adjustable support for long pieces

**DRILL DOG HOLES FOR CLAMPING VERSATILITY**
Hold parts in place without clamps

**TACK ON A TOOL TRAY**
Keep your tools at hand but off the work surface

**ADD A FIDDLE**
A perfect belt-sanding helper

**SLIP IN SOME SHELVES**
Narrow shelves add a little extra storage

**ADD A STACK OF DRAWERS, OR TWO OR THREE**
Simple drawers keep stuff at hand and protected

**MEET THE BUILDER**
Brad Holden, a senior editor at *Family Handyman*, has built custom cabinets and furniture for 30 years.

# Figure A  Basic Bench
**OVERALL DIMENSIONS: 33" H x 60" W x 24" D**

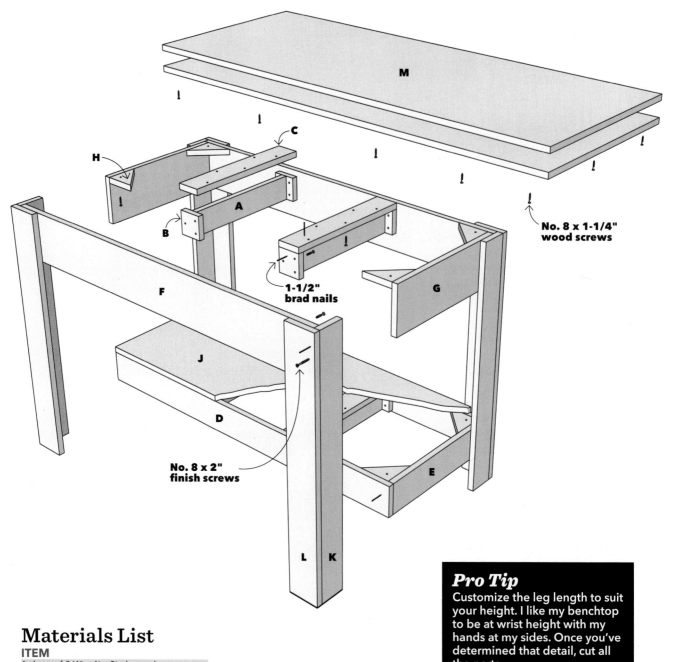

No. 8 x 1-1/4"
wood screws

1-1/2"
brad nails

No. 8 x 2"
finish screws

**Pro Tip**
Customize the leg length to suit
your height. I like my benchtop
to be at wrist height with my
hands at my sides. Once you've
determined that detail, cut all
the parts.

## Materials List

### ITEM
1 sheet of 3/4" x 4' x 8' plywood
1 sheet of 3/4" x 4' x 8' MDF (for parts J & M)
No. 8 x 2" finish screws
No. 8 x 1-1/4" wood screws
18-gauge 1-1/2" brad nails
Wood glue
1 qt. polyurethane

### OPTIONAL
Woodworking vise
1/2" x 4' x 8' plywood (for drawers)
4" fixed casters
36" piano hinge
1/4-20 threaded inserts
1/4-20 jig knobs
5mm bullet catches
1-1/4" dowel
3/4" dowel

## Cutting List

| KEY | QTY. | DIMENSIONS | PART |
|---|---|---|---|
| A | 4 | 3/4" x 3" x 15-1/2" | Brace web |
| B | 8 | 3/4" x 3" x 3" | Brace flange ends |
| C | 4 | 3/4" x 3" x 17" | Brace flange top |
| D | 2 | 3/4" x 4" x 46-1/2" | Lower platform sides |
| E | 2 | 3/4" x 4" x 17" | Lower platform ends |
| F | 2 | 3/4" x 6" x 46-1/2" | Upper platform sides |
| G | 2 | 3/4" x 6" x 17" | Upper platform ends |
| H | 8 | 3/4" x 4" x 4" | Corner braces |
| J | 1 | 3/4" x 18-1/2" x 46-1/2" | Lower platform top |
| K | 4 | 3/4" x 3-1/4" x 31-1/2" | Leg 1 |
| L | 4 | 3/4" x 4" x 31-1/2" | Leg 2 |
| M | 2 | 3/4" x 24" x 60" | Top base and work surface |

# 1 BUILD THE PLATFORMS

Assemble the braces (A–C), then build the platform frames (D–G). Attach the braces using glue and screws. Glue and screw the corner braces (H) in place. Attach the lower platform top (J) by driving screws through the brace flanges and corner braces. (See **Figure A**.)

# 2 BUILD THE LEGS

Glue and nail leg parts 1 and 2 (K and L) together in an "L" shape. To make assembly easier, support leg part 2 with a scrap the same width as leg part 1. Once the parts are tacked together with brad nails, add a few screws for strength.

# 3 ATTACH THE LEGS

Attach the upper platform flush with the tops of the legs, using glue and screws. Glue and screw the lower platform to the legs at whatever height you like. The top of my lower platform is 8 in. high. Drive screws from the inside of the legs if you prefer that they don't show.

# 4 ADD THE TOP

Fasten the layered top (M) in two steps. With the top base and work surface upside-down on sawhorses, center the assembled bench framework on the top. Drive screws through the brace flanges and corner braces into the top base only, and then predrill screw holes in the top base for attaching the work surface. Drilling these holes after attaching the top base guarantees that they'll be accessible if you need to replace the work surface. Fasten the work surface to the base with wood screws.

*You can stop right here and have a great basic bench—or add the handy upgrades you'll see on the following pages. They're easy to adapt to an existing workbench, too.*

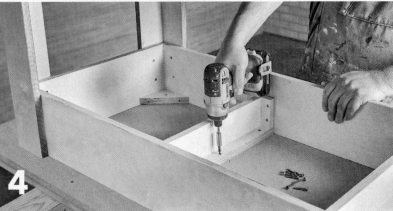

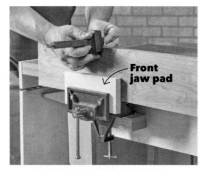
Front jaw pad

# INSTALL A VISE

Holding your work steady is essential, and the best way to do that is with a woodworking vise. You can get by with a small, inexpensive vise like this ($25 at Harbor Freight), or spend a couple hundred bucks for a larger, deluxe model. With a cast-iron vise like the one shown, line at least the front jaw with a wood pad to prevent marring your workpieces. I mount vises so the tops of the jaws or jaw pads are flush with the work surface.

**1**

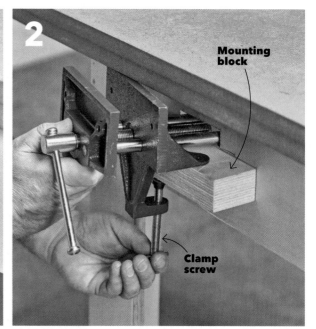
**2**
Mounting block

Clamp screw

Plywood

2x4

## MAKE A PORTABLE TOOL MOUNT

Fasten a 2x4 on edge to a piece of plywood. Bolt on a bench grinder or other tool you use only occasionally. When you're ready to use the tool, clamp the 2x4 in your vise.

## 1 MAKE ROOM FOR THE VISE

Vises have different mounting methods. For this one, I cut a hole in the platform side to allow the vise screw and rods to pass through. I like the back jaw of my vises to be flush with the edge of the workbench, essentially making the entire edge of the bench an extension of the back jaw. This way, I can clamp one end of a long workpiece in the vise and clamp the other flat against the edge of the bench using a pipe clamp.

## 2 ATTACH THE VISE

Glue up a plywood mounting block for the vise. Glue and screw the mounting block to the platform side. If you plan to upgrade vises later, skip the glue. Bolt the vise to the mounting block or just use the built-in clamp screw. Screw on the front jaw pad, making its top edge flush with the work surface.

# ADD A STACK OF DRAWERS, OR TWO OR THREE

Drawers tucked neatly under the bench create storage for all the stuff you like to have close at hand. Each finger pull in these drawers serves double duty, also acting as a hole for a "dead man" (see p. 134).

## 1 BUILD THE DRAWER CABINET

Cut the parts (N-S), and assemble the cabinet as shown, using glue and screws. The part dimensions can vary according to your bench dimensions, but the construction is simple—it's an open-front plywood box with a back. You can install drawer slides, but wooden runners work just fine. The bottom runners are 1/8 in. thick; the rest are 1/2 x 1/2 in. They provide a gliding surface and keep the drawers from tipping. This type of runner also makes it easy to take a drawer and its contents wherever you need it.

## 2 BUILD THE DRAWERS

Cut the drawer parts (T-W), allowing for 1/8 in. of play from side to side when installed. Drill 1-1/4-in.-diameter finger holes in each drawer front, then assemble the drawers with glue and finish nails.

## Cutting List

| KEY | QTY. | DIMENSIONS | PART |
|-----|------|-----------|------|
| N | 2 | 1/2" x 16-3/4" x 18-1/2" | Drawer cabinet sides |
| P | 2 | 1/2" x 11" x 18-1/2" | Drawer cabinet top and bottom |
| Q | 4 | 1/2" x 1/2" x 17-1/2" | Standard drawer runners |
| R | 2 | 1/8" x 1/2" x 17-1/2" | Bottom drawer runners |
| S | 1 | 1/2" x 11" x 15-3/4" | Drawer cabinet back |
| T | 6 | 1/2" x 4-3/16" x 17-1/2" | Drawer sides |
| U | 3 | 1/2" x 4-3/16" x 9-7/8" | Drawer backs |
| V | 3 | 1/2" x 5" x 10-7/8" | Drawer fronts |
| W | 3 | 1/4" x 10-7/8" x 17-1/2" | Drawer bottoms |

## Figure A
### Drawer Cabinet

## Figure B
### Drawers

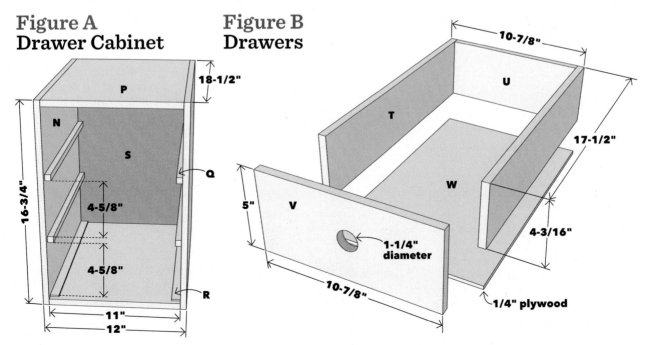

**Bench dog**

**Wedge**

# DOG HOLES FOR CLAMPING VERSATILITY

Bench dogs are a time-tested method for holding parts. You'll drill a series of holes through the benchtop and then use wedges to hold parts in place between the bench dogs. Bench dogs also work with a tail vise or fiddle (see p. 134). You can buy bench dogs or make your own (see below).

**Drilling guide**

**1**

## 1 DRILL THE HOLES

Lay out the dog holes on the work surface, placing them so you won't drill into any braces. If you're nervous about drilling straight holes freehand, make a drilling guide out of a block of wood approximately 2 x 2 x 4 in., with square edges. On your drill press, drill a hole through the block the diameter of your drill bit or its shank. Use a jigsaw to make a cutout to accommodate the bit's cutting head and to see where you're drilling. To use the guide, slip the bit's shank through the hole, then chuck it in your drill.

## 2 MAKE BENCH DOGS

Cut 3/4-in.-diameter dowels to length. For this 1-1/2-in.-thick top, I made the dogs 2 in. long. Cut a 1/8 x 3/4-in. flat face at the top using a handsaw and chisel. Drill a hole and glue in a bullet catch ($10 per 20-pack on Amazon) roughly centered on the dog's height. When you slide the dog into its hole, the bullet catch holds it in place at the desired height. If your dowels fit snugly in the dog holes, you'll need to very slightly recess the bullet catches.

**2**

**Bullet catch**

# ADD A SAW PLATFORM

If your miter saw doesn't already have a permanent home, customize your workbench to accommodate it with this flip-up platform. The platform sets your saw's table level with the benchtop to accommodate long workpieces. Depending on which end of your workpiece needs support, you can spin the saw around to work from either side of the bench.

## 1 ATTACH THE PLATFORM

Cut the platform (BB) to the size you want and attach it to the mounting strip (AA) with a length of piano hinge. Leave the mounting strip wide for now. Set the assembly on the workbench, and set the saw on the platform. Flip up the mounting strip and mark where it'll be flush with the saw table as shown. Remove the strip, cut it to width and reattach it to the platform. Attach the platform assembly to the edge of the bench with 2-in. wood screws.

## 2 INSTALL THE SUPPORTS

Make the support wings as long as possible within the span of the bench legs. For the right support wing (EE), screw the spacer (CC) directly to the leg, then attach the wing to the spacer with a length of piano hinge. The spacer allows the left support wing (DD) to fold in behind the right. Attach the left support wing directly to the leg using a length of piano hinge. Cut the tip off the left support wing so it folds in completely.

## Figure A
## Saw Platform

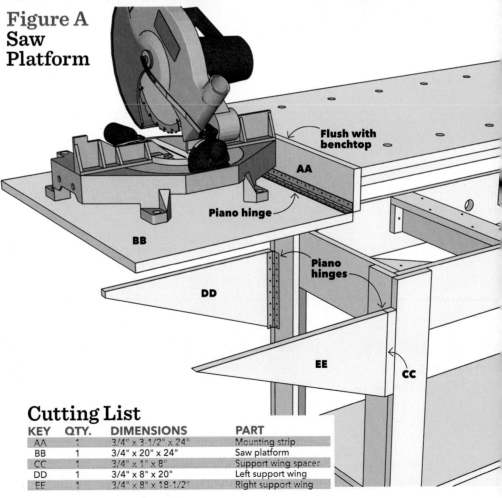

Flush with benchtop

AA

Piano hinge

BB

Piano hinges

DD

EE

CC

## Cutting List

| KEY | QTY. | DIMENSIONS | PART |
|-----|------|------------|------|
| AA | 1 | 3/4" x 3-1/2" x 24" | Mounting strip |
| BB | 1 | 3/4" x 20" x 24" | Saw platform |
| CC | 1 | 3/4" x 1" x 8" | Support wing spacer |
| DD | 1 | 3/4" x 8" x 20" | Left support wing |
| EE | 1 | 3/4" x 8" x 18-1/2" | Right support wing |

Fiddle

# ADD A FIDDLE

When you're belt-sanding a workpiece, it may want to shoot off the end of the bench unless it's held in place. Clamps work, but you need to relocate them to get at the entire surface. A fiddle stops the piece from moving, without getting in the way.

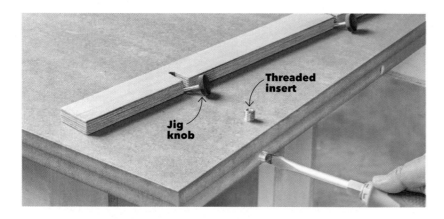

Threaded insert

Jig knob

## MOUNTING THE FIDDLE

Predrill pilot holes in the bench edge for 1/4-20 threaded inserts (eight for $8 at Rockler), then drive them in flush. Typically, the pilot hole is about 1/32 in. less than the insert's outer thread diameter. Cut the fiddle from 3/4-in. plywood, sized to match the bench end. Cut slots in the fiddle to line up with the inserts and attach it with 1/4-20 jig knobs ($2 each at Rockler).

Dead man

# GET SUPPORT FROM A "DEAD MAN"

When I'm working on a door, shelf or any long workpiece, it's nice to have someone to hold up the other end. In this case, that helper is called a dead man. All you need is a length of 1-1/4-in.-diameter dowel. Stick the dowel in the drawer finger hole or apron hole that's the right height and you're set. Drill extra holes in the apron or drawer fronts as needed.

# TACK ON A TOOL TRAY

A tool tray—standard on a traditional cabinetmaker's bench—provides a place to keep the stuff I'm using close by and off the work surface. Build the tray whatever size you like (mine is 4 x 4 in.), then screw it to the back edge of the benchtop.

# SLIP IN SOME SHELVES

The combination of the drawer boxes and the leg construction leaves a shallow cavity. Don't waste it. Cut shelves to fit the space. Install shelf standards to make the shelves adjustable, or just nail in cleats to support the shelves.

**3/4" plywood**

# POWER UP

Mount a power strip to one of the legs so you never have to search for an extension cord again.

# MAKE IT MOBILE

I like my workbench to stay put, until I need to move it. This caster mounting method keeps the legs firmly on the floor. Mounted with bolts, nuts and washers, the wheels don't quite touch the floor. Reinforce the legs with 3/4-in.-thick plywood where the casters bolt on. To move the bench, lift the end opposite the casters until the casters contact the floor.

# REFRESH WITH PLANTS

## Create a calming place with this stylish planter

### BY JAY CORK

**B**eing surrounded by greenery relieves stress and brightens your mood. Set in this custom-size planter, foliage can brighten your decor, too. Why not add one to your bathroom, bedroom or any living space? Fitted with pots, it lets you easily change out your plants whenever you'd like.

### WHAT IT TAKES

| TIME | COST | SKILL LEVEL |
|------|------|-------------|
| 2 days | $200 | Intermediate |

**TOOLS**
*Table saw or circular saw, jigsaw, router, orbital sander, brad nailer, basic carpentry tools*

Deck stain
applicator pad

# 1 PREFINISH SHEET GOODS

It's faster to prefinish a 4 x 8-ft. sheet than to do several small parts, and the finish is more consistent. After whitewashing the Baltic birch with white gel stain, I topcoated with a water-based polyurethane. Unlike an oil-based finish, it won't yellow over time.

# 2 PROFILE THE EDGES OF THE TRIM CAP

Using a router, profile the nose of the cap. For this project I used a 3/8-in. round-over bit to create a simple, classic line. Sand all the parts to 180 grit.

# 3 STAIN TRIM

Poplar is a good choice for the trim on this planter box—it's readily available and works easily. I started with iron oxide stain, followed by amber shellac.

# 4 APPLY FINISH TO THE TRIM BOARDS

Once all the trim boards are stained, apply two coats of clear finish. I chose an oil-based topcoat because it will imbue a slight yellow tone.

Homemade iron oxide stain

**MEET THE BUILDER**
Associate editor Jay Cork enjoyed designing this planter for indoors.

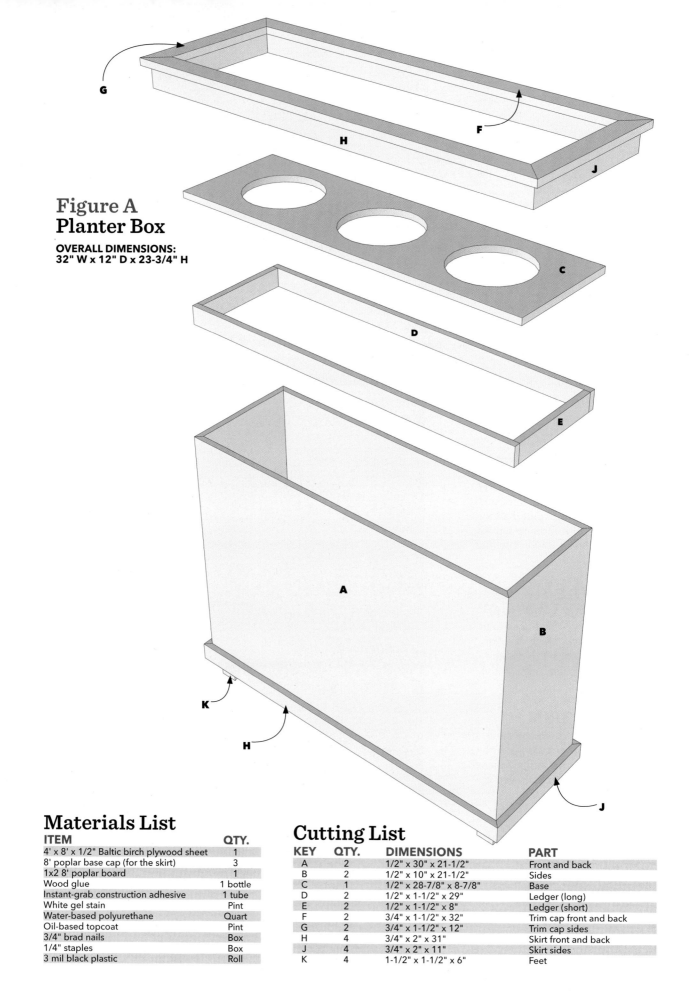

## Figure A
## Planter Box

**OVERALL DIMENSIONS:**
**32" W x 12" D x 23-3/4" H**

G
H
F
J
C
D
E
A
B
K
H
J

## Materials List

| ITEM | QTY. |
|------|------|
| 4' x 8' x 1/2" Baltic birch plywood sheet | 1 |
| 8' poplar base cap (for the skirt) | 3 |
| 1x2 8' poplar board | 1 |
| Wood glue | 1 bottle |
| Instant-grab construction adhesive | 1 tube |
| White gel stain | Pint |
| Water-based polyurethane | Quart |
| Oil-based topcoat | Pint |
| 3/4" brad nails | Box |
| 1/4" staples | Box |
| 3 mil black plastic | Roll |

## Cutting List

| KEY | QTY. | DIMENSIONS | PART |
|-----|------|-----------|------|
| A | 2 | 1/2" x 30" x 21-1/2" | Front and back |
| B | 2 | 1/2" x 10" x 21-1/2" | Sides |
| C | 1 | 1/2" x 28-7/8" x 8-7/8" | Base |
| D | 2 | 1/2" x 1-1/2" x 29" | Ledger (long) |
| E | 2 | 1/2" x 1-1/2" x 8" | Ledger (short) |
| F | 2 | 3/4" x 1-1/2" x 32" | Trim cap front and back |
| G | 2 | 3/4" x 1-1/2" x 12" | Trim cap sides |
| H | 4 | 3/4" x 2" x 31" | Skirt front and back |
| J | 4 | 3/4" x 2" x 11" | Skirt sides |
| K | 4 | 1-1/2" x 1-1/2" x 6" | Feet |

## 5 ASSEMBLE THE PLANTER BOX

You could use pocket holes and screws for this job, but the plywood end grain would show on the corners of the box. With a lock miter joint, you can get a continuous grain pattern as well as a strong glue joint. This method requires a router table and a lock miter bit—and some patience. But it is a great joinery method to learn for this and other projects.

## 6 CUT HOLES IN PLANTER BASE

Using a jigsaw, cut three evenly spaced holes in the planter base. Size them according to your planter pots. Once the holes are cut, sand any rough edges and check the fit. The planter pots should slide in right up to the rim.

## 7 ATTACH THE LEDGER

Position the ledger 1 in. down from the top. It will hold the planter base and you'll staple the plastic liner to it in Step 9. Using a combination square as a guide, I used instant-grab construction adhesive and 3/4-in. brad nails to fasten the ledger parts.

## 8 ATTACH THE FEET

Position the feet to raise the planter box off the ground about 1-1/4 in. I used scrap wood from my shop and attached the feet with instant-grab construction adhesive.

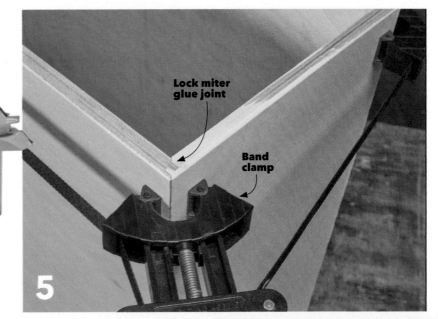

Lock miter glue joint

Band clamp

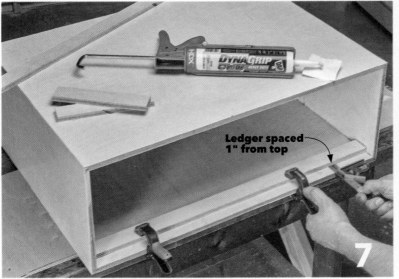

Ledger spaced 1" from top

Use scrap wood for legs

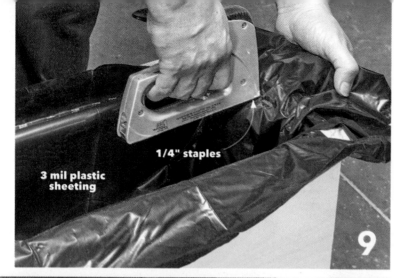

1/4" staples

3 mil plastic sheeting

**9**

## 9 LINE THE BOX WITH PLASTIC

This is an indoor planter box; line it with 3 mil plastic to prevent damage from overwatering. Staple the plastic to the front ledge first, then the back, leaving plenty of slack. Do the sides last. Trim the excess with a utility knife.

Oil-based paint adds protection

**10**

## 10 PAINT THE INTERIOR AND THE BASE

Because I planned to fill the top of the planter with black river rocks, I applied two coats of black oil-based paint to the base and inside edges of the box to make them less noticeable. Paint the inside to match the rock you choose.

## 11 ATTACH THE TRIM

Using construction adhesive and brad nails, attach the skirt trim pieces. Do the cap first, then attach the upper and lower skirts.

## 12 FILL PLANTER TOP WITH RIVER ROCK

I found inexpensive black river rock at *dollartree.com* ($1 per 32 oz.). Cover the pots completely for a traditional planted look.

3/4" brad nails

**11**

**12**

# DISCOVER GEL STAIN

## Get greater color control and better finishes

BY JAY CORK

I n Kevin Southwick's world, matching color is a daily challenge, with exacting standards. Kevin doesn't own a single can of liquid stain; he uses gel stains only. I dropped in to Kevin's shop to find out why gel stains are his favorite and asked him to share his best staining advice.

**MEET THE EXPERT**
Kevin Southwick is a furniture conservation specialist. He has been the in-house finishing expert at his local woodworking store for the past 25 years.

## Four Reasons to Use Gel Stain

### 1. GAIN GREATER COLOR CONTROL

Gel stain is more similar to paint than it is to stain; it contains significantly more pigment than liquid stain does. It also contains gel polyurethane, which helps fix the pigments to the surface of the wood. This allows gel stain to be applied in layers, giving you the ability to fine-tune the tone and depth of color.

### 2. EASILY STAIN VERTICAL SURFACES

Unlike liquid stains, which run and drip when used on vertical surfaces, gel stains, with their yogurt-like consistency, cling to vertical surfaces.

### 3. ELIMINATE THE BLOTCHY LOOK

Woods such as pine, cherry and birch don't absorb pigment evenly; they tend to look blotchy when stained. Because of the greater color control you get with gel stain, you can virtually eliminate blotching, especially if you apply two or more coats.

### 4. STAIN END GRAIN EVENLY

End grain readily soaks up liquid, making that part of a project much darker than adjacent surfaces. This occurs with gel stains, too, but less so. Gel stain can be wiped off from the end grain soon after it's applied, which helps you get a uniform color.

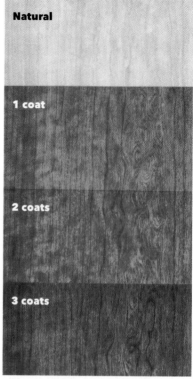

Natural

1 coat

2 coats

3 coats

## ADD LAYERS OF COLOR

Because gel stain contains urethane, you can add layers of color as long as you let the previous coat dry completely. Liquid stains don't do this very well, if at all. You can use this technique to get an extremely dark stain color on your wood.

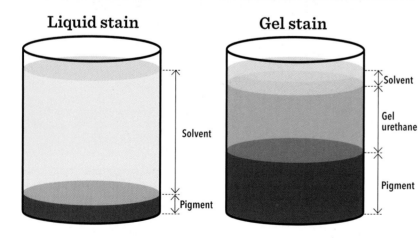

Liquid stain

Gel stain

Solvent

Pigment

Solvent

Gel urethane

Pigment

## LIQUID STAIN VS. GEL STAIN

Liquid stain contains a lot of solvent with a little bit of pigment. Gel stain is mostly pigment and gel urethane with a small amount of solvent.

Start with just a little color

## ADJUST COLOR WITH ARTISTS' OIL PAINTS

Artists' oil paints are highly concentrated pigments, and Kevin uses them to fine-tune the color. Adding a little at a time, he'll blend in oil paint with the gel stain and test the results on a piece of scrap wood. Once he's found the color he's looking for, he applies it to the whole project.

## CREATE AN ANTIQUE LOOK

Kevin takes advantage of the level of color control offered by gel stain to create an antique look. Smearing some gel stain on the detailed areas and lightly wiping off the excess with a cloth leaves more stain in the details, creating the effect he wants.

### Test your stain!

To make sure you get the look you're after, test your stain on a piece of scrap wood from your project, or the underside of a table, for example. Sand test pieces to the same grit as your project, then stain and topcoat them before making any final decisions.

## USE GEL STAIN AS A GLAZE

Kevin defines the term "glazing" as adding color over an existing finish. Gel stain excels at this. To add new life to that flea market find, gently scuff the existing finish with "0000" steel wool and apply gel stain. Lightly wipe off the excess and let dry.

## CLEAN DETAILED PROFILES

When you're removing stain from fine details in molding, use a stiff-bristle brush to get at the stain a rag wouldn't reach. Kevin usually has two brushes on hand for this purpose. As one brush gets loaded with excess stain, he switches to a clean one.

**Mineral Spirits**

## THIN GEL STAIN WITH SOLVENT

To extend the working time of gel stain, which is typically five minutes, add a little solvent. Put some gel stain in a jar or cup, add a dash of mineral spirits and mix it well. You can apply the stain as usual, but you'll have an extra few minutes of working time.

## WORK IN SMALL SECTIONS

Liquid stain can be applied liberally with a rag or a brush to cover large surfaces before wiping it off. Gel stains need to be wiped off in five minutes or less, so Kevin suggests working in sections roughly 10 ft. square at a time.

It's not dry if color comes up

## LET IT FULLY DRY

It's important to wait for gel stain to dry completely before you apply the next coat of stain, especially for the topcoat. If it's not dry, the solvent in the topcoat causes the stain to lift and get smeared around on the surface of your project. Kevin recommends a full 24 hours between coats.

More wiping = more color removed

## FINE-TUNE THE COLOR

Applying more or less pressure when you're wiping off gel stain lets you control how much color is left behind. Wiping lightly will produce a bolder color. For less color depth, wipe harder and repeatedly. This technique is perfect for getting even color on wood prone to blotches.

Color being removed

## ERASE YOUR MISTAKES

Undoing liquid stain is difficult. But with gel stains, you can "erase" the color as long as you act quickly. Get to it before it dries, wet a rag with mineral spirits and wipe off the stain.

## *Dispose of rags properly!*

Rags full of oil finish can self-ignite if they're crumpled and thrown into the garbage before they're completely dry. Best practice is to drape rags over the rim of a garbage can until they feel stiff, usually overnight but maybe longer. Then they're safe to throw away.

# Kevin's favorite finishing gear

Achieving a fine finish is challenging work. Here are some of the tools Kevin relies on to produce the best results with gel stain.

**PAPER TOWELS**
These paper towels feel and work like real cloth towels. A box of 200 Sellars TOOLBOX white rags costs about $12.

**JULEP SPOON**
Never one to shy away from fancy things, Kevin uses a julep spoon to scoop stain out of the can when mixing custom colors.

**GEL STAIN**
Kevin uses General Finishes gel stain for its quality of pigments. It's available in half pints ($16.99) and quarts ($39.99).

**CAN OPENER**
One of the most important tools in the shop, it opens cans of stain as well as your favorite beverages!

**FOAM PADS**
Kevin uses stiff foam pads to grip sandpaper or steel wool during the finishing process.

**KNIVES**
A palette knife (or even a butter knife) works well for stirring oil pigments into stain.

**CHIP BRUSH**
Kevin uses chip brushes to clean stain out of small details.

**SASH BRUSH**
Sash brushes allow you to work color into the details and crevices of molding and carvings.

**ACID BRUSH**
These cheap, disposable brushes are good for applying stain in hard-to-reach areas.

# 5 Exterior Repairs & Improvements

# SIDING

## How to install durable & stylish steel siding

BY BILL BERGMANN

**Y**our choice of siding defines your home and protects it from all that nature throws its way. Choose well, and your vacation home will blend in with nature while maintaining the architectural style you admire—for years to come.

Within the wooded setting of the *Family Handyman* Getaway, we wanted it all: modern style, durability and low maintenance. We chose Vesta Steel Plank from Quality Edge. Steel siding is gaining popularity, mostly in the form of vertical corrugated panels. We favored the look of Vesta's steel lap-siding products; you can install the material vertically or horizontally. The style was born out of traditional and proven wood shiplap, common on older houses. This modern adaptation in steel has a permanence we couldn't find with other products.

In our budget calculations, this splurge was well worth the upcharge compared with more conventional siding products. What sealed the deal was not only Vesta's warranty and non-fading, rustproof finish, but also its sustainability. Steel is 100% recyclable.

## Working with steel plank siding

Installing Vesta Steel Plank siding is similar to installing vinyl or aluminum siding. Many of the components are the same profile, and you install them in the same manner. Vesta does employ some unique components and methods that aid its durability. Its support trim, for example, maintains the rigidity of the siding where it tucks into the J-channel at the top of a wall or below a window.

The Getaway was designed with generous 3-ft.-wide soffits and a 2x8 subfascia on the sides and the front. A soffit this wide would often require additional support framing in the center. However, with a 29-gauge thickness, the plank is stiff enough to bridge that distance. Beyond the subfascia, the only additional soffit framing needed was a 2-by nailing flange against the house. We used a lighter color of Vesta Steel Plank for our soffit material to contrast with the darker siding and to coordinate with our roof material. We oriented these soffit planks and our outdoor porch ceiling in the same direction

J-channel installed around windows

Starter strip

The starter strip is crucial. Measure twice before snapping a chalk line.

as our decking. The 8-in. fascia trim pieces hide the subfascia and the ends of the soffit planks. The ends against the house are hidden by the J-channel, installed later, that caps the top course of our sidewall planks.

Depending on a home's roof design, you'll need to consider venting the roof and soffit. Our Getaway has vaulted ceilings and therefore no attic, so we insulated the ceiling with closed-cell spray foam. This "hot roof" construction method doesn't require soffit venting. If your roof system requires venting, be sure the framing and the soffit material allow proper airflow.

To begin the bottom-to-top installation of siding, first measure down from the soffit. Setting the starter strip for the first course is crucial. After calculating to be sure we wouldn't end up with a skinny course at our windows or in the final top row, we snapped a chalk line to indicate the placement of our starter strip. Even with new construction, this line may not be level. It's more important that your siding be parallel to your soffit and windows. With our starter course line established, we set multiple

parallel lines above it for reference as we sided our way up the wall. The planks fit together consistently, requiring little course adjustment and making for a fast installation.

Making weatherproof, attractive siding joints can be time-consuming, whether the ends of the planks butt together or overlap. With other types of siding, these joints often require caulking or priming, and some tooling for a good fit. The Vesta Plank system uses a clean overlapping interface on the ends of each panel to provide a tight fit and nearly invisible seam.

To allow panels to expand and contract, and

1/8" to 3/16" gap

to hide variations in the exterior sheathing, proper fastening is vital. A 1/8- to 3/16-in. gap is required between the nail head and the panel's nail flange. Each nail must be driven into a wall stud, not just into the sheathing. We marked the locations of our wall studs on the exterior house wrap so we knew where to nail.

2x8 subfascia

3'-wide soffits

# Cutting steel siding

Cutting steel siding is easier than you might think, as long as you use the proper tools. A sliding miter saw and a circular saw with a ferrous metal blade are best. Cutting thin steel requires a saw blade with many teeth: An 80-tooth carbide blade yields the cleanest cuts. A grinder or an abrasive type of saw can damage the siding's protective finish, and use of those tools could void the product's warranty.

For making long horizontal cuts or rips, we chose power shears. This tool makes quick work of long cuts of up to 12 ft. We used hand metal shears for precise cuts with J-channel sections, corner pieces and other components.

We finished this siding installation with a bit of color-coordinated caulking around utility, plumbing and electrical penetrations. The tall lakeside exterior of the Getaway was something to behold with its completed siding. Although a modern design, the structure keeps an organic look; the earthy finish on the siding makes our Getaway appear as if it simply grew out of the woods.

# A GOOD FIRST IMPRESSION FOR A FAST SALE

**O**f course, the best home-selling advice is to fix everything that needs fixing. But pay special attention to the things a buyer will see first. Anything needing repair or replacement will put a buyer off. Here are the top items you should focus on:

- The front door or storm door should have a nice fresh finish and operate smoothly.
- A doorbell that isn't working sends a clear message that you're not on top of household maintenance. Fixing it is easy (search for "doorbell repair" at *familyhandyman.com*), and installing a new battery model is even easier.
- A weather-beaten mailbox and old exterior light fixtures just look sad. One trip to the home center and you can update both. For all the how-to, search for "install a mailbox" and "exterior light fixture" at *familyhandyman.com*.

**MEET THE EXPERT**
**Melanie Zaelich is a certified home stager and stylist, and the owner of Happy Place Interiors** (*happyplace interiors.com*).

# METAL ROOFING

## Get the layers right for a long-lasting roof

Ice-and-water barrier

Eave trim

Inside foam closure strip

24"

BY MIKE BERNER

**W**ith its sleek, modern look, metal panel roofing was our first choice for the *Family Handyman* Getaway. It has no visible seams and is maintenance free—just a light rain will wash leaves and sticks off the roof. Even better, it won't grow moss and algae in the shade of the Wisconsin woods. A metal roof will reduce cooling costs by reflecting heat and will last 50 to 70 years. Armed with a basic understanding of the anatomy of a metal roof, along with a few tips, you can install one yourself in just a few days.

Adhesive backing

6" to 8" overlap

Adhesive backing

## Apply the underlayment

The first layer on top of the plywood or OSB roof deck is the underlayment. For this we chose a self-healing ice-and-water membrane to protect the shallow-pitched roof deck. The tricky part in laying the underlayment is keeping it flat and wrinkle-free. Unroll the underlayment across the roof while removing the bottom half of the adhesive backing. Overlap the previous layer by 6 to 8 in. Once the underlayment is rolled out, cut it flush and pull the rest of the adhesive backing out from underneath.

**Outside foam closure strip**

**Ridge cap**

**Gable trim**

**Metal roofing panel**

It's all about the layers. When it rains, a roof sheds water from one layer to the next until the water runs off the roof. Build roof layers the right way and your home will stay dry inside its entire life.

**Eave trim**

**Gable trim**

## Bend trim ends closed

Before you install the trim, you need to cut and bend the leading end to wrap it around the corner. Make a series of 1-in. cuts with aviation snips at each bend to create tabs. Fold the tabs in with a hand seamer to meet a wall or a corner, or to close a gap created by the trim. Each trim is a different shape, requiring unique cuts and bends.

## Fasten eave trim

Install the eave trim tight to the fascia, and fasten it to the roof deck over the underlayment with 1-in. roofing nails. In warmer climates, the eave is attached before the underlayment. In northern Wisconsin, where ice dams are common, we install these atop the underlayment to protect the entire roof from those ice dams.

**Mono pitch ridge cap**

## Splice and overlap trims

Where two trim ends meet, you'll splice them together. First, cut the bottom hem of the underlapping trim at an angle. After installing the underlapping trim, apply sealant on top. Pry open the bottom hem of the overlapping trim and slide it over the angle-cut hem of the underlapping trim.

**Sidewall flashing trim**

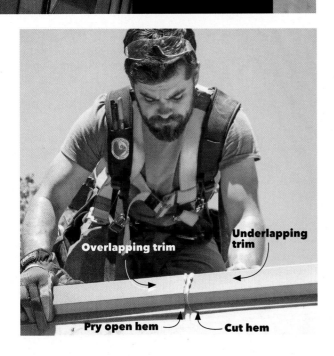

**Overlapping trim**

**Underlapping trim**

**Pry open hem**

**Cut hem**

**Second mark**

35'

28'

## Snap a square reference line

A square reference line is important for installing roofing panels evenly. Use the 3-4-5 method to establish a reference line 90 degrees to the eave. First, make a mark along the eave 3 ft. (or any multiple of 3) from the corner. At that mark, measure 4 ft. (or the same multiple of 4) toward the ridge. Then, from the original corner, measure 5 ft. (or the same multiple of 5) and mark where it intersects the second mark. Snap a line from the first 3-ft. mark through the intersection of the second and third marks. Since the Getaway roof is larger, I measured to 21 ft., 28 ft. and 35 ft. (7 times 3, 4 and 5) to make my square reference line.

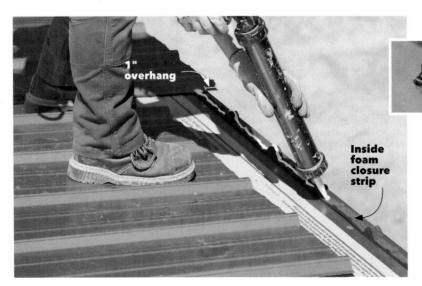

**1" overhang**

**Inside foam closure strip**

**Rubber gasket**

## Drive screws just right

Fastening the panels just right is the key to a watertight roof. Here is what you should know:

■ At the eave, place screws on both sides of every rib and lined up to go through the foam closure strip.

■ Each row should be spaced no more than 24 in., with one screw at each rib on the overlapping side.

■ Start at the bottom, fastening across the panel in rows, working toward the ridge.

■ Drive screws to sit flat on the roof; a crooked screw won't seal.

■ Don't overtighten or undertighten. Tighten just enough to compress the rubber gasket to the edge of the screw head, not past it.

■ Clean up any metal shavings or burrs right away. They will rust.

## Set the first panel

Place each metal panel on an inside foam closure strip. A strip is shaped to fit the corrugated underside of the panel and to keep bugs and water from getting underneath. Position the closure strip along the eave about 1 in. from the edge, and stick it to the panel with butyl tape. Run a bead of sealant on top of the closure strip, then set your panel so it overhangs beyond the eave by 1 in. Adjust the panel so any measurement from it to the reference line is the same at the top and bottom.

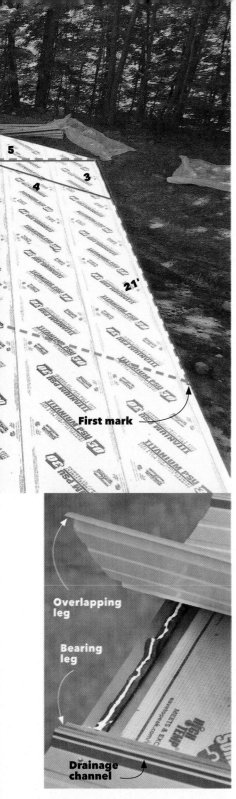

First mark

Gable trim

Butyl tape

## Cover the rake edge

After all the panels are fastened, it's time to attach the gable trim. This cleans up the edge of the panel and keeps rain and snow from getting under the roof panels and siding. After you bend the end of the trim to meet the corner at the eave, apply butyl tape on the underside of the trim, where it lands on the flat part of the roof panels. Press it in place and drive screws every 12 in. right over the butyl tape.

Overlapping leg

Bearing leg

Drainage channel

## Overlap the panels

The two edges of the metal panels are different. The overlapping edge has a shorter rib leg that doesn't contact the roof surface when laid flat. The rib on the underlapped side has a drainage or anti-siphon channel to keep water moving toward the eave. Overlap the last rib on each panel; they should nest together perfectly.

### SECURE THE RIDGE CAP

To cap the roof, adhere a line of outside closure strips with butyl tape 4 in. from the top of the peak; this is where you'll fasten the ridge cap to the roof with screws. Apply a bead of sealant on the foam closure, then fit the ridge cap on the peak and fasten it through every rib to the roof deck with 2-in. screws. With the cap of the roof complete, all the water that lands on the roof will be able to exit the roof without ever touching the underlayment.

Sealant

Outside foam closure strip

Mono pitch ridge cap

Butyl tape

# ROLL-UP DOOR

## Experience open-air living

BY JOE CRUZ

At the *Family Handyman* Getaway, we wanted a full view of the scenery. We love to see the colors of the forest, hear the song of a loon on the lake and smell the fresh air in the morning, and we wanted to be closer to it all. A simple screen door was not enough.

We decided that a roll-up glass wall opening to our deck would enhance each of these senses and nearly double the square footage of our main living area. Many cafes, brew-pubs and homeowners are opening up to the industrial chic style of a glass panel roll-up wall instead of a smaller sliding patio door.

**A SCREEN**
Keeping out the bugs is a definite concern in the North Woods of Wisconsin. If necessary, we can install a full fiberglass net screen, available for about $60.

**THE APRON**
Like a garage floor, the apron is slanted, allowing water to flow out and away.

**THE BOTTOM SEAL**
The bottom rubber seal is designed to keep out pests and debris, and to save on energy costs.

**THE DOOR**
To get a full view, we installed a 9 x 12-ft. Wayne Dalton Contemporary Aluminum Model 8850 garage door with 12 insulated clear glass panels. Staying on point with the contemporary style of the Getaway cabin, the door frame and tracks were treated with a black powder-coat finish.

## THE OPENER

To complement the open floor plan, we installed a Genie model 6170 wall-mount garage door opener. Because this opener doesn't require a traditional rail and power head hanging from the ceiling, it's ideal for this application. It attaches directly to the garage door's spring tube. This opener has the Aladdin Connect smart garage feature, which enables you to monitor your garage door from a smart device. It also features a wireless wall console and a Bluetooth LED light and door lock.

## THE R-VALUES

The 1/2-in. insulated argon-filled glass has an R-value of 3.125. The stiles and rails of the door frame are extruded aluminum alloy and are filled with polyurethane insulation, giving the door an R-value of 4.06.

## THE ROLLERS

We chose nylon rollers with bearings because they're quiet, rust resistant and long-lasting.

## THE TRACK

Your roll-up door track can be attractive if it gets a powder-coat finish, as it should when it's in a living area.

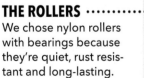

## Go with a Pro

No doubt about it, installing a garage door yourself could save you hundreds of dollars. But even for an experienced DIYer, this project would take a good 8 to 12 hours to complete. Let's not forget the danger involved in installing the torsion springs for a roll-up door. Some jobs are best left to the pros who do things like this every day.

# QUICK & EASY
# STORM DOORS

## Install a storm door kit in just 30 minutes

BY MIKE BERNER

**A** storm door with a roll-away screen makes it easy to let in the breeze on a beautiful day and keep out the weather when it's not so nice. Most door companies make an easy-to-install version that has a precut frame and adjustable parts. If your door opening is mostly square, the install is a cinch. In about a half hour, and without altering the opening, I had a perfect new door.

**MEET THE BUILDER**
Mike Berner, an associate editor at *Family Handyman*, is a big fan of anything quick and easy.

### WHAT IT TAKES

| TIME | COST |
|------|------|
| 1/2–1 hour | $250 |

| SKILL LEVEL | TOOLS |
|-------------|-------|
| Beginner | Drill, chisel |

Placeholder screw

Hinge rail

## 1 SET THE PLACE-HOLDER SCREW

Hold the hinge rail tight to the door trim and drive a screw into the top hole. Leave a 1/8-in. gap between the screw head and the trim. Remove the hinge rail by sliding it over the screw.

## 2 ASSEMBLE THE DOOR

Set the door on a pair of sawhorses and screw the hinge rail to the door. Cover the unused mortise hole with the provided plug, then slide on the adjustable door sweep and slip on the rail extender cap.

Door sweep

Rail extender cap

Mortise plug

Hinge rail

## 3 HANG THE STORM DOOR

Hang the door by the hinge rail onto the placeholder screw and tighten it to hold the door in place.

## 4 FASTEN THE HINGE RAIL

Drive screws along the inside of the hinge rail. Slide the rail cap down to the door's sill, then fasten the outside of the hinge rail to the trim.

## 5 INSTALL DRIP CAP AND LATCH RAIL

Line up the drip cap with the edge of the hinge rail, hold it tight to the trim and fasten it with screws. Install the latch rail tight to the drip cap, lined up with the edge of it.

Fasten hinge rail on inside

Slide rail extension to sill

Line up edges

Drip cap

Latch rail

### 6 DRILL HOLES FOR THE LATCH

Snap the drilling guide onto the door and drill the holes from both sides with the provided spade bit.

### 7 INSERT THE LOCK BODY

Slide the lock body into the mortise and fasten it with a screw. If the latch isn't facing the right direction, you'll have to unscrew the front of the lock body and spin the latch.

### 8 MOUNT THE HARDWARE

Position the faceplates on each side of the door. Push the handle rod through the faceplate and lock body, and secure the other handle with a setscrew.

**Drilling guide**

**Lock body**

**Tighten setscrew**

**Faceplate**

**Handle rod**

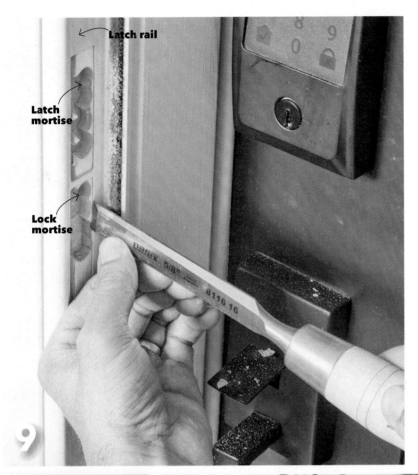

Latch rail

Latch
mortise

Lock
mortise

**9**

## 9 MAKE ROOM FOR THE LATCH AND DEAD BOLT

The latch and dead bolt should be able to extend all the way into the latch opening. If not, you'll have to drill and chisel out a mortise in the trim.

## 10 INSTALL THE CLOSER

Screw the side-jamb bracket to the hinge-side jamb, then insert the closer with the short connecting pin. Pull out the closer rod slightly, then attach the door bracket to the door. Connect the closer to the door bracket with the long pin. If your door has two closers, repeat this step at the top of the door.

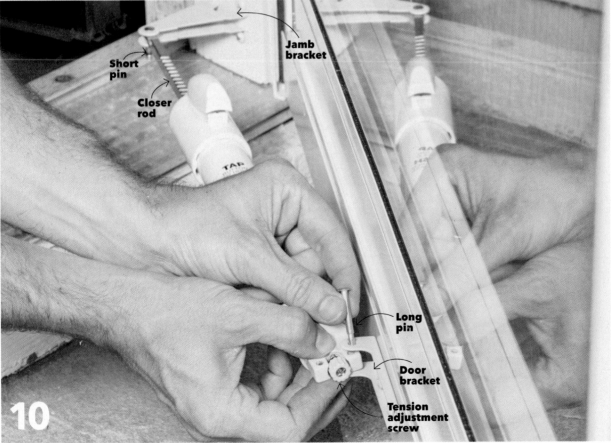

Jamb
bracket

Short
pin

Closer
rod

Long
pin

Door
bracket

Tension
adjustment
screw

**10**

# WINDOWS

## Decoding the numbers to make a good decision

BY BRAD HOLDEN

Whether you're standing in the window aisle at a home center or studying window specs online, the wide variety of options and add-ons available may seem daunting. You can choose windows that control solar heat gain, let in more or less light, resist condensation and more. Here, I'll outline the important numbers and terms you need to know to make informed choices.

## WHAT SHOULD YOU PAY FOR?

You can choose plenty of add-ons for your windows, but you'll need to decide what's worth the upcharge.

■ When it comes to windows, price isn't always an indicator of performance. Shop around using the selection tool at *efficientwindows.org*. You can find quality windows below the top price tier.

■ Stock sizes or custom? You might think you can save a little money buying in-stock sizes from a home center. Most manufacturers, however, build windows to order, so the idea of "stock sizes" isn't always relevant. Order the sizes you need instead of just grabbing what's available at the store.

■ If you're thinking about upgrading to triple-glazing to save on energy bills, consider it carefully. It'll take a long time to recoup the expense. In most cases, double-glazed insulating windows are sufficient. However, if you enjoy sitting by the windows in the winter, compare the cost of double-glazed to triple-glazed and decide if the price difference—sometimes as much as 30%—is worth it.

■ Grilles, high-end hardware and exotic wood species are decorative only and cost extra. You'll need to weigh the look you want against the added cost. Be aware that grilles might raise the U-factor number slightly.

■ Buying windows prepainted does cost extra, but it's a huge time-saver. If I had to choose one thing from this list to splurge on, this would be it.

STEVE URICH

# Choose windows that suit your climate and location

When you're window shopping, understanding these terms will help you find windows that will perform well in your climate. For in-depth, location-specific information for your house, use the window selection tool from the National Fenestration Rating Council at *efficientwindows.org*. What is *fenestration*, you ask? Generally, it means any opening in a surface, such as a wall.

**1 INSULATING GLASS**

Insulating glass adds a layer of energy efficiency and comfort to your living space. Most new windows have two panes of glass with gas–typically argon–in between the panes.

**2 U-FACTOR**

The U-factor tells you a window's rate of heat loss. The lower the number, the better the window will keep heat in. In a cold climate like Wisconsin's North Woods, chose windows with a U-factor of 0.27, which meets Energy Star ratings for northern zones. If your windows have a higher U-factor number, you'll want to increase the solar heat gain coefficient **(see #6)**.

**3 VISIBLE TRANSMITTANCE**

Expressed as a number between 0 and 1, visible transmittance signifies the fraction of the visible sunlight spectrum allowed through a pane of glass. The higher the number, the more light the window lets in. Generally, most people prefer to let in all the light they can, so be aware that a lower solar heat gain coefficient typically means a slight reduction in visible transmittance.

ENERGY STAR® Certified in Highlighted Regions

■ Certified

**World's Best Window Co.**
Series "2000"
Casement
Vinyl Clad Wood Frame
Double Glazing•Argon Fill•Low E
XYZ-X-1-00001-00001

National Fenestration Rating Council®
CERTIFIED

**ENERGY PERFORMANCE RATINGS**

| U-Factor (U.S. / I-P) | Solar Heat Gain Coefficient |
|---|---|
| **0.35** | **0.32** |

**ADDITIONAL PERFORMANCE RATINGS**

| Visible Transmittance | Air Leakage (U.S. / I-P) |
|---|---|
| **0.51** | **≤0.3** |
| Condensation Resistance | |
| **51** | **–** |

Manufacturer stipulates that these ratings conform to applicable NFRC procedures for determining whole product performance. NFRC ratings are determined for a fixed set of environmental conditions and a specific product size. NFRC does not recommend any product and does not warrant the suitability of any product for any specific use. Consult manufacturer's literature for other product performance information. www.nfrc.org

**4 CONDENSATION RESISTANCE**

The higher this number, the better your windows are at resisting condensation. This is greatly affected by interior relative humidity.

**5 COATINGS**

A low-E coating is standard on most windows. The coating is transparent to allow in all the light, but it reflects heat. In warm climates, it's applied to the outer glass to keep heat out. In cold climates, it's applied to the inside glass to retain heat.

**6 SOLAR HEAT GAIN COEFFICIENT**

Typically a bigger concern in warm climates, solar heat gain is also a consideration in northern climates where summers are hot. The lower the number, the better the window is at blocking heat from the sun. Most people buy windows with the same ratings for the whole house, but it's possible to fine-tune your windows to suit your needs. For example, you can choose windows with a lower number for your south-facing windows and windows with a higher number for your north-facing ones. Some people even buy two sets of sashes for their windows, changing them seasonally.

**7 AIR LEAKAGE RATING**

An air leakage rating from 0.10 to 0.30 is good; most new windows easily meet that standard.

**MEET THE EXPERT**
**Steve Urich is the senior director of programs at the National Fenestration Rating Council.**

# REPLACE A CRACKED STORM WINDOW

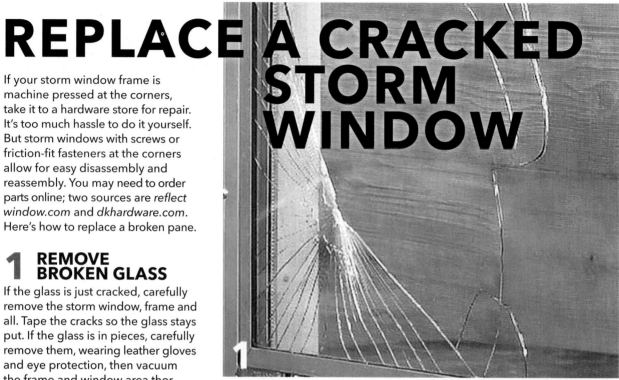

If your storm window frame is machine pressed at the corners, take it to a hardware store for repair. It's too much hassle to do it yourself. But storm windows with screws or friction-fit fasteners at the corners allow for easy disassembly and reassembly. You may need to order parts online; two sources are *reflectwindow.com* and *dkhardware.com*. Here's how to replace a broken pane.

## 1 REMOVE BROKEN GLASS

If the glass is just cracked, carefully remove the storm window, frame and all. Tape the cracks so the glass stays put. If the glass is in pieces, carefully remove them, wearing leather gloves and eye protection, then vacuum the frame and window area thoroughly before removing the frame.

## 2 MEASURE FOR NEW GLASS

Before you disassemble the frame, measure the inside width and height. Measure the depth of the channel using a flat ruler and add that to the height and width of the frame's interior dimensions.

## 3 DISASSEMBLE THE FRAME

For friction-fit frames like this one, clamp one frame side to a work surface. Separate the frame parts using a hammer and a wood block. Remove any remaining glass and the rubber gasket, being careful not to tear it. If the gasket is in good shape, reuse it. Vacuum the work area.

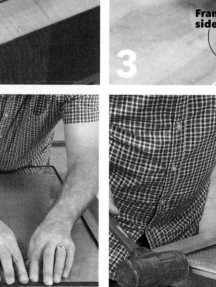

Frame side

## 4 INSTALL THE GLASS

Apply the gasket over the edge of the new glass. If it's a new gasket, make small cuts at the corners to help make the turns. Tap the frame sides on first, using a rubber mallet. Align the corner keys on the frame top and bottom with the corners of the sides, and gently tap the frame pieces home.

**JOE CRUZ**
ASSOCIATE EDITOR

Rubber gasket

4a    4b

# CHOOSING WINDOW SCREEN

Screens are no longer a one-size-fits-all category. If you've never replaced your window screens and they're nearing the end of their service life, know you can choose from several options. You'll still find the classic aluminum, but a different screen material might be a better choice for you.

**ALUMINUM SCREEN** is very durable, allows great visibility, and is available in many colors and different mesh sizes. On the downside, it's more expensive than fiberglass and is susceptible to dents.

**SUN OR SOLAR SCREENS** block light and absorb heat, making them a good choice for a warm-climate patio. Typically, they reduce natural light by 30% to 40%. They can help reduce air conditioning costs, add privacy and slow the fading of patio furniture. But they'll darken your space.

**VISIBILITY SCREEN** is all about the view. When you want to be able to see through a screen clearly without even noticing it, this light mesh screen is a good choice. The downsides are that this screen doesn't offer any privacy or block sunlight, and it is less durable.

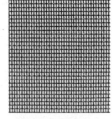

**PET-RESISTANT SCREEN** is typically made from heavy-duty polyester coated with vinyl. It might not stop your St. Bernard from a tempting squirrel chase, but this type of screen definitely resists tears from an errant paw.

**SMALL INSECT SCREEN** has tiny mesh to keep out the smallest gnats and no-see-ums. If you live in a marshy, wooded or coastal area and your screened porch is plagued by tiny pests, this is a good option. On the downside, small insect screen does decrease visibility.

# GRILL REVIVAL

## 8 ways to make your old grill good as new (or even better)

BY JAY CORK

**I**f your grill cooks as shabby as it looks, a new model is probably on your wish list. But before you start shopping, consider this: There's a solution for almost any grill problem, and the fixes are easy.

Winter is the perfect time to recondition a grill. I know—I tackled two of mine as the snow flew, and the next spring, they were set to go. All it took was a little elbow grease and DIY ingenuity. Now, these grills will be cooking for many seasons to come.

**MEET THE EXPERT**
**Jay Cork is an associate editor at** *Family Handyman*. **Over the past decade, he's rescued many grills from the scrap pile.**

## *Grilling since 1951*

The grill that did the most to popularize backyard grilling was born the same year as this magazine. In fact, *Family Handyman* was one of the first to introduce the Weber grill, and we've been featuring projects, tips and fixes for it ever since. The invention of the Weber grill is an inspirational DIY story, too.

Seeking to improve on the brazier grill he was using at home, George Stephen Sr. was inspired by a product he made at Weber Brothers Metal Works in Chicago: buoys for the U.S. Coast Guard. He cut the bottom off a buoy and added a leg stand. With the addition of a vented lid, the kettle grill was born. He called it "George's Barbecue Kettle" and started selling them in 1952. By the late '50s, his shop had stopped making buoys. Weber grills are still made in Illinois and are sold in more than 70 countries.

**Each igniter is mounted to a burner tube with two screws**

**Cleaned and straightened, the igniter is ready to be reattached**

## ◄ A GAS GRILL THAT WON'T IGNITE

When a gas grill won't ignite, it could mean that the battery is dead or that the igniters have gone bad and need to be replaced. I was prepared to replace mine when upon inspection I discovered that they weren't actually bad. Instead, two had somehow gotten bent, and the gap between the igniter tips and the burner tubes must be 1/8 in. or less for a spark to occur. After cleaning and straightening the igniters, I reattached them and made sure they were properly positioned to create a spark.

## UNEVEN FLAMES ▼

If the burners aren't severely rusted, they can be cleaned. First, clean the burner tubes with a wire brush or an abrasive pad, then clean out each burner hole with a toothpick. Doing this once a year will extend the life of any gas grill burner. But if the holes get too big or have rusted through in some places, it's time to replace the burners.

Try cleaning first—
a toothpick is
the perfect size
and won't harm
the steel

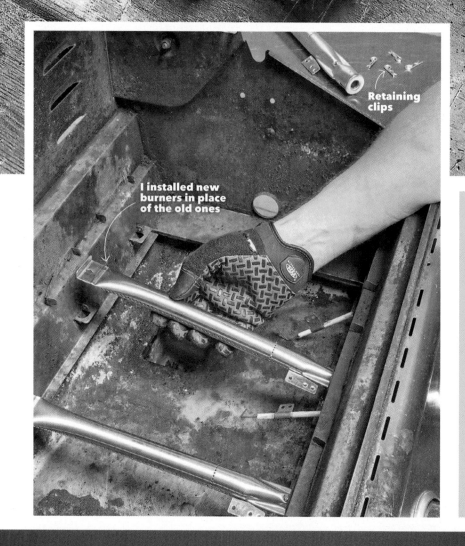

Retaining
clips

I installed new
burners in place
of the old ones

## WHERE TO FIND GRILL PARTS

Most home centers and garden centers carry one or two brands of grill parts, but I've always had difficulty finding parts for my particular grill. The good news is that parts for virtually any grill ever made are available online. I found several websites that cater to grilling fanatics. The folks at *grillparts.com* and *bbqguys.com* were happy to chat with me and help me find what I was looking for.

## COALS KEEP LOSING HEAT OR GOING OUT ▶

The vent on my charcoal grill was rusted shut. I couldn't find an exact replacement, so I decided to restore it.

The easiest way I've found to remove rust is to use cleaning vinegar, which is available at home centers (a half gallon costs about $2). Cleaning vinegar is about 20% more acidic than the type you have in the kitchen cupboard. There are no harsh chemicals or acids to deal with, and you don't have to spend hours with a wire brush and sandpaper.

I soaked the parts in vinegar overnight, and by the next morning the rust rinsed right off. After a quick coat of high-temperature paint, the vent was ready to be reinstalled. The refurbished vent looks great, and now my grill has proper airflow again.

I soaked the hinges and other parts in cleaning vinegar

## ▲ WORN-OUT SIDE TABLES

The side tables on my charcoal grill were showing their age and had started to rust. So, I purchased bamboo cutting boards for about $20 each online. After using the old side table as a template to trace the shape, I made a quick cut with the band saw and screwed them on. They look fantastic, and to keep them looking that way, I'll apply butcher block oil at the beginning of every grilling season.

I used auger-tip screws because they don't require predrilling

## ◄ INCONSISTENT HEAT OR FLAMES

Once I replaced the burners, the burner closest to the fuel tank burned well, but the one farthest away had either a small flame or none at all. This meant the regulator needed to be replaced.

Home centers and garden centers carry basic regulators for about $20, but online I found this regulator with a stainless steel braided jacket for about $30. It was longer than the original, which was nice; the old one was so short that it was hard to attach to the tank. Replacing the regulator was easy; after wrapping Teflon tape around the male threads on the manifold, I used an adjustable wrench to tighten it down.

**A 3/8" female flare has an actual inside diameter of 5/8"**

I used one self-tapping screw per leg

I reused the old washer but used a new cotter pin

## ▲ LOOSE LEGS

When the legs on a kettle grill become loose, the grill can be a pain to move. Here's a permanent fix that took me about 10 minutes: I drilled a pilot hole in each leg and screwed in a self-tapping stainless steel screw. Go slow; the legs are aluminum and can easily strip out.

## ▲ BROKEN WHEELS

The plastic wheels on my charcoal grill were broken. I decided to replace them with heavy-duty rubber wheels (about $30 a pair online). The ones I found were a little larger than the originals. To make sure the grill still sat level, I added a small rubber foot on the other end of the frame using self-tapping screws.

## ADDING TEMPERATURE SENSORS

When the temperature sensors on my grills broke, I replaced them and added a few more. The additional sensors will give me a much clearer indication of what's going on inside my grill. I used a step drill to pierce the lid and then attached the new sensors with a threaded nut. I love step drills: perfectly round holes, automatically deburred. Step drill bits cost about $40 at home centers.

**Step drill bit**

**These temp sensors are available online for about $15 each**

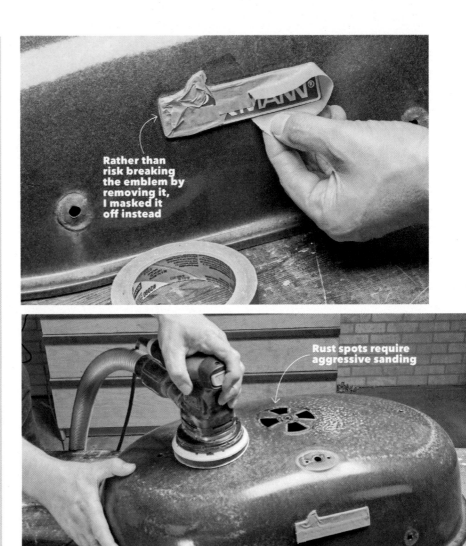

**Rather than risk breaking the emblem by removing it, I masked it off instead**

**Rust spots require aggressive sanding**

## ▲ CHIPPED AND RUSTY PAINT

Repainting a grill takes time—time I didn't want to take during grilling season. In the winter, though, I could take my time to completely repaint it while I performed other repairs and upgrades. My grill had only a few rust spots to fix; most of it just needed to be degreased and cleaned with mineral spirits before being sanded.

I found I had to be aggressive with the sandpaper; I had to use 40 grit on some spots! But, in the end, I sanded the grill up to 180 grit. After one more wipe-down with mineral spirits, it was ready to paint.

I used high-temperature paint in "Charcoal Metallic" from *kbs-coatings.com*. It's good to 1,500 degrees F. Because spray-painting indoors requires careful ventilation, I set up a fan behind me on low to help guide the overspray to the vent fan (set on high) in the wall.

This paint needs heat to cure, so I filled the firebox with coals, lit them and let it sit. It stayed at about 450 degrees for almost two hours. Perfect.

**Aerosol coatings from KBS cost about $20**

# NEXT-GENERATION
# GRILLING

The outdoor grill, reinvented

## BY BILL BERGMANN

**W**e've been grilling food since the domestication of fire. By the 12th century, this outdoor ritual went indoors when we devised ovens for our "modern" kitchens. In the 1950s, cooking went outdoors again with the postwar boom that brought us the Weber-style charcoal grill. Today, we're enjoying an outdoor cooking renaissance, with the grill becoming an essential extension of our indoor kitchens and dining rooms.

Knowing how your grill works is the secret recipe for great food. Here, you'll learn about the operation and cooking characteristics of three popular grill types—from a few modern grilling masters.

> *"I think finally we're at the point where the grill is an appliance and people aren't going to just go get that poorly made $200 grill that happened to be at the corner hardware store. They want something that's going to last and yields consistent results year-round."*
> **DIVA Q**

# PELLET GRILL

Traeger pellet grills are highly regarded and are the choice of many celebrated outdoor chefs. Diva Q is one of those chefs, and I caught up with her to find out what makes her such a devotee.

"When I first started in competitive BBQ, lots of guys were put off by a woman with a pellet grill. But once I proved myself, those same guys are now asking advice on how to use the pellet grill, wishing they'd listened when I said, 'You know I'm working smarter, not harder, right?'" For Diva Q, her pellet grill yields the "most consistent results with the easiest learning curve," opening the door for grilling newbies and enabling veterans to experiment. While the new app-controlled pellet grills are easy to use, there are some essentials to learn.

"One of the key things is not all pellets are created equal." Diva Q says the compression rate, moisture content and sourcing of the wood all play key parts in a quality pellet. Softwood is not great and is usually what's in cheap pellets. All-natural hardwood gives the best fire and flavor. The flavor profiles of apple, cherry, hickory and oak are all different. Diva Q feels it's best to establish a base flavor that's softer and then mix in a harder one like mesquite. Also, the hotter a pellet grill gets, the less smoke it produces. This is good for baking and high-temperature dishes that don't need smoke. But at temps less than 250 degrees F, "they produce all kinds of beautiful mild smoke that brings that great flavor to the food."

Most pellet grills don't sear a steak as well as a gas or charcoal grill. But Diva Q says she's learned a lot about the science of grilling, and she now knows that caramelization for the desired char from searing still happens with low, indirect heat. With a pellet grill, you can still get what's called the "Maillard reaction," which gives browned food its singular flavor, but it is not done with the same high-heat char as on a direct heat charcoal or gas grill.

Diva Q says that she can smell when the sugars are changing with low heat and that she doesn't really need an app to cook. She will use the Traeger app if she leaves the grill unattended. She says the real benefit of the app is its library of recipes. They designate timing, temperature and serving size, enabling anyone to execute exceptional grilled food.

**Charwood pellets**

**Cherry pellets**

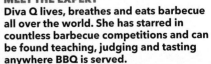

**MEET THE EXPERT**
**Diva Q lives, breathes and eats barbecue all over the world. She has starred in countless barbecue competitions and can be found teaching, judging and tasting anywhere BBQ is served.**

## A SMOKING OVEN

Pellet grills/smokers resulted from the 1973 oil crisis, as we searched for alternative fuel sources for furnaces. Joe Traeger figured out how to use compressed sawdust pellets to fuel a grill. His original design shines through in today's pellet grills. The pellets go in a hopper, from which a motorized auger delivers them to a firepot, which has an electric heating element. A fan then aids combustion and circulates the hot air. Traeger held the patent on this grill until 2006. Then mass production brought a wave of innovation, tranforming them into sophisticated appliances.

Most modern pellet grills employ digital automation for app-based control. A thermostat in the cooking chamber automates the fan and auger operation. You can program your grill to cook at a specific temperature for a determined length of time. Some grills integrate leave-in meat probes to hold a temperature once the food reaches a set point.

## How it works

1 Auger
2 Fan
3 Igniter
4 Firepot
5 Heat baffle
6 Grease dome
7 Grease bucket

→ Convection heat airflow

→ Cool intake airflow

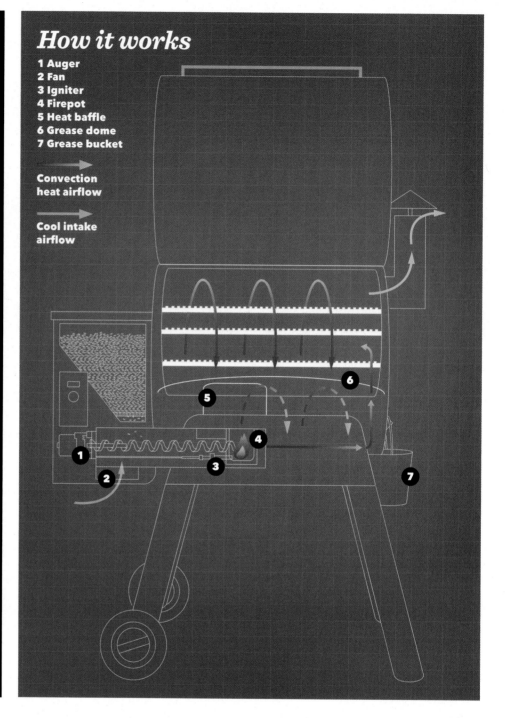

# Recommended wood pellet pairings

|  | BEEF | POULTRY | PORK | LAMB | SEAFOOD | BAKING | VEGETABLES | WILD GAME |
|---|---|---|---|---|---|---|---|---|
| ALDER | X | X | X |  | X | X | X |  |
| APPLE |  | X | X |  |  | X | X |  |
| CHERRY | X | X | X | X |  | X |  |  |
| HICKORY | X | X | X |  |  |  | X | X |
| MAPLE | X |  | X | X |  | X | X |  |
| MESQUITE | X | X |  |  | X |  |  | X |
| OAK | X |  |  |  | X | X |  |  |
| PECAN | X | X | X | X |  | X | X |  |

> *"It's a primal way to cook, which is a beautiful thing these days. You're in the moment, you're interacting with the charcoal, you're building that fire, you're present. It's about mindfulness and, hopefully, not thinking about your cell phone."*
>
> **CHEF ERIC**

# KAMADO GRILL

These grills have been around for thousands of years, but only since WWII has the Japanese kamado been grilling deliciousness in the United States. The kamado grill's ceramic outer shell and inner parts retain heat far better than a steel grill. This results in a slower, more efficient and controlled burn. Their popularity coincided with the rise of "foodie" culture, and they're now available at most home centers and hardware stores. I spoke with kamado guru "Chef Eric" Gephart to glean some knowledge about this archaeologic treasure of a grill.

Many say a kamado heats up slower than other charcoal or gas grills. Chef Eric says that if you have quality lump charcoal and the right approach, you'll have a usable fire in 10 to 15 minutes. Once you have flame, close the lid and adjust the draft door and control cap to find your desired temp. This is a crucial point of control with a kamado. If you leave that cap and draft door open too long, the draft will stoke the coals and the temp can quickly climb as high as 750 degrees F. A kamado is so efficient at holding heat that it's difficult to drop temperature quickly. If you want a slow, low-temp cook, increase the temperature gradually. The upside of the kamado's quick flash heat is that you can slow-smoke food and then finish it with a quick sear by opening up both vents and even the lid for immediate, high heat.

The most popular kamado grills are 18 to 22 in. in diameter, but they come as large as 42. Chef Eric says all grill sizes perform the same way. The only difference is what he calls "grill estate." The more grill space you have, the greater the options for different cook zones, or "heat signatures," as he refers to them. Banking the charcoal to one side creates separate areas of direct and indirect heat, allowing you to cook different foods simultaneously. Larger grills often have secondary grates or racks for even more "grill estate." Combine this with a rotisserie or other accessories and "you can have a culinary jungle gym," says Chef Eric.

Chef Eric sees more and more culinary aspirants drawn to kamado grills. He has used a kamado grill to execute everything from Bretagne-style apple cake to triple cream beer bratwurst and, yes, of course, some serious BBQ brisket.

**Wood chunks**

**Lump charcoal**

**MEET THE EXPERT**
**Chef Eric Gephart is the "Live Fire Culinary Expert" at Kamado Joe. He has taken his high-performance grilling adventures around the world, spreading his passion for food, sustainability and mindfulness to everyone he meets.**

# GRILLING

## THE CLAY POT COOKER

Other than the lid, a kamado grill has two moving parts: the lower draft door, and the top control or chimney cap. Chef Eric sees the draft door as a heat pump, sucking in ambient air to create convection. Closing that draft door is like putting on the brakes; this is where you execute big temperature changes. The chimney cap regulates smaller changes in temperature. The cooking grate sits on the fire ring above the firebox, also ceramic. An optional heat deflector aids indirect cooking. All these ceramic components retain temperature for an even distribution of heat.

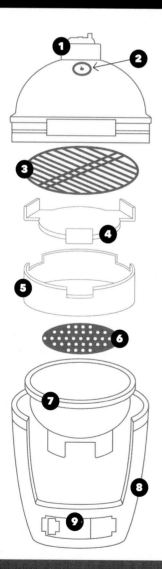

## *How it works*

1 Chimney cap vent
2 Thermometer
3 Standard grate
4 Heat deflector
5 Fire ring
6 Fire grate
7 Firebox
8 Ceramic base
9 Lower draft door

➡ **Convection heat airflow**

➡ **Cool intake airflow**

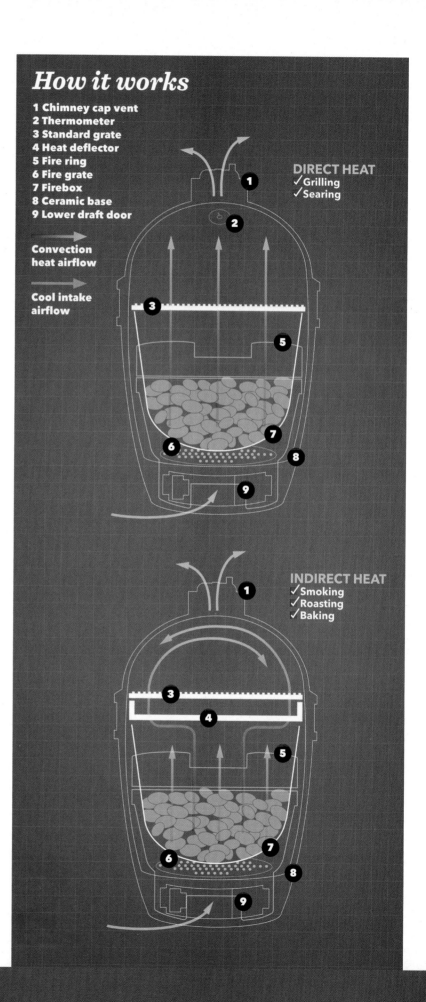

**DIRECT HEAT**
✓ Grilling
✓ Searing

**INDIRECT HEAT**
✓ Smoking
✓ Roasting
✓ Baking

> *"The design of this grill allows both the novice and the seasoned grill chef to execute more creative and adventurous recipes because their focus is on the food, not the flame."*
> **DANIEL MERCER**

# GRAVITY-FED CHARCOAL

Gravity-fed charcoal smokers came on the competitive barbecue scene in the 1990s. Their self-feeding mechanism put an end to staying up all night stoking smokers. Initially these were custom DIY builds, made by a handful of boutique manufacturers. But their popularity quickly put them into the home consumer market.

Until recently, most gravity-fed units were for serious barbecue enthusiasts with big budgets. But design innovations have made these units more user-friendly and affordable. Adam Carter and Daniel Mercer from Masterbuilt have taken gravity-fed charcoal to a new level of "set it and forget it" with automation technology, bringing capabilities not previously seen on this grill type. A fan stoking the firebox automatically adjusts to maintain temperature. It's linked to your phone, so you can monitor your grill remotely. This adds convenience and pinpoint temperature control but also means fast temperature change—up to 700 degrees F within 15 minutes—no fussing with fuel or airflow dampers. With this temperature control, you can sear a steak just as easily as slow-cook a rack of ribs.

Does all this convenience remove the art and craft from grilling? Daniel says, "The creativity with this grill comes in how you layer wood chips in with your fuel or use the fast temperature control to cook several different things for a meal." The ability to use technology to dial in that delicious charcoal flavor without tending a fire removes the barrier to having a great grilling experience every time.

↖ **Charcoal briquettes**

↖ **Wood chips**

**MEET THE EXPERTS**
**Daniel Mercer (left) and Adam Carter are the masterminds behind Masterbuilt's gravity-fed charcoal grills. Their passion for engineering is as strong as their appetite for good southern BBQ.**

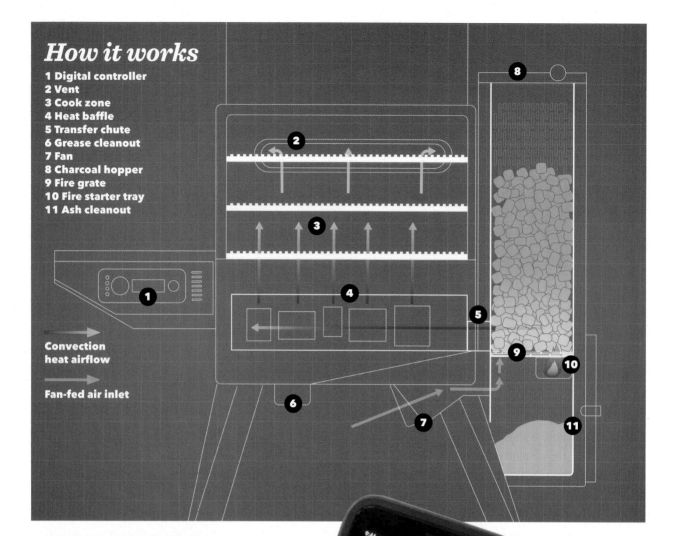

## How it works

1 Digital controller
2 Vent
3 Cook zone
4 Heat baffle
5 Transfer chute
6 Grease cleanout
7 Fan
8 Charcoal hopper
9 Fire grate
10 Fire starter tray
11 Ash cleanout

Convection
heat airflow

Fan-fed air inlet

## MORE THAN JUST GRAVITY

The basic design of gravity-fed charcoal cookers is simple: A tall charcoal hopper sits to one side of the cooker, gravity-feeding fuel into the firebox. An air inlet in the firebox regulates oxygen. Heat and smoke from the firebox flow through a transfer chute and hit the heat baffle that's centered below the cooking zone.

Below the heat baffle sits a grease shield or drip pan with a cleanout tray. The cook chamber has a cooking grate directly over the heat baffle and two or more cooking racks above it. At the top of the chamber, a chimney vents heat and smoke from the firebox up around the cooking zone. There's typically an ash cleanout below the fire grate.

## GRILL APPS

Some might see grilling as a good reason to get off your phone, but monitoring and modulating cooking temperature remotely means you don't have to babysit that slow-cooked meal; you can prepare your side dishes or tend to other chores. Our pros say that the biggest benefit of an app is the recipes, which are created specifically for your grill and the community that shares them.

# Great Goofs®

## Laughs and lessons from our readers

## IF THE TREE FALLS, WILL ANYONE HEAR YOU YELL?

A storm toppled the oak tree next to my house, but amazingly it ended up leaning against the edge of the roof without causing any damage. I climbed on the roof to push the tree away. Just as I was going to start pushing, I realized that as the tree gave way, my momentum might carry me right off the roof! So, instead, I got on my back, inched my way to the edge of the roof, put my feet up on the trunk and pushed as hard as I could.

Success! The tree fell harmlessly to the ground. Only then did I realize that my legs were hanging precariously from the roof's edge. With nothing to push off from, I couldn't inch myself away from the edge! I spent two hours stranded in that position until a friend showed up. Two hours is plenty of time to think about ALL the ways I could have done this better.

**BERNIE SCUTARO**

## ONE STEP FORWARD, THREE STEPS BACK

We hired a contractor to replace our front step. Once it was removed, he attached an auger to his skid loader and told one of his workers where to drill holes for the footings, then he left. After lunch, he returned to pour the concrete.

All seemed well and good until after supper, when we noticed that our laundry room floor drain had backed up. I thought that tree roots had grown into the sewer line again—it happens every year. But when city workers inspected it, they discovered something else: The contractor and his guys had drilled through the sewer line and filled it with concrete. Replacing the line involved digging up 40 ft. of our yard and 12 ft. under the house (taking out our basement floor), and cutting down a 50-year-old tree. What I learned is this: Anytime you're planning to dig big holes, have everything marked, including the sewer line.

**ROD STAPLETON**

# 6 Outdoor Structures, Landscaping & Gardening

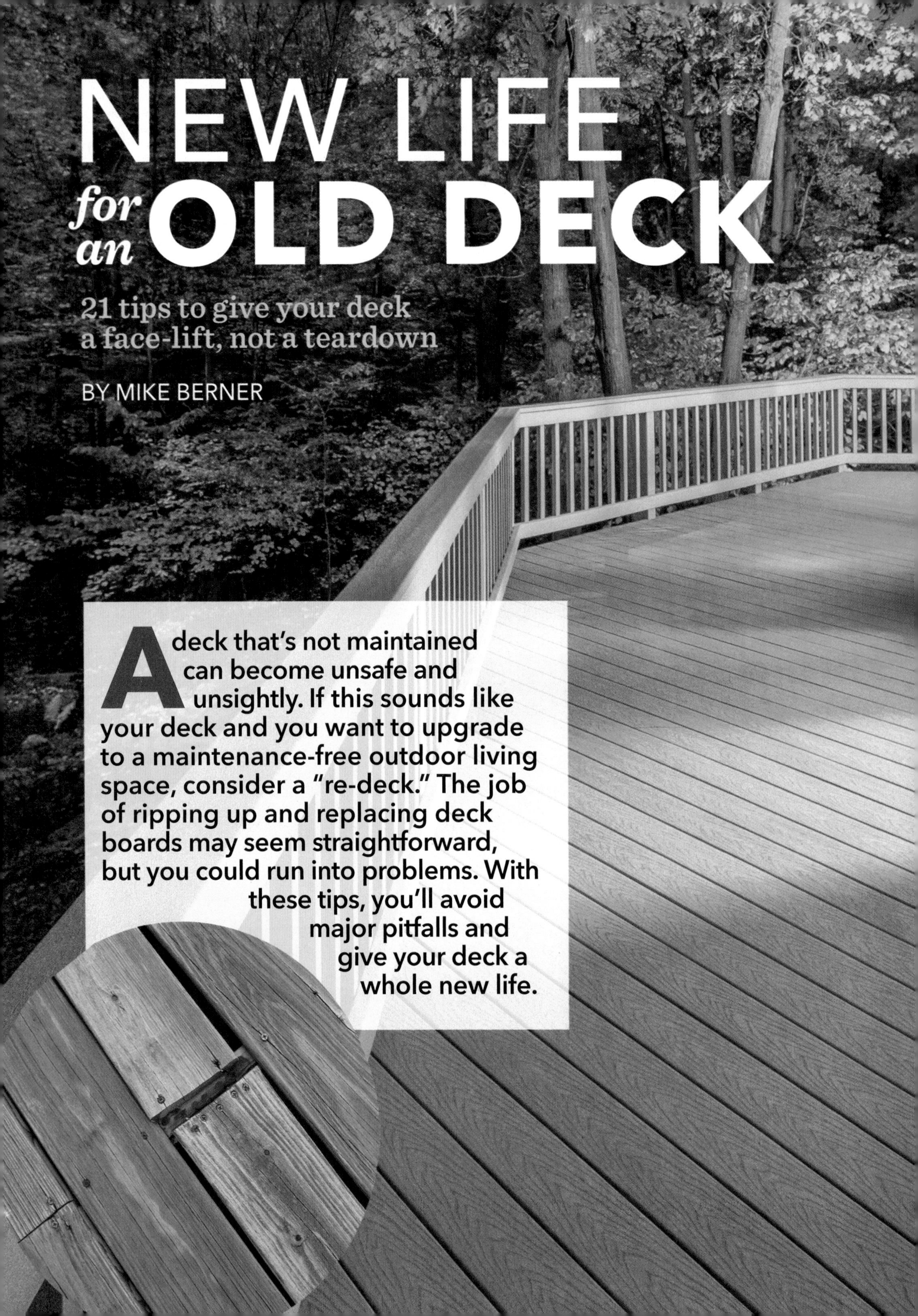

# NEW LIFE
## *for an* OLD DECK

### 21 tips to give your deck a face-lift, not a teardown

BY MIKE BERNER

**A** deck that's not maintained can become unsafe and unsightly. If this sounds like your deck and you want to upgrade to a maintenance-free outdoor living space, consider a "re-deck." The job of ripping up and replacing deck boards may seem straightforward, but you could run into problems. With these tips, you'll avoid major pitfalls and give your deck a whole new life.

## Demo the decking

Pulling up deck boards is a chore. If your wooden decking was nailed on, demo will be a bit easier. If it was screwed on, don't expect to back out the screws one by one. Instead, pry up the boards, then break off any screws left in the joists by hitting them at the base with a hammer. A purpose-built pry bar like this Duckbill Deck Wrecker will ease this job.

Z-flashing

## Flash the ledger board

Install Z-flashing over the ledger board that holds the deck to the house. Older decks may not have flashing, but with the decking off, it's the perfect time to add it. Tuck the Z-flashing under your home's weather-resistant barrier to protect the ledger board and send water away from the house.

**Support the deck on both sides of the rotten post**

**Rotten post**

**Hydraulic jack**

**New post**

**Post base**

## Replace rotten posts

Check the bottoms of the posts that support your deck. If they're rotting, it's time to replace them. And it's pretty easy. First, using hydraulic jacks, place temporary posts on both sides of the rotten post. Make sure jacks are on firm, flat ground, then slowly jack up the deck framing enough to remove the post. Install a new post on a post base to keep it from rotting.

**Fill all nail holes**

## Missing hanger nails

With the deck boards off, check the joist hangers. They should be rust-free and full of nails. If you see holes that are missing nails, hammer in hanger nails. Pound 1-1/2-in. nails into the ledger board and 3-in. nails at a 45-degree angle into the joists.

## Protect the joists from rot

Composite decking will last a long time. To make sure the structure of your deck lasts, adhere joist tape on the tops of the joists before fastening the deck boards. The tape will seal around all the deck screws, helping to keep out water and prevent rot.

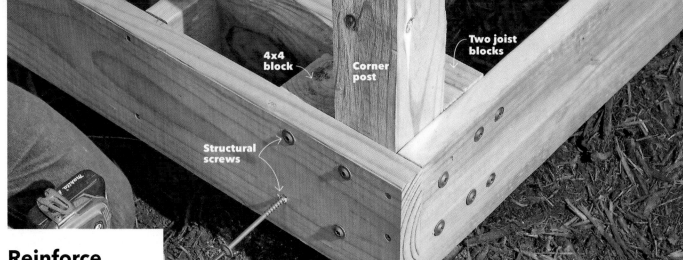

Two joist blocks

4x4 block

Corner post

Structural screws

## Reinforce railings

If your deck is higher than 30 in., it will need a railing. Whether you're using wood, composite or aluminum railing, building code requires it to withstand a minimum of 200 lbs. of force applied anywhere. This is difficult to measure, so it's best to beef up the rails so they don't budge.

### ■ CORNER POSTS

Fasten the corner posts with 5-in. structural screws. Then add two blocks between the joists against the post and a 4x4 block cut to the same height as the joist right behind the post.

### ■ EDGE POSTS

For posts along the edge of the deck, fasten blocks on both sides of the post. Then fasten a 4x4 block against the post and between the blocks.

### ■ SURFACE-MOUNTED RAILINGS

For surface-mounted railings, secure a double-layer block flush to the top of the deck framing. If the joists are perpendicular to the edge, add a block across the joists, then use 8-in. structural screws to fasten them. The grain of the blocking should run perpendicular to the edge of the deck.

Joist blocks

Edge post

4x4 block

Structural screws

Joist block

Double-layer block

Stagger
the blocks

Supports
picture
frame
border

Supports deck
board ends

## Stiffen up the joists

Here's an easy fix for a bouncy deck: Snap a chalk line down the middle of the deck and add tight-fitting blocks between the joists. Stagger them so they're easier to screw in.

## Add a picture frame border

A great way to hide the cut ends of your deck boards is to wrap the entire deck with a picture frame border. You'll need additional blocking to support the deck boards, but the clean look is worth the extra effort. Add an extra joist 3 in. away from the end joist and add blocks every 12 in. between. This will support the picture frame board and the decking that runs into it.

## Work from the outside in

The first row of decking you install should be away from the house. This will ensure that the most visible deck boards are full width and any skinny boards are hidden against the house.

**Toe-screw into the groove**

**Centermost joint**

## Pin the middle

Composite decking expands and contracts with fluctuating temperatures, and decking manufacturers include an installation step, but it's often missed: Toe-screw each deck board into the centermost joist. This way, if a board expands a total of 1/4 in., it will move 1/8 in. in either direction, which is much less noticeable than 1/4 in. in one direction.

**Hidden fastener**

## Run the boards long to avoid butt joints

Deck boards come in lengths up to 24 ft. Cut deck boards to span your entire deck, when possible, in order to avoid butt joints. Keep the deck boards long instead of trying to cut them, and line them up individually as you lay them. See "Trim the edges" on p. 189.

## Hidden fasteners for a clean surface

The brand of decking you choose will dictate the fasteners used. Screwing through the top is an option, but the clean surface you get by using hidden fasteners is worth the upcharge. Plus, hidden systems space the deck boards perfectly, so usually they install just as fast.

## Butt joint seam fix

If you can't avoid a seam in your deck boards, choose one of these two options:

**1.** Stick with a butt seam. You'll need to leave a gap between the boards and fasten each end down. To do this, add a block into which you can screw the hidden fasteners for each board.

**2.** Place a pattern board perpendicular to the rest of the decking. You'll need extra blocking to support the pattern board and the ends of the deck boards on both sides.

Hidden fastener

Support a board end with a block

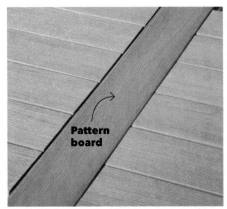

Pattern board

Add a stringer

## Easy stringer replacement

Most composite decking requires shorter spans between the framework supports, especially on stairs. Check with the manufacturer of the decking for the required stringer spacing; some require stringers to be as close as 8 in. apart. If you need to add new stair stringers, use an existing stringer as a template. Trace its shape onto a new 2x12 and cut it out.

## Trim the edges

Trim the edges after you've installed all the decking. Snap a line and cut the boards all at once. This is faster than cutting each board when you're installing it, and it will ensure the ends line up.

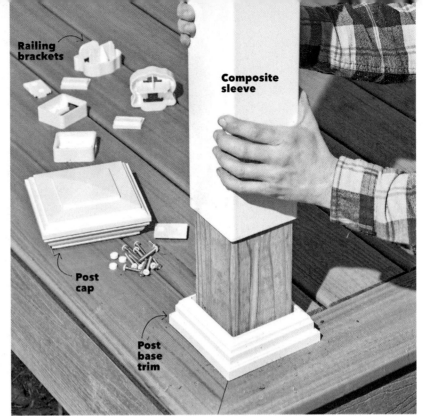

Railing brackets

Composite sleeve

Post cap

Post base trim

## Update wood posts with sleeves

To protect your wood posts and give them a new look fast, you can just slide a sleeve over the top of each. Combine sleeves with an 8-ft. railing kit and you'll get a maintenance-free section of railing and two covered posts for just under $200. Find the sleeves and railing kits at home centers.

## Modernize with aluminum rail

Upgrade the style of your deck with aluminum railing. Install aluminum posts on the surface of your deck and choose from a variety of railing options, including glass and steel cable. Expect to pay at least $250 for 6 ft. of aluminum railing and posts at home centers.

# *demystifying* DECKING

## Need help choosing deck boards? We've got you covered

BY MIKE BERNER

**W**hether you're building a new deck or replacing old, worn deck boards, you'll find an overwhelming number of decking options. The two main categories, wood and composite, include dozens of choices. I'll walk you through them to help you choose the right material for your deck.

# Wood ▶

Wood decking is beautiful and typically much more economical than composite. However, it loses its warm tone and turns a dull gray after a few years if it's not meticulously maintained, which increases lifetime cost.

### PRESSURE-TREATED
■ The boards are soaked with chemicals and put under pressure so the treatment permeates an entire board. This makes them resistant to rot and insects.
■ Copper, a common element in treatments, gives treated boards their green tint.
■ When you're sanding or cutting any treated lumber, respirators are a must.
■ This lumber is readily available in many red and brown tones.
■ Cut ends of pressure-treated boards must be treated with an exterior sealer, such as Woodlife CopperCoat.
■ Boards must be thoroughly dry before you apply a stain or protective finish.

### CEDAR
■ It is naturally rot and insect resistant.
■ It has a beautiful bright tone and can be stained easily.
■ This wood is long lasting and easy to work with.

### EXOTICS: IPE, CUMARU
■ Naturally rot and insect resistant, exotic woods have a beautiful, high-end look.
■ The installation is labor intensive. The boards are very heavy, dense and need to be predrilled for screws.
■ The boards are available with or without grooved edges to accommodate hidden fasteners.

# PVC ▶

Cellular PVC is an all-plastic decking. Its core is a porous (cellular) lightweight plastic that's capped just like other composite decking. PVC contains no organic material to rot, grow mold or swell when exposed to moisture, and it comes with a 20-plus-year warranty from staining and fading.

■ Boards can be bent for curved designs using heat.
■ As the temperature shifts, PVC expands and contracts more than wood and WPC.
■ It may become stained with exposure to some rubber products, like grill mats and water shoes.
■ PVC is the most expensive option, ranging from $4.40 to $7.50 per lin. ft.

PRESSURE-TREATED

PRESSURE-TREATED CEDAR TONE

CEDAR

IPE

CUMARU

TIMBERTECH AZEK, VINTAGE COLLECTION, COAST LINE

TIMBERTECH AZEK, HARVEST COLLECTION, KONA

TREX ENHANCE, ROCKY HARBOR

MOISTURESHIELD VISION, SPANISH LEATHER

DECKORATORS, VOYAGE, KHAYA

DECKORATORS, VOYAGE, TUNDRA

## ◄ Wood Plastic Composite

Made with up to 95% recycled plastic that encapsulates the wood fibers, wood plastic composite (WPC) decking is very strong and often comes with a 20-plus-year warranty against staining and fading. Unlike natural wood, it won't crack or splinter. Aside from an easy annual soap-and-water cleaning, it's pretty much maintenance-free.

- WPC is much heavier than wood.
- Some WPC decking requires shorter joist and stringer spans because it's less rigid than solid wood.
- Ranging from $2.90 to $6 per lin. ft., WPC is more expensive than wood.

## ◄ Mineral-Based Composite

Mineral-based composite (MBC) decking is the newest type of composite decking. It's as lightweight as PVC but twice as strong and carries a 25-year stain and fade warranty. There's virtually no temperature-induced shrinking or swelling, and MBC decking is highly resistant to moisture.

- MBC is more rigid than WPC and PVC, so it can be used on longer joist and stringer spans.
- It can withstand ground and water contact.
- It can maintain smaller gaps at miters and seams.
- Ranging from $4 to $6 per lin. ft., MBC is comparable in price to WPC.

## CAPPED VS. UNCAPPED

**M**ost modern decking has a hard plastic cap for better UV, weathering, scratch and dent protection. Capped deck boards provide color variations and the appearance of textured wood grain. But uncapped decking has improved and still has a place. Uncapped boards are cheaper and are available with wood grain patterns. Because uncapped deck boards are uniform throughout, you can round over their cut ends or edges with a router without noticeably changing the board's sheen or color. And scratches or dents can be "healed" with a heat gun or left to heal naturally over time under the sun's heat.

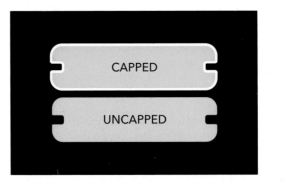

CAPPED

UNCAPPED

# Profiles

The profile and cross section of your deck boards may seem insignificant, but they're important in regard to how your deck is built and how it will look.

### SQUARE EDGE

Use square profile boards on your deck's borders to hide cut ends or as a pattern board to avoid seams. With square profile boards, you'll typically drive fasteners through the faces of the boards. However, some fastening systems let you hide the fasteners by using a jig to drive them into a board's edge at an angle. CAMO has a system like this.

### GROOVED EDGE

Use grooved-edge boards in the middle of the deck, anywhere the edge isn't visible. Hidden fasteners fit in the grooves for a clean look.

### SCALLOPED BOTTOM

The scalloped underside makes each board lighter weight and a bit less expensive. Face-screwing scalloped boards can be difficult; screws angle toward the grooves, pull the board and leave an oblong hole that's hard to plug.

### NONSTANDARD BOARD WIDTHS

Standard deck boards are 5-1/4 in. wide, but many companies offer different widths, from 3 in. up to almost 12 in. wide. This lets you achieve a completely different look from standard decking and opens the door to many design possibilities. Wide boards also make single-board stair treads possible.

**TREX ENHANCE, ISLAND MIST**

**TIMBERTECH PRO, RESERVE COLLECTION, DARK ROAST**

**TREX ENHANCE, FOGGY WHARF**

**TREX ENHANCE, BEACH DUNE**

Scalloped boards are made with solid edges or grooved edges

**FOLLOW FASTENER RECOMMENDATIONS**
Whichever decking you choose, be sure to follow the manufacturer's fastening instructions. The warranty typically depends on your use of the recommended fasteners, including face screws, fascia screws and hidden fasteners.

Cedar skirt board

Matching composite skirt board

## MATCHING SKIRT BOARDS

Most decking manufacturers offer a 1/2-in.-thick version of decking for use as skirt boards (11 in. wide) and stair risers (8 in. wide). These skirt boards and stair risers are typically available in all of a manufacturer's color options.

# Design Options

Today, it's easy to get the look you're after. The color, grain pattern, size and shape of the boards give you countless design options.

## ◀ GRAIN PATTERN

Every board of natural wood has a unique grain pattern. Even though the "grain" in composite decking mimics real wood, the pattern repeats from board to board. The grain options vary, from a deep embossed texture to tight, straight grain.

## ▲ COLOR

Almost any tone of wood or stained wood is available in composite decking. In addition, some of the more expensive composites have realistic color streaking that mimics the natural colors of real wood. Typically, you won't see this in the more economical options, but you'll still find a wide range of colors.

**GET A GRIP**
Although all decking meets a minimum requirement for grip, if you're concerned about slippery conditions, consider decking with deeper grain.

## ▲ TEMPERATURE

Composite decking gets hot in the sun, so if your deck gets full sun, consider lighter-colored deck boards or be prepared to wear shoes. Some manufacturers claim their decking has special properties that resist heat retention and remain cooler even in darker colors.

## WHAT'S IT GONNA COST?

You can find economical, mid-range and high-end choices for each type of decking. A typical deck (16 x 20 ft.) covers about 350 sq. ft. For that size, the cost of decking alone can range from $450 up to six times that at $2,700.

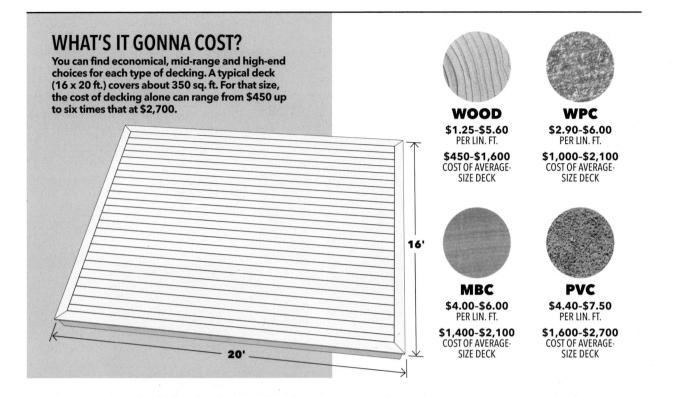

16'

20'

### WOOD
**$1.25–$5.60**
PER LIN. FT.

**$450–$1,600**
COST OF AVERAGE-
SIZE DECK

### WPC
**$2.90–$6.00**
PER LIN. FT.

**$1,000–$2,100**
COST OF AVERAGE-
SIZE DECK

### MBC
**$4.00–$6.00**
PER LIN. FT.

**$1,400–$2,100**
COST OF AVERAGE-
SIZE DECK

### PVC
**$4.40–$7.50**
PER LIN. FT.

**$1,600–$2,700**
COST OF AVERAGE-
SIZE DECK

# DECK FRAMING ON ANOTHER LEVEL

BY GLENN HANSEN

Our lead carpenter, Josh Risberg, is very particular about building materials. I couldn't understand why he chose to frame his deck with laminated veneer lumber (LVL). It's more expensive than conventional 2-by framing, and it's really heavy. Yet I soon realized Josh was on to something, especially with his choice of Pacific Woodtech (PWT) LVLs.

PWT's TRU-CORE treating system is different; the treatment permeates the entire board to its core. That's not the case with most conventionally treated lumber. This makes the company's LVLs more effective at preventing decay, rot and insect damage. Although these LVLs aren't rated for ground contact, they do work for exterior columns and sill plates.

These joists may be heavier to put in place, but they're dead flat and straight as an arrow, with no bad edges. They'll also support longer spans, meaning fewer support columns and longer cantilevers. Josh put a 6-ft. cantilever on his deck to provide a walk-through area below. These are other benefits:

■ There's no need to re-treat ends after cuts.
■ It's noncorrosive to framing hardware.
■ The joist sizes are consistent.
■ You can stain it immediately.

You do need to use joist sealing tape, but that's good practice for any deck framing. PWT makes these joists in nominal lumber sizes from 2x6 to 2x12 and offers beams in the same material from 1-3/4 x 9-1/2 in. up to 5-1/4 x 18 in. Also, the product is backed by a 25-year warranty.

# ATTACH A DECK LEDGER TO BRICK, THE RIGHT WAY

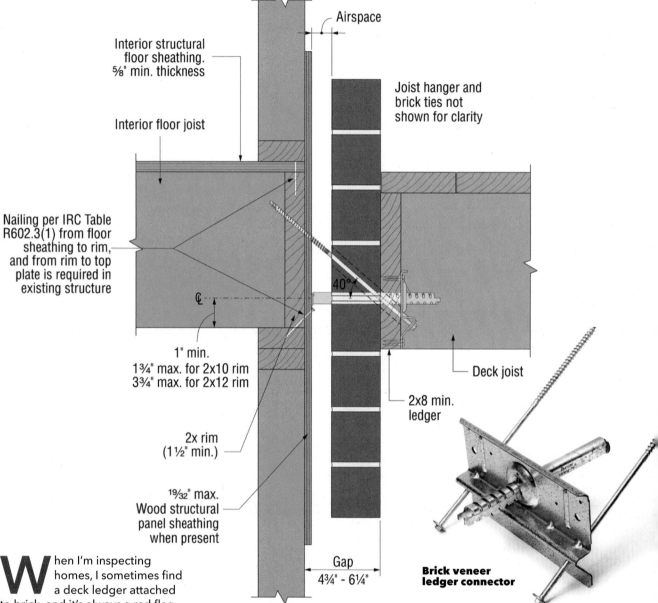

Airspace

Interior structural floor sheathing. ⅝" min. thickness

Interior floor joist

Joist hanger and brick ties not shown for clarity

Nailing per IRC Table R602.3(1) from floor sheathing to rim, and from rim to top plate is required in existing structure

40°

Deck joist

1" min.
1¾" max. for 2x10 rim
3¾" max. for 2x12 rim

2x8 min. ledger

2x rim (1½" min.)

¹⁹⁄₃₂" max. Wood structural panel sheathing when present

Gap
4¾" - 6¼"

**Brick veneer ledger connector**

W hen I'm inspecting homes, I sometimes find a deck ledger attached to brick, and it's always a red flag. Chances are, it's not a solid brick wall but instead a standard wood-frame wall with a layer of brick on the outside called "brick veneer."

Brick veneer isn't structural, so you can't attach a ledger to it. Here's why: Bricks absorb water, and as they dry, the water escapes on the back side of the bricks as condensation. So, to allow that condensation to drain through "weep holes," there's an air gap behind the brick. Because of that gap, you can't just run lag screws

through the bricks and into the house's rim joist. Doing so would suck the brick veneer in toward the house, potentially causing the veneer to crumble.

You could chisel out the bricks to attach the ledger directly to the rim joist, but that's a lot of work. Simpson Strong-Tie offers a brick veneer ledger connector (BVLZ; $120 for a four-pack) specifically for this situation. A BVLZ works for new ledgers or as a retrofit to correct a ledger that was attached

improperly. Long lag screws driven at an angle suspend the ledger from the rim joist. An adjustable post threads through a steel plate, maintaining the gap behind the brick veneer so there's actually no weight or force on the brick veneer.

**MEET THE EXPERT**
**Reuben Saltzman is the owner of Structure Tech Home Inspections.**

# INSTALL MODERN CABLE RAILING

BY MIKE BERNER

## 1 SURFACE-MOUNT POSTS

I first determined the post locations while I was framing the deck, and I added extra blocking to fasten the surface-mounted posts. When the decking was done, I positioned the posts over the blocking, fastened them with structural screws and plumbed them with the supplied setscrews. Then I hid the screws by sliding on the post base trim.

## 2 INSTALL THE RAIL AND SPACERS

Trim the rails with a miter saw so they're 1 in. shorter than the distance between posts. Then fasten a rail bracket to each end, with the cable spacers attached equidistant along the bottom of the rail. Level the rail between the posts, then predrill the posts and fasten the rail.

## 3 FEED THE CABLE

This Deckorators ALX Contemporary Cable Railing System consists of stainless steel cable with a threaded bolt on one end. I fed the cable end through the posts and the rail spacers, then attached a locking nut onto the threaded end.

## 4 TENSION AND TRIM THE CABLE

At the opposite end, I twisted the provided Pull-Lock fitting onto the cable. I pushed the fitting into the predrilled hole in the post and pulled the cable tight while holding the fitting in place. This Pull-Lock fitting locks onto the cable to hold the tension. Thread and tighten all the cables, starting from the center and working toward the top and bottom alternately. To tension them, hold the threaded stud in place with a hex key and turn the locking nut. Trim the excess cable and threaded stud, and cover both ends with the threaded caps included.

Leveling setscrew

**1**

| WHAT IT TAKES | | |
|---|---|---|
| **TIME** | **COST** | **SKILL LEVEL** |
| *1 day* | *$65/ft.* | *Intermediate* |

**TOOLS**
*Drill/driver, level, miter saw, screwdriver, hex key, wrench*

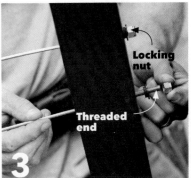

Locking nut

Threaded end

**3**

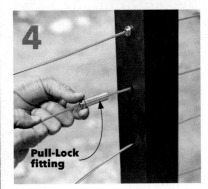

**4**

Pull-Lock fitting

**2**

Rail

Cable spacer

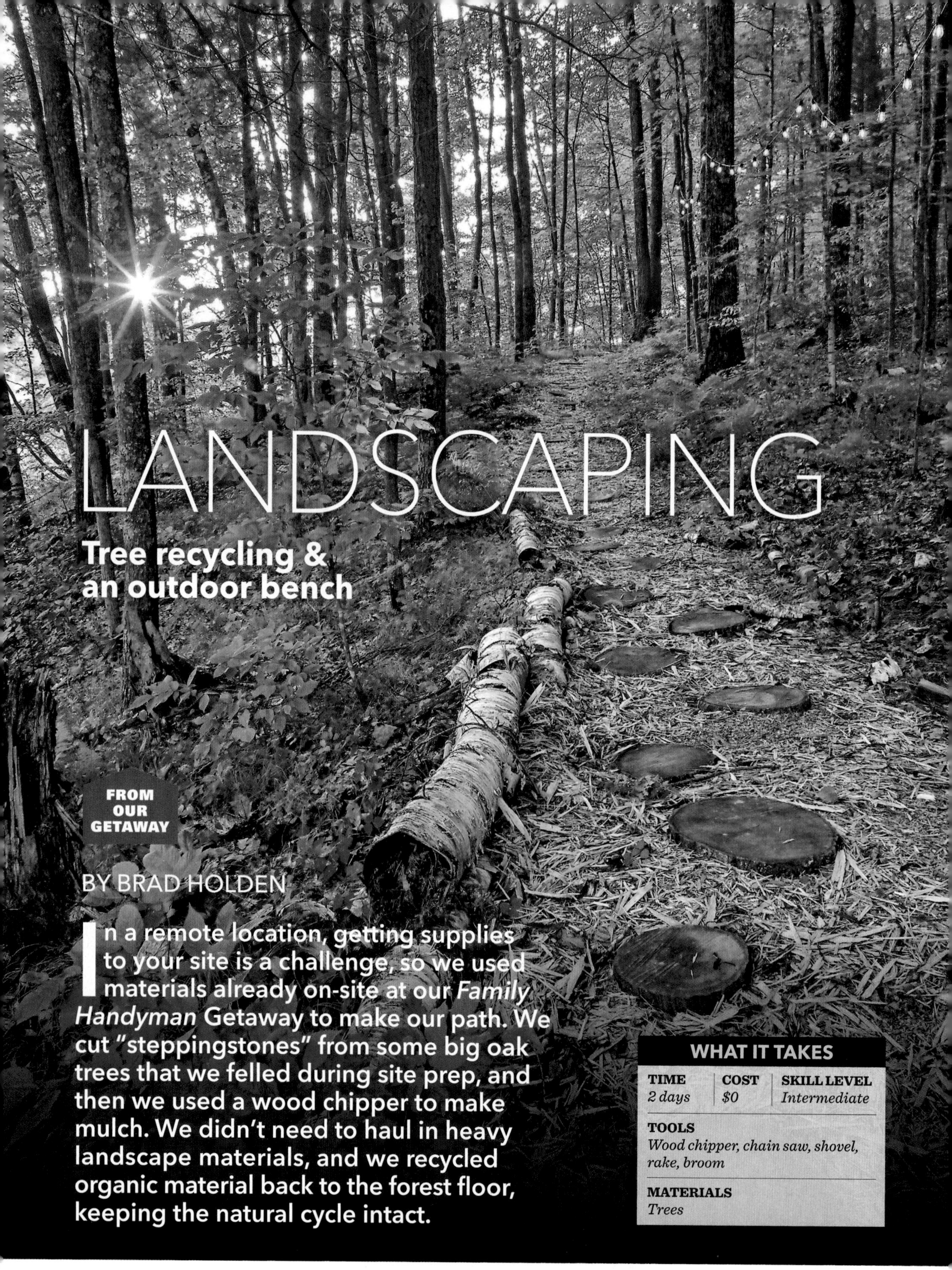

# LANDSCAPING

## Tree recycling & an outdoor bench

**FROM OUR GETAWAY**

BY BRAD HOLDEN

In a remote location, getting supplies to your site is a challenge, so we used materials already on-site at our *Family Handyman* Getaway to make our path. We cut "steppingstones" from some big oak trees that we felled during site prep, and then we used a wood chipper to make mulch. We didn't need to haul in heavy landscape materials, and we recycled organic material back to the forest floor, keeping the natural cycle intact.

**WHAT IT TAKES**

| TIME | COST | SKILL LEVEL |
|---|---|---|
| *2 days* | *$0* | *Intermediate* |

**TOOLS**
*Wood chipper, chain saw, shovel, rake, broom*

**MATERIALS**
*Trees*

# 1 SET THE STEPPINGSTONES

Bust out your chain saw—with a new, sharp chain—and slice a pile of steppingstones. We cut these about 2 in. thick. Any thinner than that and they crack easily. Set them in your path, spaced at an easy walking pace. It'll take some shuffling to get this just right. You might need to dig out a bit of soil underneath some of the stepping-stones to get them to sit level and not rock as you walk on them.

# 2 LET THE CHIPS FLY

Our DR Power PRO 400 wood chipper is an easily portable 4-in.-capacity unit. We wheeled the chipper down the path, filling in as we moved along so the chips would fall where we needed them. We used both deadfall from the woods and split logs from felled trees.

# 3 RAKE OUT THE PATH

Once you're done chipping, rake and sweep the wood chips to expose the steppingstones.

## A Simple Bench

You need a place to sit at the end of the path, right? Here's a simple DIY bench. Make concrete forms for the legs from 2x4s and plywood—our forms allow space for a seat of two 2x8s. Fill the forms, allowing the legs to cure. Remove the forms and attach the seat using lag screws and concrete anchors. For our bench seat, we split and smoothed a slab of oak from the property.

# QUICK TUNE-UP FOR HEDGE TRIMMER BLADES

A dull hedge trimmer doesn't cut cleanly, making an easy job far more work. You can have your trimmer professionally sharpened, but doing it yourself is easy. Using a rotary tool and a diamond paddle, you'll be back in business in about 30 minutes. You can file the teeth, but it takes a bit longer.

# 1 LOOSEN THE BLADES

Remove the nuts that secure the blades to the bar. I don't remove the blades on this trimmer because it involves disassembling the entire machine. Removing the nuts lets me separate the blades enough for sharpening.

# 2 CLEAN THE TEETH

Wipe off as much pitch and sap as you can using a blade cleaning liquid such as Red Armor from Echo ($10 for a 12-oz. bottle). Your grinding stone cuts faster if the teeth are clean.

# 3 GRIND THE BEVELS

With the blades clamped to a work surface, carefully grind each beveled edge using a small grinding stone in a rotary tool. Use a light touch and stop when the bevel is shiny all the way down to the edge and you can feel a slight burr under the edge. A small wood spacer block clamped between the blades maintains clearance for grinding.

# 4 HONE THE UNDERSIDES

Hone the underside of each tooth to remove the burr created by grinding. My favorite tool for this is an EZE-LAP diamond paddle ($20 for a set of three). Wipe off the teeth with blade cleaner again to remove any metal dust. Then reinstall the nuts that secure the blades to the bar.

**BRAD HOLDEN**
SENIOR EDITOR

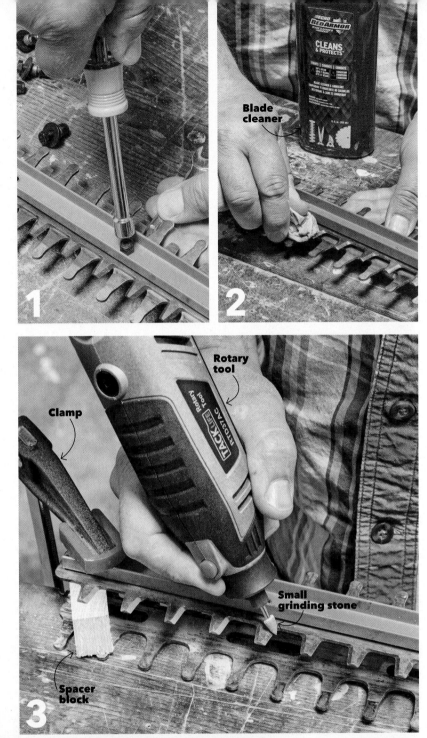

Blade cleaner

Rotary tool

Clamp

Small grinding stone

Spacer block

Diamond paddle

# START A GARDEN

## Expert advice for growing healthy plants

BY JAY CORK

There's more to starting a healthy garden than just grabbing a shovel and digging in. First, you need to test the soil and cultivate the ideal conditions for whatever you plant to thrive. I spoke with Ashley Hansen from Bachman's Garden Center to get her best advice for creating a garden from scratch.

**MEET THE EXPERT**
Ashley Hansen is a certified Minnesota Nursery & Landscape Association professional and a sales consultant at Bachman's Garden Center. She loves to grow zinnias for their amazing colors.

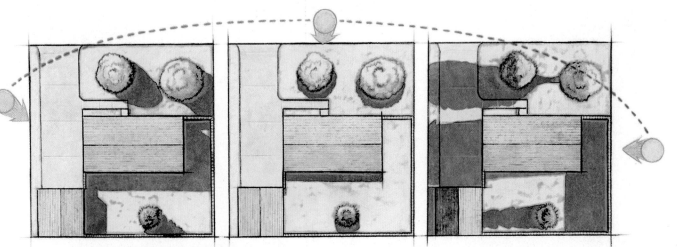

## TRACK THE SUNLIGHT

Take photos of your desired garden location in the morning, at noon and again in the evening to see how much sun it gets. To provide ideal sunlight for the widest selection of plants, place your garden in full sun to light shade. A vegetable garden requires full sun.

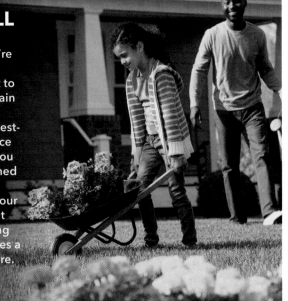

## START SMALL

Consider how much time and money you're willing to devote to your garden—not just to install it but to maintain it as well. By starting small, there's less investment and more chance of success because you won't get overwhelmed by maintenance. You can always expand your garden over time, but starting big and losing control of it guarantees a weed-infested eyesore.

## OUTLINE THE GARDEN BED

Outline your garden's perimeter with marking paint ($7 at home centers). Gentle curves are visually pleasing and easier to mow around than sharp corners.

## TEST THE SOIL

A soil test tells you whether you need to work in nutrients such as nitrogen, potassium or phosphorus. Test kits are available at home and garden centers, but you'll get more comprehensive results from a university extension service or state-certified soil testing lab. You'll pay $20 to $50 for these tests and get the results in just a few weeks.

Take samples from several areas. For a good sample, shovel a 6-in.-deep, V-shaped hole. Take a slice off one side of the hole, remove all the plant matter and put the soil in a clean plastic bucket. Thoroughly mix all the samples in the bucket.

One to 1-1/2 cups of soil is enough for a lab to run the tests. Some labs even supply a special bag for your soil sample; just fill the bag and return it.

6"-wide trench

## DEFINE THE EDGE

Once you've determined the placement of your garden, define the perimeter. With a spade, follow the outline of the garden bed, slicing down about 6 in. When you've sliced the entire perimeter, create a 3- to 6-in.-wide trench. This prevents the sod cutter or herbicide from straying into your yard when you remove or kill the grass.

## REMOVE THE GRASS

The grass has got to go, but clearing sod by hand is hard work! So rent a sod cutter from a local rental center instead. It'll cost about $100 per day, and the cutter will cleanly cut the sod below the roots. Once the sod is cut, you can roll the strips into easy-to-carry bundles.

Till the top 6" to 10" of soil

## ENRICH YOUR SOIL

Adding organic matter such as compost or manure improves drainage in heavy clay soils and the water-holding capacity of sandy soils. It also makes the soil more permeable, which encourages root growth and attracts organisms that add nutrients. Spread 2 to 4 in. of organic matter over the garden and, with a digging fork, work it into the top 6 to 10 in. of soil. Consider renting a power tiller (about $70 a day) if your garden is too big to do by hand.

## Grass killing methods

A sod cutter is the fastest way to remove grass, but if you can't get your hands on one, you can kill the grass and till it instead. Here are three options:

**PLASTIC.** Lay down black plastic that's at least 3 mil thick over the garden for six to eight weeks. When the grass is dead, power till the soil.

**MULCH.** Cut the grass as short as possible. Cover the area with at least 2 in. of leaves or wood mulch and keep it wet. The covering and the grass will naturally decompose, leaving a rich compost. This process can take several months, so plan ahead.

**HERBICIDE.** Spray the area with a non-selective herbicide. Do this only after you've edged the garden so the weed killer won't harm the adjacent lawn. If there is anything still growing after seven days, spray it again and wait another week.

## CUSTOM-FERTILIZE YOUR PLANTS

Your soil test helps you determine the type of fertilizer you need to add to suit your plants. There are three main nutrients needed for plant growth: nitrogen, phosphorus and potassium. Fertilizer labels list them in order as a series of numbers. For example, 10-20-10 contains 10 percent nitrogen, 20 percent phosphorus and 10 percent potassium. If your soil needs only one nutrient, don't bother adding the others. Buy a slow-release granular fertilizer that contains the appropriate percentage of nutrients your soil needs, and add it just before planting.

## *Consider a raised bed*

If your yard has a lot of heavy clay, rocky soil or poor drainage, then a raised garden bed is the perfect solution. It lets you bring in good soil and create the ideal garden bed. It also lets you garden without bending over as far or working on your hands and knees. A raised garden bed should be built at least 12 in. deep and filled with topsoil.

## ADJUST THE SOIL pH

The pH level of your soil determines your plants' ability to absorb nutrients and can affect their yield. A pH level in the 6.0 to 7.0 pH range is perfect for most home gardens. A pH tester ($25 online) lets you monitor and maintain proper pH levels in your garden.

Adding lime or wood ash improves acidic soil. If your soil is alkaline, add ground sulfur or calcium sulfate.

Paver bricks

## KEEP THE GRASS OUT

Add a border to keep grass from getting a start in your garden; it's hard to get rid of grass once it invades. Strips of steel or heavy-duty plastic edging are unobtrusive and work well on fairly even terrain. But pavers and brick are an attractive alternative, forming a wide border that provides a flat surface to mow over. To keep grass from intruding, be sure your border extends at least 4 in. into the ground.

# Ashley's favorite gardening gear

Ashley works at a garden center and devotes a lot of time to her own garden. Here are some of the tools she loves and has come to rely on.

**SPADE OR FLAT SHOVEL**
A spade usually has a shorter handle and a flat blade. It's handy for cutting sod and edging. Pick one up for about $20 at a garden center.

**HORI HORI MULTI-TOOL**
The hori hori knife is a heavy, serrated steel blade used for digging, cutting, weeding and planting. They're available for $20 and up.

**GRIPPY GLOVES**
Ashley likes these polyurethane coated gloves from MUD. Their form-fitting stretch shell is breathable and has an outstanding wet/dry grip. They cost about $10 online.

**ROUND-POINT SHOVEL**
A full-length round-point shovel is best for digging large holes and working over large areas of soil.

**BYPASS PRUNERS**
Ashley prefers Felco bypass pruners. They give smooth, clean cuts without damaging her plants. Every gardener should have a pair. Expect to pay at least $60 for these.

**KNEE PADS**
Gardening can be hard on the knees. Ashley prefers these waterproof memory foam knee pads from Kneelo. At just over $40, they're a little expensive, but your knees will thank you!

**HAND TROWEL**
A hand trowel is a must-have. There are many sizes to choose from. Ashley recommends searching for one that feels good in your hand, as it's the one tool you're likely to use every time you work in your garden. Expect to pay about $20 for a good hand trowel.

**DIGGING FORK**
For cultivating compost and turning over soil, Ashley recommends a digging fork. They cost about $40 at home and garden centers.

# Is treated lumber safe for vegetable gardening?

Many articles online claim that it isn't safe to grow edible plants in containers made of treated lumber. But read closer and you'll see that they're talking about wood treated with arsenic (CCA), which was banned for residential use back in 2003. The treated lumber sold today contains no arsenic and is considered safe for food contact and growing food. Some common types of treated lumber are ACQ, CA and MCQ.

# LIGHT UP
## YOUR GARAGE

A combination of showroom
and task lighting does it best

BY JAY CORK

**L**et's face it; most garages are poorly lit, often by just a single bulb or fluorescent fixture. To give this garage plenty of light for project work, I installed a task light above the work surface and designed two ceiling islands to provide even more direct light. To add some showroom flair, the islands include indirect lighting that complements the illuminated countertop and the accent lighting along our garage walls.

**MEET THE BUILDER**
Jay Cork, an associate editor at *Family Handyman*, is an inventor at heart.

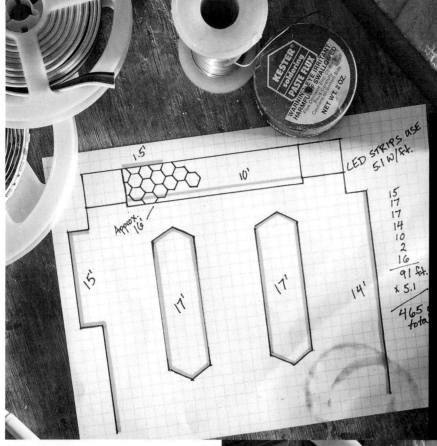

## LIGHTING DESIGN

**■ MAKE A DRAWING**

A sketch is my most important tool for designing a lighting project. It helps me conceptualize the design and gets me to the next step—the math.

**■ DO THE MATH**

To figure the power draw, I multiplied the total length (91 ft.) by the wattage per foot (5.1). The result: 464 watts. I chose to double up; two 400-watt, 24-volt power supplies means I'll have plenty of power now and when I add more lights down the road.

**■ BUY YOUR POWER CABLE**

A lighting project like this requires running power cable. Always order extra; if I think I'll need 100 ft., I order 140.

## MAKE THE CEILING ISLANDS

**1" pocket hole screws**

### 1 ASSEMBLE THE FRAMES

Each ceiling island uses 1/2-in. MDF for the face and 3/4-in. pine for the sides. After assembling them with pocket hole joinery and construction adhesive, chamfer the edge of the face with a router bit. I sanded the islands lightly and painted them to match the ceiling.

### 2 DRILL HOLES FOR THE SPOTLIGHTS

Using a hole saw, drill 3-in. holes for the spotlights. Because these ceiling islands were 8 ft. long, it was easy to evenly space the five lights at 16-in. on center.

### 3 ADD THE ACCENT LIGHTS

Line the inside of each island with an LED strip, using a wood block as a guide to keep the strip centered on the sides. The controller for the LED strips sits inside the islands and is connected to the power supplies with low-voltage cable fished through the ceiling and the walls.

**3" hole saw**

### WHAT IT TAKES

| TIME | COST | SKILL LEVEL |
|------|------|-------------|
| 2 to 3 days | $1,300 | Intermediate |

**TOOLS**

Table saw, sander, drill, pocket hole jig, router, basic carpentry tools, basic electrical tools, soldering iron

## Figure A  Ceiling Island

**OVERALL DIMENSIONS: 8' L x 2' W x 4" H**

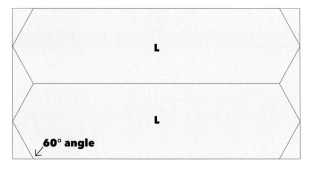

## Figure B  Cross Member

**OVERALL DIMENSIONS: 23" L x 3-1/2" W**

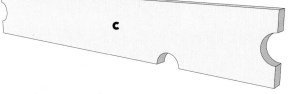

## Figure C  Hanger

**OVERALL DIMENSIONS: 9-3/8" L x 5-1/2" W x 3-3/4" H**

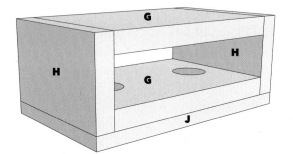

## Figure D  Cutting Diagram

**OVERALL DIMENSIONS: 8' L x 4' W**

60° angle

Each island has five spotlights ($60 for six online) that connect to 110v service. Hidden inside are LED strips for indirect accent lighting.

## Materials List

| ITEM | QTY. |
|---|---|
| 1/2" x 4' x 8' MDF sheet | 1 |
| 1x4 x 8' select pine | 4 |
| 1x6 x 8' select pine | 2 |
| 16' LED strips | 6 |
| LED light controllers | 7 |
| 24v power supplies | 2 |
| Remote control | 1 |
| Spotlights | 10 |
| 1" pocket hole screws | Box |
| No. 8 1-1/4" wood screws | Box |
| No. 8 2" wood screws | 12 |
| 4" lag bolts | 8 |

## Cutting List

| KEY | QTY. | DIMENSIONS | PART |
|---|---|---|---|
| A | 4 | 3/4" x 3-1/2" x 82-1/8" | Sides–long |
| B | 8 | 3/4" x 3-1/2" x 13-7/8" | Sides–short |
| C | 6 | 3/4" x 3-1/2" x 23" | Cross members |
| D | 2 | 3/4" x 5-1/2" x 9-1/2" | Cantilever arms–long |
| E | 2 | 3/4" x 5-1/2" x 6-1/2" | Cantilever arms–short |
| F | 4 | 3/4" x 5-1/2" x 5" | Cantilever posts |
| G | 8 | 3/4" x 5-1/2" x 7-7/8" | Hanger box tops/bottoms |
| H | 8 | 3/4" x 5-1/2" x 3-1/4" | Hanger box sides |
| J | 4 | 1/2" x 5-1/2" x 9-3/8" | Hanger box backers |
| K | 4 | 1/2" x 5-1/2" x 5-3/4" | Cantilever post backers |
| L | 2 | 1/2" x 24" x 96" | Island faces |

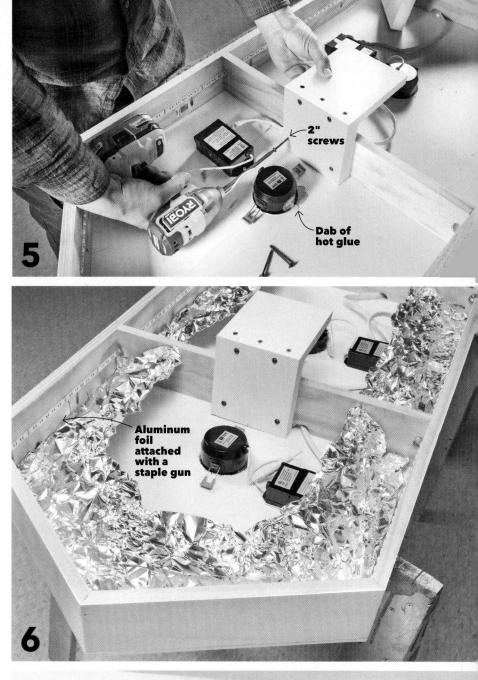

**Spring clip**

**2"**
**screws**

**Dab of**
**hot glue**

**Aluminum**
**foil**
**attached**
**with a**
**staple gun**

## 4 WIRE THE SPOTLIGHTS

After you mount and wire the individual transformers for the spotlights inside the island, the lights easily mount through the holes on the face. The spring clips on the lights allow a little movement, so use hot glue to help them stay put.

## 5 MAKE THE HANGERS

Here's a super simple method to hang the ceiling islands. First, bolt two open-ended boxes (see **Photo 7**) to the ceiling joists. Attach L-shaped brackets to the island's cross members, then slide each "L" into a box.

## 6 CREATE A SPECIAL EFFECT

A crinkled layer of aluminum foil inside creates random reflections on the ceiling, diffusing the light.

## 7 HANG THE ISLANDS

After connecting all the wiring, grab a friend to help you hang the islands. The front bracket is longer, so slide it in first. This allows you to easily see where the rear bracket needs to go.

### Pro Tip
You can find LED systems at home centers, but I found a much more robust selection of LEDs, power supplies, controllers and wiring at *superbrightleds.com*.

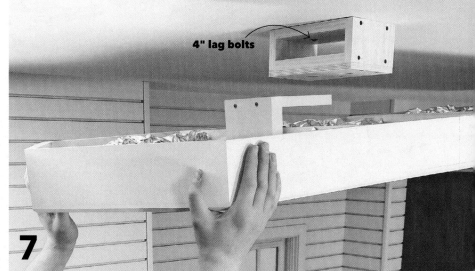

**4" lag bolts**

# INSTALL ACCENT LIGHTING

To power all the LED strips, I used two separate power supplies that feed seven individual channel controllers. This gives me control over the color and brightness of each individual run of LED strips. Too much? Not at all. Remember what I said about showroom flair?

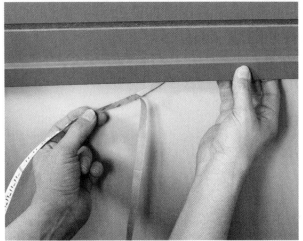

## 1 HIDE AN LED STRIP ALONG THE WALLS

A piece of trim applied to the bottom of the slat board provides a perfect space for an LED strip. I stuck one strip along each wall.

## 2 HIDE THE CABLES

For some LED strips, I had to get creative on running the power cables. A piece of scrap wood helped me tuck the power cables out of sight. I gave it a gentle push so I wouldn't damage the cables.

**PROGRAM THE REMOTE** ·············•

Before installing all the LED controllers and tucking them away, I paired them to the remote and tested all the connections.

## WORK SPACE TASK LIGHT

Most of the LEDs I installed are for accent lighting, but I also wanted direct light on the main work surface. I attached an aluminum U-channel ($40) to the underside of the upper cabinets with double-sided tape. I snapped a frosted lens into the channel to diffuse the light.

I learned something important in this step: The aluminum channel absorbed the heat of the LED lights, causing the double-sided tape to partially fail. Lock your lights into place with a bead of hot glue on the back of the channel. That fixed it for me.

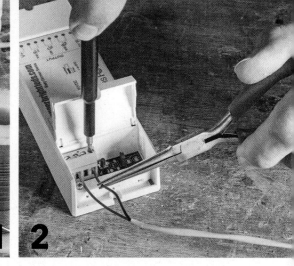

## 1 TIN THE LEADS WITH SOLDER

When you connect braided copper wire to screw-type terminals, tin the leads with solder. This provides a better connection and keeps the strands of the braid from fraying.

## 2 CONNECT THE CABLE

I used a two-conductor 18-gauge braided copper cable to connect the power supplies to the LED controllers. With screw-type terminals, always give wires a little tug after tightening the screw to make sure they are secure.

## 3 SKIP THE QUICK CONNECTORS

The LED strips connect to the controllers using a five-conductor cable. There are solderless quick connectors available, but they can be difficult to use and unreliable. Instead, I solder the wire leads directly to the LED strips.

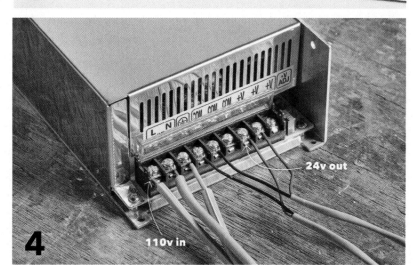

24v out

110v in

## 4 CONNECT THE POWER SUPPLIES

Once you've run all the cables into the cabinet, it's time to connect the controllers to the power supplies. The power supplies should not be plugged into an outlet while you do this. Plug them in only after all the controllers have been connected.

## 5 KEEP THINGS NEAT

Keep multiple wires and cables neat and organized with cable clips, zip ties and even hook-and-loop fasteners. This way, troubleshooting and adding or removing components will be much easier.

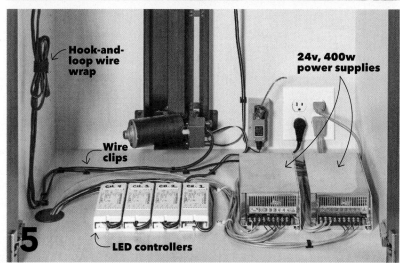

Hook-and-loop wire wrap

24v, 400w power supplies

Wire clips

LED controllers

# FULLY CHARGED

This sliding station keeps your tools ready to go

BY MIKE BERNER

**H**ow many times have you picked up a battery-powered tool, only to find that it was put away with a dead battery? I came up with this sliding panel and drawer charging station built into a tall garage cabinet. It lets me store everything in one place. With tools organized and easy to access, a bin for charged batteries and a charger at the ready, you won't be stuck waiting for a charge.

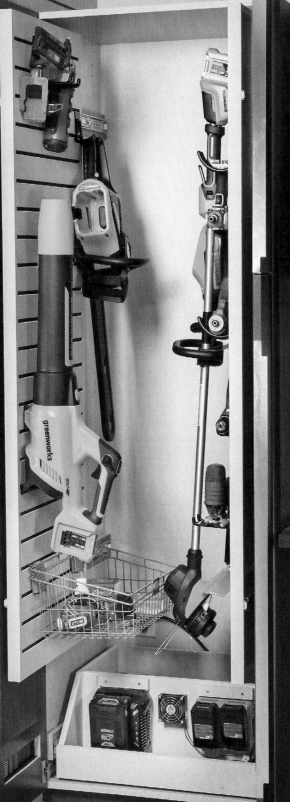

## WHAT IT TAKES

| TIME | COST | SKILL LEVEL |
|------|------|-------------|
| 1 day | $250 | Beginner |

**TOOLS**
*Table saw or circular saw, miter saw, jigsaw, drill, 18-gauge nailer, basic carpentry tools*

## 1 FRAME AROUND SLAT WALL PANELS

Cut the slat wall panel to size and attach a frame around it. The poplar frame stiffens the panel and hides the raw edges. I glued and nailed the frame parts to the edges of the panel, flush with the face, starting with the top and bottom. I cut the sides to fit and fastened them the same way.

### Pro Tip
The slats in the panels I bought ran the long way, so I had to put two pieces together to make the panels tall enough. The frame held the edges together, and I added an extra batten on the back to support the seam.

## 2 BATTEN THE BACK

Glue and nail battens about 6 in. from the top and bottom of the panels. Both the frame and the battens stiffen the panels; the battens also give you a place to screw in drawer slides.

## 3 MARK YOUR STORY STICK

I made a mark 2 in. from the top of the story stick and lined it up with the top of my panel. I made a mark for the centerline of the slides on the spacers and the story stick, then rotated the stick and marked the locations for the cabinet spacers.

### MAKE A STORY STICK TO PLACE THE SLIDES
The locations of the spacers and slides are arbitrary, but they *do* need to line up. For this I make a story stick; it's a custom ruler marked with all my important measurements. I mark one side of the stick for spacers, a second side for slide locations, and the other sides for the drawer width and depth.

Slat wall

Poplar frame

Battens

Slide spacer marks

Slide centerline

Top of panel

2"

Top of cabinet

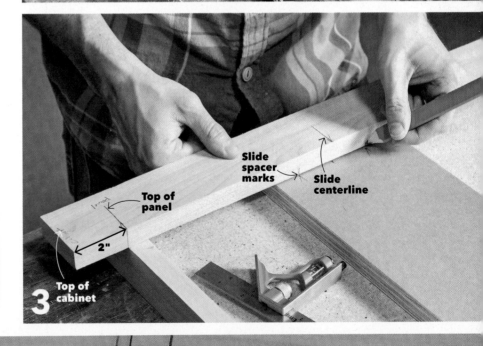

Story stick

Drawer width measurements

cabinet front → Drawer front Drawer Bottom

Drawer depth measurements

Drawer Side Drawer Side Drawer Bottom

## 4 SHIM SLIDES WITH SPACERS

I used the story stick to locate the 3-in.-wide slide spacers in the cabinet. These spacers allow the slides to clear the door hinges.

**No. 6 1-1/4" wood screws**

**Slide spacer**

## 5 TRANSFER SLIDE MARKS TO SPACERS

To mark the slide locations on the spacers, hold the story stick to the top of the cabinet and transfer the drawer slide centerline marks from the story stick to the spacers. Mark both ends of the spacers, then connect the marks to make the slide centerline.

**Story stick**

**Drawer slide centerline**

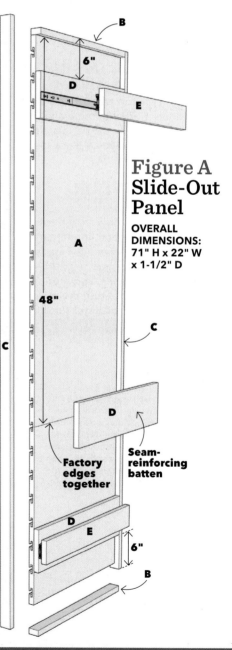

**B**

**6"**

**D**

**E**

# Figure A Slide-Out Panel

**OVERALL DIMENSIONS: 71" H x 22" W x 1-1/2" D**

**A**

**48"**

**C**

**C**

**D**

**Seam-reinforcing batten**

**Factory edges together**

**D**

**E**

**6"**

**B**

## Cutting List

| KEY | QTY. | DIMENSIONS | PART |
|-----|------|------------|------|
| A | 2 | 3/4" x 20-1/2" x 69-1/2" | Slat wall panels |
| B | 4 | 3/4" x 1-1/2" x 20-1/2" | Frame tops/bottoms |
| C | 4 | 3/4" x 1-1/2" x 71" | Frame sides |
| D | 6 | 3/4" x 5-1/2" x 20-1/2" | Battens |
| E | 6 | 3/4" x 3" x 21-1/4" | Slide spacers |
| F | 1 | 3/4" x 21-1/4" x 24-1/2" | Drawer bottom |
| G | 2 | 3/4" x 10-3/4" x 21-1/4" | Drawer sides |
| H | 2 | 3/4" x 10-3/4" x 24-1/2" | Drawer back/divider |
| J | 1 | 3/4" x 3-1/2" x 26" | Drawer front |
| K | 2 | 3/4" x 3/4" x 6" | Charger cleats |
| L | 1 | 1/4" x 12-1/4" x 80" | Door-joining panel (Photo 12) |

## 6 ATTACH THE DRAWER SLIDES

Place the slides so their screw holes fall right on the slide centerline and the fronts of the slides are flush with the front of the panel and drawer. Drill a pilot hole and drive in the screw right on the centerline. Use this same technique for attaching each part of the slide: the cabinet member and the drawer member.

## 7 ASSEMBLE THE DRAWER

Drill pocket holes in the drawer bottom and back. Glue and clamp the parts together. Then flip the drawer upside-down and drive the pocket screws. The clamps keep the drawer parts from shifting while you drive the screws.

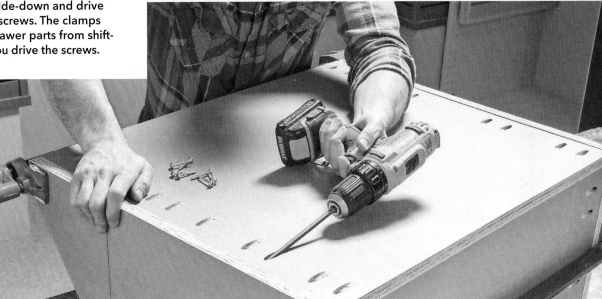

## Figure B
## Drawer

**OVERALL DIMENSIONS:**
10-3/4" H x 26" W x 22" D

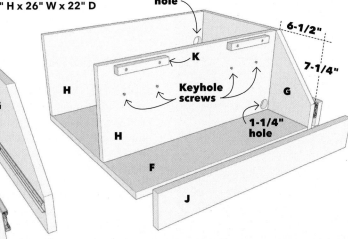

1-1/4" hole

6-1/2"

7-1/4"

**Keyhole screws**

1-1/4" hole

K

H

G

G

H

F

J

E

**MEET THE BUILDER**
Mike Berner is an associate editor at *Family Handyman*. He enjoys spending time relaxing in his yard, not waiting for batteries to charge.

## Materials List

| ITEM | QTY. |
|---|---|
| 3/4" x 4' x 8' MDO sheet | 1 |
| 4' x 8' slat wall sheet | 1 |
| 1/4" x 4' x 8' hardboard sheet | 1 |
| 1x2 x 8' poplar | 4 |
| No. 6 1-1/4" wood screws | |
| No. 8 2-1/2" pan head screw | 4 |
| No. 8 3/4" wood screws | |
| 1-1/4" pocket hole screws | |
| No. 10 1" bushing | 4 |
| Cabinet vent | 2 |
| Wood glue | |
| Small cooling fan | |
| Slat wall accessories | |

# TRICKED-OUT GARAGE

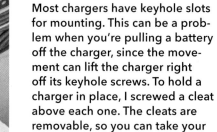

**8**

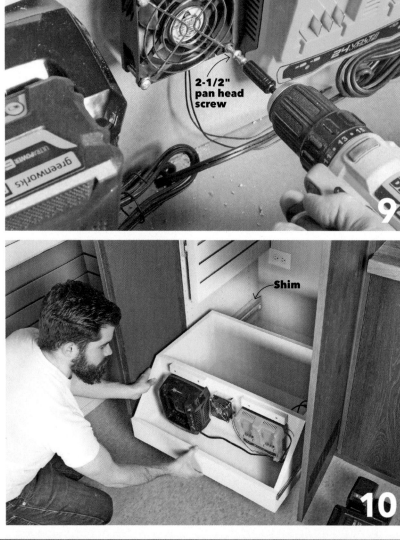

## 8 SECURE THE CHARGERS

Most chargers have keyhole slots for mounting. This can be a problem when you're pulling a battery off the charger, since the movement can lift the charger right off its keyhole screws. To hold a charger in place, I screwed a cleat above each one. The cleats are removable, so you can take your charger with you if necessary.

## 9 COOL CHARGERS WITH A FAN

To help prevent heat buildup inside the drawer, I mounted a fan between the chargers. I slid 1-in. bushings over 2-1/2-in. screws to keep the fan away from the divider for better air circulation.

## 10 INSTALL THE PANELS AND DRAWER

I removed the chargers and fan, primed and painted the panels and drawer, and then slid the panels and drawers into place. That's when I realized I'd built the drawer too narrow—the slides wouldn't catch. To fix it, I backed out the screws in the spacer, slipped in a couple shims behind it and then tightened it back up.

1" bushing

2-1/2" pan head screw

Shim

3/8"
starter
holes

## 11 VENT THE CABINET

I wanted to add vents to the door bottoms so warm air could escape. I wrapped the area with painter's tape to minimize chipping the laminate as I cut, then I marked the opening for the vent. I drilled 3/8-in. starter holes in the corners and cut the opening with a jigsaw.

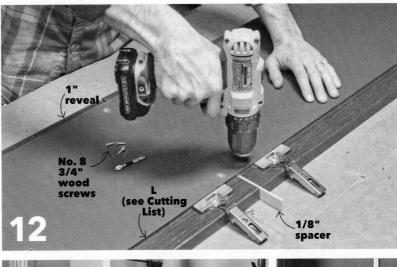

1"
reveal

No. 8
3/4"
wood
screws

L
(see Cutting
List)

1/8"
spacer

12

## 12 JOIN THE DOORS

Our cabinet has four doors: a pair for the top portion and a pair for the bottom. I didn't want to open two doors on each side to access the panel or drawer. So I joined the top and bottom door pairs using a piece of painted 1/4-in. hardboard cut to fit inside the hinges, with a 1-in. reveal around the other edges. With the door pairs on a flat table and a 1/8-in. spacer between them, I screwed the hardboard to the doors. Leave the spacers between the doors until the doors are installed.

## 13 ARRANGE ACCESSORIES

Slat wall accessories include a variety of hook types and sizes as well as baskets and shelves. I was able to hang a lot of lawn and yard tools on the panels. The best part of this slat wall system for storing battery-powered tools is how easy it is to rearrange them as needed.

13

## TRICKED-OUT GARAGE

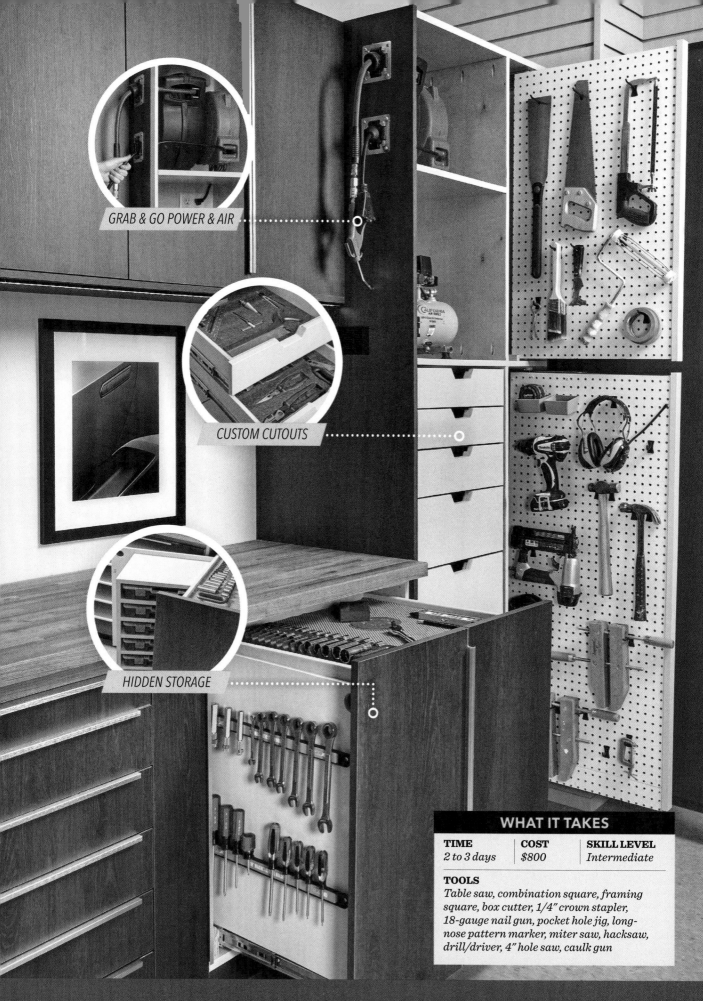

GRAB & GO POWER & AIR

CUSTOM CUTOUTS

HIDDEN STORAGE

## WHAT IT TAKES

| TIME | COST | SKILL LEVEL |
|------|------|-------------|
| 2 to 3 days | $800 | Intermediate |

**TOOLS**
*Table saw, combination square, framing square, box cutter, 1/4" crown stapler, 18-gauge nail gun, pocket hole jig, long-nose pattern marker, miter saw, hacksaw, drill/driver, 4" hole saw, caulk gun*

# ULTRA-ORGANIZED
# GARAGE CABINETS

## Modify your cabinets for greater storage and convenience

### BY BILL BERGMANN

**O**ur garages are multitaskers—vehicle protectors, workshops, tool organizers and hangout spaces for friends and family. For a garage to serve all those purposes, it must be highly organized. I customized two typical kitchen cabinets for maximum storage—think Swiss Army knife caliber organization and convenience.

## TALL CABINET

### 1 INSTALL SHELVES

Use a clamp to temporarily support the middle shelf (C) in its approximate location, and use the lower divider panel (B) as a support and spacer. Attach the shelf with pocket screws. After attaching one side of the shelf, slide the divider to the other side, remove the clamp and attach that side. You'll repeat this process for the upper shelf (D) once the upper divider panel (A) is in place.

**MEET THE BUILDER**
Bill Bergmann spends too much time in his garage building projects, rehearsing with "garage bands" and hosting man cave happy hours. This project shows his skill at modifying cabinets.

Upper shelf (D) used as spacer

Vertical staples

Horizontal staples

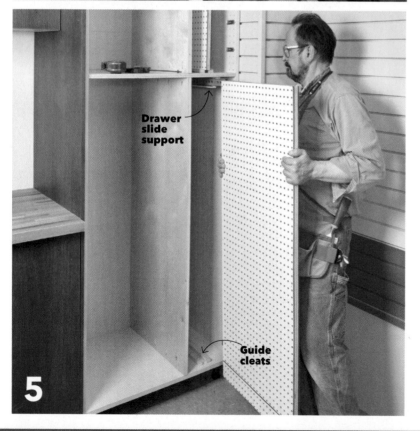

Drawer slide support

Guide cleats

## 2 INSTALL THE DIVIDER PANELS

Using the upper shelf (D) as a spacer, attach the top and bottom of the lower panel. Repeat the process for the upper divider panel (A), then install the upper shelf. Use pocket screws for all these connections.

## 3 ASSEMBLE DRAWER BOXES

After completing the Cutting List, assemble the drawer boxes (N-W) using crown staples and wood glue. Do this on a flat table to ensure the parts stay flush on the bottom.

### Pro Tip

Staple horizontally to attach the sides, fronts and backs to the base. Staple vertically to connect the sides to the front and back. Keep the staples slightly away from the outer edge to avoid splintering the plywood's veneer.

## 4 BUILD PEGBOARD PANELS

Make a pullout pegboard panel (J and K) sandwich using nails for the mitered corners of the frame (E-H) and crown staples and construction adhesive for the panels.

## 5 INSTALL THE PULLOUT PANELS

Attach the drawer slide inner rails to the panels and the slides to the supports (L). Install the supports and the guide cleats (M) with adhesive and brad nails, centering each panel in its space.

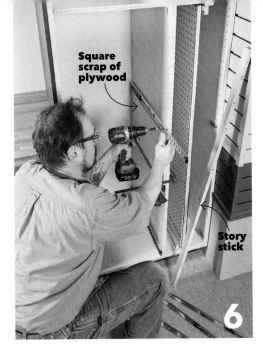

**Square scrap of plywood**

**Story stick**

**6**

## 6 LAY OUT AND INSTALL DRAWER SLIDES

Rip a scrap of plywood to make a story stick, and mark the drawer spacing on it. Stand the stick in the cabinet and transfer those marks to the cabinet side and the lower divider. Install the first pair of slides at the bottom of the cabinet. Set the slides back the thickness of the drawer face plus 3/16 in.

### Pro Tip

Cut a scrap of plywood the same size as the distance between the bottom slide and the next slide up. Use that plywood to position the second set of slides. As you work your way up with the drawer slides, cut the plywood to match the layout and support each set of slides for installation.

## Figure A  Tall Cabinet

**OVERALL DIMENSIONS: 94" H x 30" W x 24" D**

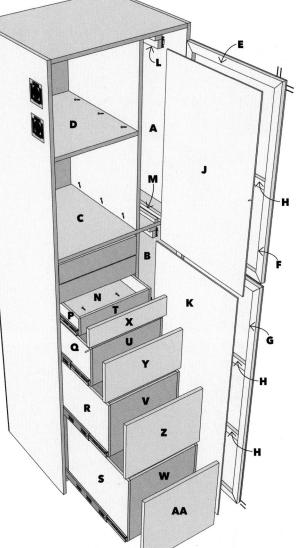

## Materials List

| ITEM | QTY. |
|---|---|
| 3/4" x 4' x 8' fir-core birch plywood | 2 |
| 1/2" x 5' x 5' Baltic birch plywood | 2 |
| 1x4 x 4' clear pine | 1 |
| 3/4" x 16" x 4' S4S laminated spruce panel board | 2 |
| 1/4" x 2' x 4' pegboard | 4 |
| 1/4" x 4' x 8' hardboard | 1 |
| 22" heavy-duty over-travel drawer slides | 1 pair |
| 22" soft-close drawer slides | 8 pairs |
| 3/4" x 2' piano hinge | 2 |
| Biometric cabinet lock | 1 |
| 1/4" crown staples: 1" and 1/2" | |
| 1-1/2" 18-gauge nails | |
| 1-1/4" pocket screws | |
| 1-1/2" trim screws | |
| 1" cabinet screws | |
| 3" corner braces | 4 |
| Construction adhesive | |
| Wood glue | |
| Heavy-duty double-sided tape | |
| Polyurethane finish | |
| Latex enamel | |
| 50' cord reel | 1 |
| 50' hose reel | 1 |
| 4" hose ports | 2 |
| 1-1/8" x 2' x 4' Kaizen foam | 1 |
| Heavy-duty 30-mm cup hinges | 5 |

## Cutting List

| KEY | QTY. | DIMENSIONS | PART |
|---|---|---|---|
| A | 1 | 3/4" x 23" x 36" | Upper divider panel |
| B | 1 | 3/4" x 23" x 51-3/4" | Lower divider panel |
| C | 1 | 3/4" x 23" x 28-1/2" | Middle shelf |
| D | 1 | 3/4" x 23" x 18" | Upper shelf |
| E | 4 | 3/4" x 1-1/2" x 22" | Pegboard frame rails |
| F | 2 | 3/4" x 1-1/2" x 36" | Upper pegboard frame stiles |
| G | 2 | 3/4" x 1-1/2" x 50-3/4" | Lower pegboard frame stiles |
| H | 3 | 3/4" x 1-1/2" x 19" | Panel crosspieces |
| J | 1 | 22" x 36" | Upper pegboard panels |
| K | 2 | 22" x 50-3/4" | Lower pegboard panels |
| L | 4 | 3/4" x 1-1/2" x 22" | Slide support top and vertical |
| M | 4 | 3/4" x 3/4" x 22" | Pullout guide cleats |
| N | 6 | 3/4" x 16" x 20-1/2" | Drawer box bases |
| P | 6 | 1/2" x 3-3/4" x 21-1/2" | Small drawer box sides |
| Q | 2 | 1/2" x 8-1/2" x 21-1/2" | Medium drawer box sides |
| R | 2 | 1/2" x 12-1/2" x 21-1/2" | Large drawer box sides |
| S | 2 | 1/2" x 16" x 21-1/2" | X-large drawer box sides |
| T | 6 | 1/2" x 3-3/4" x 16" | Small drawer box fronts and backs |
| U | 2 | 1/2" x 8-1/2" x 16" | Medium drawer box front and back |
| V | 2 | 1/2" x 12-1/2" x 16" | Large drawer box front and back |
| W | 2 | 1/2" x 16" x 16" | X-large drawer box front and back |
| X | 3 | 3/4" x 4-1/8" x 17-7/8" | Small drawer face |
| Y | 1 | 3/4" x 8-7/8" x 17-7/8" | Medium drawer face |
| Z | 1 | 3/4" x 12-7/8" x 17-7/8" | Large drawer face |
| AA | 1 | 3/4" x 6-3/8" x 17-7/8" | X-large drawer face |

## 7 POSITION AND INSTALL DRAWER FRONTS

Using heavy-duty double-sided tape and shims, position the drawer faces (X-AA), keeping about a 1/8-in. gap around the perimeter. Attach each face from the inside of the drawer box using cabinet screws. The cabinet doors leave little space for drawer pulls. Drill 1-1/2-in. holes for finger pulls or make a hand-pull cutout as I did.

## 8 INSTALL THE CORD/HOSE PORTS

Drill two 4-in. holes through the side of the cabinet, then attach the ports to the outside of the cabinet with panhead screws.

### Pro Tip

Start the hole-saw cut from the inside. Once the guide bit comes through the outer cabinet, finish the cut from the outside to avoid any tear-out or splintering. The port covers will help hide sloppy cuts, but better to avoid them in the first place.

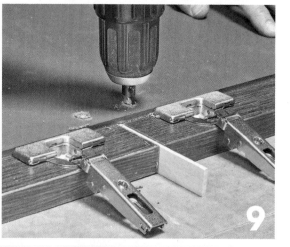

## 9 ATTACH CABINET DOORS TO TALL CABINET

I joined the doors of this cabinet with 1/4-in. hardboard, using an approach similar to editor Mike Berner's in the charging center project (p. 214). I upgraded to heavy-duty cup hinges for this larger, heavier door.

## 10 MAKE FOAM TOOL INSERTS

Use a box cutter and a straightedge to cut foam drawer inserts. Place your tools on the foam where you want them, and trace them with a long-nose marker. Set the depth of a box cutter blade to match each tool and score the outlines. Kaizen foam is a stack of foam layers, so you can remove layers to the approximate depth of your cut.

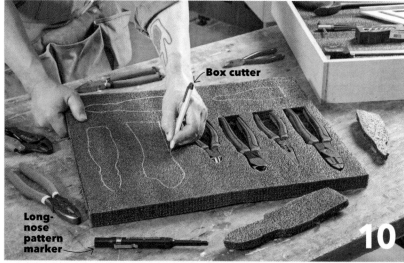

Box cutter

Long-nose pattern marker

# BASE CABINET

## 1 ATTACH DRAWER SLIDES TO LARGE PULLOUT

With the parts for the lower pullout (A-C) and storage boxes (D and E) assembled, use 1/2-in. spacers to attach the inner rail of the drawer slides to the base buildup (C) on the pullout box. Set the insert back about 3/16 in. from the front of the box. Attach the corner braces—two on the top and two on the bottom—to square and stiffen the box.

3/16"

1/2" spacer

## Figure B Base Cabinet Pullout

**OVERALL DIMENSIONS OF THE CABINET:**
**34-1/2" H x 30" W x 24" D**

F

B

D

A

E

G

3" corner brace

C

1-1/2" nail

1-1/2" trim screw

## Cutting List

| KEY | QTY. | DIMENSIONS | PART |
|-----|------|------------|------|
| A | 2 | 3/4" x 24-1/2" x 25" | Lower cabinet pullout front and back |
| B | 2 | 3/4" x 24-1/2" x 20-1/2" | Lower cabinet pullout top and bottom |
| C | 2 | 3/4" x 2" x 20-1/2" | Buildup |
| D | 4 | 3/4" x 11" x 16-3/4" | Inner storage box for lower pullout, top and bottom |
| E | 4 | 3/4" x 11" x 19-1/4" | Inner storage box for lower pullout, side |
| F | 4 | 3/4" x 2" x 23" | Slide supports for lower pullout |
| G | 2 | 1/2" x 21-1/8" x 23" | Backs for inner storage boxes |

Edges of storage box marked for nail placement

Self-centering drill bit

**2**

**3**

Electrical tape

**4**

### 2 HANG STORAGE BOXES ON LOWER PULLOUT

Cut the piano hinge to length. Install one side on the inner box, then attach the other to the lower pullout. A No. 4 self-centering bit gives quick and accurate screw placement for the hinges.

### 3 INSTALL STORAGE BOX BACKS

Mark the edges of the storage boxes on the backs (G) and fasten them using glue and brad nails. Using a 1-1/2-in. hole saw, cut a finger pull hole in the upper front corner of each back.

### 4 INSTALL LOWER PULLOUT DOORS

With the drawer slides installed on their supports (F), slide the lower pullout into place. I recommend drawer slides rated for at least 250 lbs. Loaded with tools and fasteners, this pullout pushed the limits of the 150-lb. slides I used. Place the original doors using double-sided tape, maintaining a consistent gap against the adjoining cabinets. Attach them from inside the pullout with wood screws.

> **Pro Tip**
> Use black electrical tape to black out the light plywood and create a shadow line in the gap between the two doors.

### *Finishing touches*

To safeguard valuable and heirloom tools in this tall cabinet, I installed a biometric lock. Installation was easy: I drilled a 3/4-in. hole in the door, mounted the lock and a strike plate, and then did a few simple steps to add my fingerprint. Other final touches included adding peel-and-stick edge banding for the visible plywood edges, 1-1/2-in. nosing on the pegboard pullouts, magnetic catches on the lower storage boxes and edging trim on the top of the lower pullout. I sealed the interior cabinet components with two coats of water-based polyurethane and painted others with a latex enamel.

# Great Goofs®

**Laughs and lessons from our readers**

## RUNAWAY MOWER

My old riding mower works fine, except for a weak battery that needs an occasional jump start. One day as I was riding my mower across the lawn, I had to shut it down to take a phone call. When I tried to start it again, the engine wouldn't turn over. Luckily, it had died near the street, so I pulled my car next to the mower, connected the jumper cables and waited a few minutes. Standing next to the mower, I pressed my foot down on the brake and turned the key. Sure enough, the engine started right up. I then took my foot off the brake and watched in horror as the mower sped away, ripping off the jumper cables as it went. I had forgotten to put the transmission in neutral! Thankfully, I was able to hop on and stop it before it got too far, but I got a hearty round of applause from my neighbors, who appreciated the clown show.

**CHRIS LINDSAY**

## BEE CAREFUL WITH THAT HAMMER

I was tearing down an old shed that wasn't much more than weathered lumber over a dirt floor. A fair number of bees were flying around, but I kept going until the planks were down and stacked into neat piles. There was one last piece of plywood lying on the ground. I used the claw of the hammer I had in my hand to lift up the plywood. Out from the ground came more bees!

I dropped the plywood and started running. One of the bees was gaining on me! I instinctively waved my hands to ward it off, but I had forgotten I was holding a hammer! The emergency room doc was laughing so hard that he had a tough time keeping the stitches straight as he worked on the gash above my eyebrow.

**NORMAN BULLOCK**

# 7 Using DIY Tools & Materials

# 26
# THINGS
## THAT CHANGED
# DIY
## FOREVER

## Innovations that improved home improvement

### BY THE EDITORS OF *FAMILY HANDYMAN*

**N**ew products are constantly making DIY projects faster, easier and cheaper. Introducing these products is and always has been part of our mission. In fact, many of the most important advances were first publicized in *Family Handyman*. Here are a few of our favorite DIY breakthroughs.

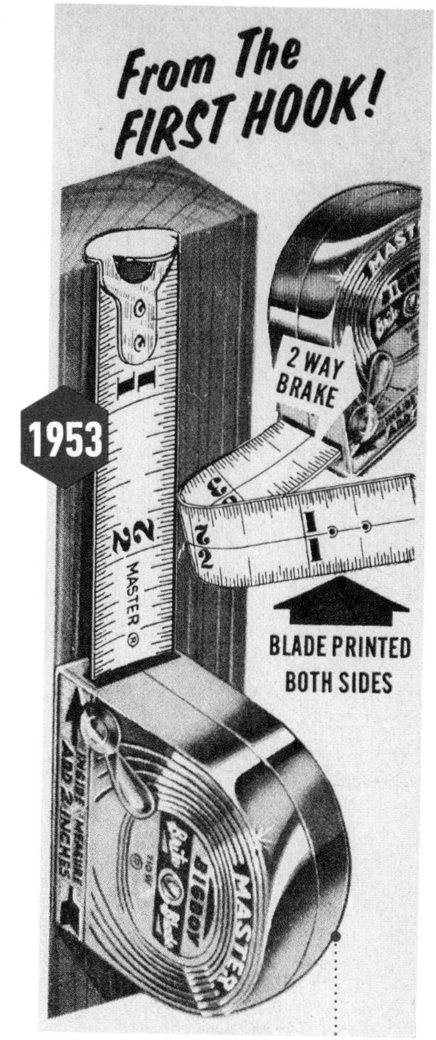

## From The FIRST HOOK!

1953

2 WAY BRAKE

BLADE PRINTED BOTH SIDES

## 3 Pegboard

It just might be the greatest organizing invention of all time. The ad in 1957 said it all: "Turn any wall into a working wall with famous Masonite Peg Board." At that time, inventors were already working on ways to keep the hooks from falling out—nobody has found the perfect solution yet.

## 1 THE TAPE MEASURE

The basic idea goes back centuries, and by the mid-1800s, there were tape measures much like the ones we use today. But early tapes were finicky and super expensive (equivalent to about $300 today). So most DIYers and pros stuck with the old "folding rule." Finally, as manufacturing became better and cheaper in the 1950s, everyone, including *Family Handyman*, made the switch to tapes.

## 2 *FAMILY HANDYMAN* MAGAZINE

In 1951, a publishing brand devoted to DIY was a radical idea. Today, that idea—and the brand that launched it all—is at an all-time high in popularity. The founders of *Family Handyman* would be thrilled. They had hoped to serve thousands of DIYers. Now their radical idea serves millions—through this magazine, how-to books and *familyhandyman.com*.

**1957**

## 4 THE MOTORIZED MOWER

The first issues of *Family Handyman* included only push-powered reel mowers, which made mowing a hard workout. But before long, ads and articles on gas-powered models appeared. Many of them were just motorized reel mowers, not the rotary mowers we use today. There was even a riding rotary mower!

## 5 Water-based paint

Acrylic latex paints hit the market in the 1950s, and *Family Handyman* quickly jumped on the bandwagon. But for decades, people held on to the notion that oil-based paints were better. As late as the 1980s, we were still trying to convince the skeptics that acrylic paints were superior—and a whole lot easier to clean up.

## 6 THE PAINT ROLLER

The first rollers produced in 1938 by David and Morris Welt were nearly worthless for applying paint. They just didn't soak up enough paint to coat a large area. But the Welts did find that their "stipple roller" was great for giving paint a consistent texture after it was brushed on. Over the next decade, manufacturers developed fabrics that held paint better, but consumers were apparently skeptical. In 1953, *Family Handyman* was still encouraging readers to "try a paint roller."

**1953**

## 7 DRYWALL

It's hard to fully appreciate drywall unless you know how bad things were before: Walls were covered with wood or metal lath (which took lots of time) and coats of plaster (which took lots of skill). A giant trowel, or "darby," was used to flatten plaster. *Family Handyman* generally recommended that DIYers steer clear of plaster work but enthusiastically endorsed drywall as "the only way to go" in 1960.

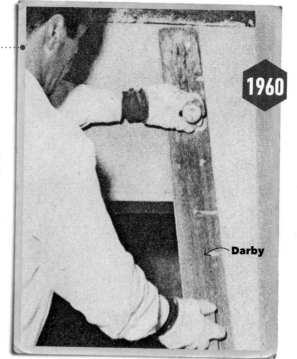

1960

Darby

1952

## Do it yourself with SpeedWay SpeedTools

Build, repair, install, finish or refinish—at your convenience, at low cost. Powerful SpeedTools take the drudgery out of work, help you do "professional" quality work in a hurry.

**No. 150 SpeedSander**
An all-ball-bearing, orbital-motion, finishing sander with powerful 3450 r.p.m., A.C. induction motor and cast aluminum body. **$34.50**

**No. 150-K SpeedSander Kit**
The Sander with Accessories including: deep contour pad, finishing plate, felts for free abrasives and wet rubbing, lamb's wool bonnet, 90 sheet abrasive covers, etc. in fitted steel carrying case **$49.50**

**No. 1000 SpeedSaw**
¼ H.P. Universal Motor, cast aluminum housing, safety shut-off switch. Cuts all angles to 45°, any depth to 1⅛" **$29.95**

**SpeedDrills**
*(for metal or wood)*
Extra power, high speed, electric drill with cast aluminum cases, and geared chucks.
No. 200-J ¼" SpeedDrill **$19.50**

No. 400 ½" SpeedDrill **$39.50**
*also other sizes, types.*

**Drill Kits**
Several fast selling kits. Painters and Householders Kit (illustrated) is typical. It has: ¼" Hornet Drill, Abrasive Discs and rubber backer plate, grinding wheel, wire brush, buff, etc. in attractive display carton **$19.95**

*Write for catalog*

**SpeedWay MANUFACTURING CO.**
1827 So. 52nd Ave., Cicero 50, Ill.

## 8 Safety gear

Apparently, nobody thought much about eye, ear and lung protection during the first decades of *Family Handyman*. Only in the 1970s did it begin to show up. We even found photos from the 1980s that made us cringe: This guy really needs a dust mask and hearing protection.

1987

## 9 SNAP-TOGETHER FLOORING

In the early days of *Family Handyman*, every option for flooring required lots of time, skill and tools. Things got a little better over the decades, but nothing simplified DIY flooring half as much as today's interlocking laminate or luxury vinyl floors.

## 10 THE SKINNY 2x4

In 1964, the American Lumber Congress set 1-1/2 x 3-1/2 in. (not 2 x 4 in.) as the standard. That may sound like a rip-off—less lumber for your money—but it made building much easier. Before the mandated standard, 2x4s from the same mill could vary in width or thickness by 1/2 in. or more.

## 11 AFFORDABLE POWER TOOLS

Nothing has made DIY faster or easier (or more fun!) than the falling cost of power tools. We took prices from 1950s ads and punched them into an inflation calculator. A typical drill cost about $200 and a circular saw about $300. Sanders were especially pricey: more than $300.

**1993**

*paslode*

## 12
### *The nail gun*

Air-powered nail guns showed up at about the same time as *Family Handyman*. But they (and compressors) were just too expensive for DIYers and didn't appear in the magazine until 1993. Even then, an inexpensive brad nailer cost the equivalent of about $200 today. Now you can get a good gun and compressor combo for less than that.

## 13 CORDLESS TOOLS

We were shocked to see that the first cordless drill hit stores way back in 1961. Great idea, but the technology of the time couldn't supply much power or run time, so the cordless revolution didn't really get energized until the late 1980s.

**1961**

**Black & Decker's first cordless drill**

## 14 THE BUNGEE CORD

Soldiers returning from World War II introduced this stretchy strap into civilian life. The era of bungee misuse soon began, with roof-rack cargo strewn across highways, bad bumper repairs and hook-shaped scarring.

## 15 PEX PLUMBING

We think PEX is simply the greatest plumbing innovation of the past 100 years. Compared with steel, copper or CPVC pipe, it's amazingly easy.

## 16 THE UTILITY KNIFE

A blade you can just toss when dull? We take that for granted. But for DIYers in the '50s, it felt like a miracle. A super-sharp blade always—no sharpening hassles.

**1960**

## 17 PLASTIC PIPE

In the old days, using steel pipe for waste lines and vents required know-how and expensive equipment. Cast iron was even worse: Connections were sealed with molten lead! Thanks to PVC and ABS pipe, we don't have to melt lead in our basements.

## 18 DRILL DRIVING

The experience of driving screws with a drill was "a pleasant surprise" to our editors in 1960. There was a problem, though: Many drills weren't reversible and couldn't remove screws.

**1960**

## 19 NM CABLE

Armored cable—wires encased in flexible metal—is still required for some jobs. But luckily for us weekend electricians, "nonmetallic" (NM) cable—wires sheathed in a plastic jacket—became the norm in the 1960s. Wiring a switch or outlet hasn't changed much, but working with NM cable is a lot faster and easier.

## 20 POCKET HOLE JOINERY

Craig Sommerfeld didn't invent pocket hole joinery when he built his own "Kreg Jig" in 1986. He did something even better: He turned an industrial method for joining wood into an easy, affordable option. Today, it's still an option used by most woodworkers (pros or DIYers).

**1986**

**The original Kreg Jig**

**1969**

## 21 THE CHAIN SAW

The first wood-cutting chain saws were big beasts that required two lumberjacks for operation. One-person models hit the market at about the same time *Family Handyman* launched. But the basic concept—a sharp chain racing around a bar—goes way back to an 1830s surgical tool designed to cut bone. Good concept for a horror movie?

**1958**

## 22 Spray paint

In 1949, Bonnie Seymour suggested to her husband, Ed, that paint could be packaged in an aerosol can, like the deodorizers she used around the house. Ed, a paint salesman, gave it a try and an entire industry was born. In 1958, spray-can wood finish debuted in *Family Handyman*.

You Can Build It With Sakrete!

*Now Concrete & Mortar in paper sacks*

PREMIXED **~~RETE~~** ~~UCTS~~ ADD ~~ER~~

~~...o~~ can patch y ~~co...~~ ~~...lk,~~ build that outd ~~...~~ fireplace, set up that clothes dr ~~...er~~

## 23
### Bagged concrete

Need to set a fence post? Here's the old process: Go buy some Portland cement, sand and gravel, then carefully measure the proportions of each, add water and mix. But soon bagged concrete came along. As the ad in the very first issue of *Family Handyman* said, "Just add water."

## 24 PUSH-ON PLUMBING FITTINGS

A ton of testing shows that push-on connectors (such as SharkBite fittings) are reliable. Still, it's hard for some of us to accept—can something so easy really be good?

## 25 SMARTPHONES

They might be the greatest DIY tool ever! You can order hardware online, check an electrical code, snap a photo of a plumbing fitting to find a match at the store or even install an app that turns your phone into a level.

## 26 DUCT TAPE

While working in an ordnance factory during World War II, Vesta Stoudt suggested that waterproof tape would provide a reliable, removable seal for ammunition boxes. Management didn't pursue the idea, but Stoudt persisted; for her this was both personal and patriotic since she had two sons in the Navy. She sent a letter and diagrams to President Roosevelt, and the War Department quickly put her idea into production. Soldiers soon discovered that the strong, super-sticky tape had a million uses. Later, HVAC installers found that it worked well to seal ductwork. Today, we have better tapes for ducts, but the name lives on.

# SHARP DRILL BITS IN 30 SECONDS

BY NICK WIESNESKI OWNER, NICK OF ALL TRADES LLC

You can tell a drill bit has become dull when it squeals, smokes or takes five minutes to bore a hole. A close look usually reveals a cutting edge that reflects light, meaning it's no longer an edge but a surface, which won't cut anything.

On too many occasions, I found myself on a job site, where running out for a new bit wasn't an option. I had to learn how to make a bit "sharp enough" in a hurry. I've used a bench grinder, a belt sander, an angle grinder and the narrow benchtop belt sander shown here.

## 1 MARK THE FACES

Color each face behind the cutting edge using a permanent marker so you have a reference to track your progress and make sure your angle is correct when you start grinding. (Wear eye protection!) The goal is to lightly grind each face evenly, from the heel to the cutting edge, without changing the angle or the size of the chisel tip. It sounds complicated, but if you're careful, you'll have a sharp bit in about 30 seconds on your first try.

## 2 FIND THE ANGLE

Before turning on the sander, looking from the top, eyeball the angle of the cutting edge. On larger bits, you can even press the bit's face against the belt and feel the angle.

## 3 FIND THE HEEL

Keeping the first angle, drop the end of the bit until the heel is touching the belt. Feel that position in your muscle memory.

## 4 GRIND AWAY!

Turn on the machine and touch the bit to the belt. Using very light pressure, rotate the bit, starting from the heel, until you've reached the cutting edge. Check your progress by looking at the colored face. When the marker ink is gone and the cutting edge no longer catches light, you're done!

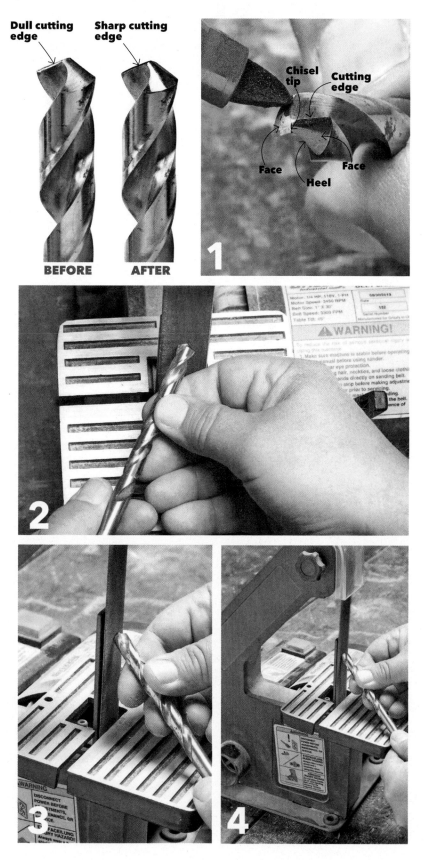

Dull cutting edge    Sharp cutting edge

BEFORE    AFTER

Chisel tip    Cutting edge
Face    Face
Heel

# CUT METAL LIKE THE PROS

## The right tools make all the difference

BY JAY CORK

To cut metal for siding, roofing and flashing, you need the right tools for the best results. As we were getting ready to roof and side the *Family Handyman* Getaway, I talked my fellow editors into trying different methods of cutting metal—shears, nibblers and saws—to see what they liked best.

### MEET THE EXPERTS

**Bill Bergmann** managed the steel siding project.

**Mike Berner** was in charge of the metal roofing.

### SAFETY FIRST

Whenever you cut metal, expect steel shavings to go everywhere. Eye protection is a must. Bill is also wearing latex-coated gloves. While no glove will prevent every cut, the coating provides a cut-resistant layer and extra grip power.

**No deformation**

## NIBBLERS FOR PROFILES

Mike loves how clean a nibbler cuts; he says it's the best tool to cut profiles without deforming them. This is also a great tool for cutting round holes for vents. One downside: It punches out tiny pieces of steel, which go everywhere. There's a risk of injury; always wear the appropriate PPE.

**One side becomes deformed**

## SINGLE-CUT SHEARS FOR SPEED

Single-cut shears cut flat stock fast. However, they won't produce smooth edges on both sides of the cut; the cutoff side will always be deformed. These shears are a good choice for trimming ends, but they won't work as well to cut through the middle of a wider sheet.

## CIRCULAR SAW FOR SIDING

**Chips collect here**

Circular saws work well for crosscutting metal siding. But don't expect good results with a woodcutting blade—always use blades made for metal. Bill also warns that a regular circular saw will throw bits of steel everywhere. He found that a purpose-built metal-cutting circular saw eliminates most of that debris with a chip catcher. No matter what type of saw you use, always wear a full face shield, not just safety glasses.

## DOUBLE-CUT SHEARS FOR FLAT STOCK

Mike says double-cut shears work well for straight cuts on flat stock; they cut fast and leave both edges nice and flat, without any curling. However, they tended to deform the shape too much when cutting across the profile. This was also the cleanest-cutting tool he used, producing an easily managed curl.

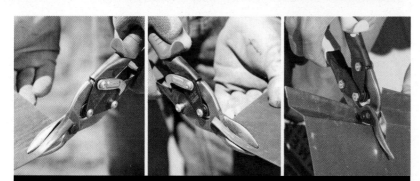

## USE THE CORRECT SNIPS

Bill taught me something: Aviation snips have colored handles for a reason. Red handles indicate that the snips cut the waste off to the left side; green ones cut it off to the right. Yellow handle snips are perfect for making small notches or cutting in either direction.

# THE GEAR WE USED

We tried a lot of tools at the Getaway—here are some of our favorites for metal work.

**EARMUFFS**
Cutting metal is loud work! Always protect your hearing with earplugs or earmuffs.

**GLOVES**
No matter how you cut steel, there are going to be sharp edges. Protect your fingers with cut-resistant gloves.

**RIDGID JOBMAX SHEAR**
The Ridgid JobMax Shear Head ($60; attachment only) has a carbide cutter that's easy to replace.

**MAKITA CIRCULAR SAW**
This model is designed to cut metal, and collect the shavings ($230; tool only).

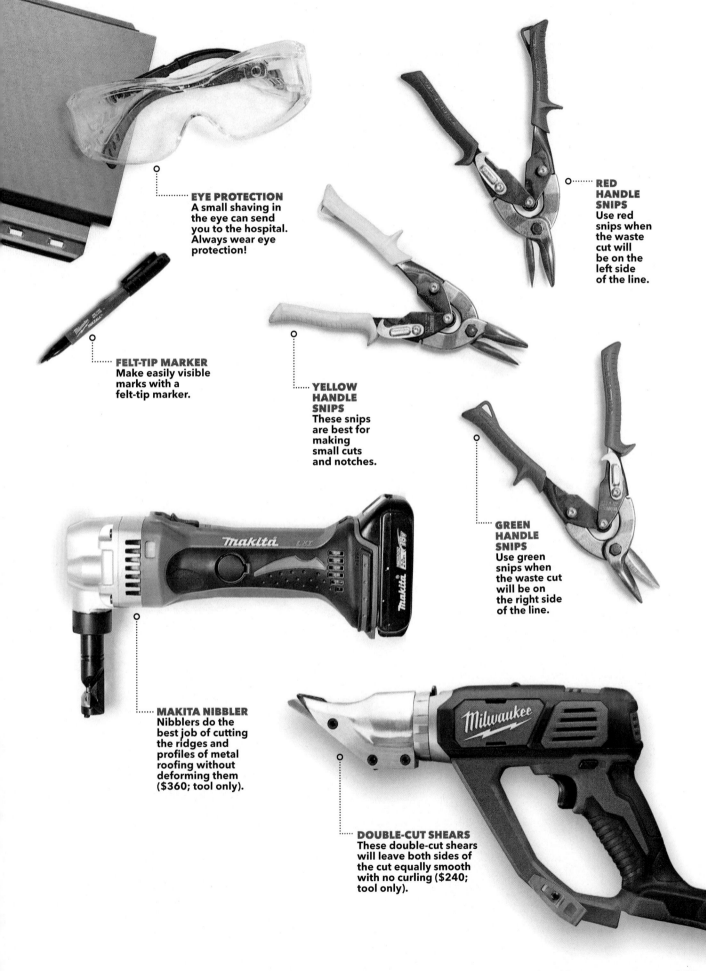

**EYE PROTECTION**
A small shaving in the eye can send you to the hospital. Always wear eye protection!

**FELT-TIP MARKER**
Make easily visible marks with a felt-tip marker.

**RED HANDLE SNIPS**
Use red snips when the waste cut will be on the left side of the line.

**YELLOW HANDLE SNIPS**
These snips are best for making small cuts and notches.

**GREEN HANDLE SNIPS**
Use green snips when the waste cut will be on the right side of the line.

**MAKITA NIBBLER**
Nibblers do the best job of cutting the ridges and profiles of metal roofing without deforming them ($360; tool only).

**DOUBLE-CUT SHEARS**
These double-cut shears will leave both sides of the cut equally smooth with no curling ($240; tool only).

# CORDLESS AND COMPACT

## These powerful trim routers make it easy to cut the cord

BY MIKE BERNER

**C**ordless tool technology has come a long way in a short time. Five years ago, I tried a first-generation cordless router and hated it, thinking some tools just weren't meant to be cordless. But I've been proven wrong. Today's cordless routers can handle 90% of my routing tasks.

## THE CASE FOR COMPACT CORDLESS

If you own a router and are considering a second, I recommend a cordless. Light edge profiles make up most of my routing, so a compact is perfect for me, and cordless is even more appealing. I grab my full-size corded router only for heavier jobs. Compact cordless routers are also a good choice for a first router. They'll do everything a corded compact can.

## DON'T WORRY ABOUT RUN TIME

For five of the six routers we tested, the manufacturers claim they'll rout at least 250 linear feet on a single charge. But run time partly depends on whether I'm trimming laminate or routing a big round-over. With two batteries, all I need is a charger that keeps pace with the job at hand. And I can't remember the last time I had to rout 250 ft. of anything! All the routers we tested had sufficient run times and speedy charging, making this rating a nonissue for me.

## PUTTING BATTERY POWER TO THE TEST

I put the battery-powered compact routers through the test shown below to evaluate their ease of use, run time and overall power. I started by cutting a 3/8-in.-deep groove and dado with a spiral bit, then I switched to a chamfer bit and made a 1/2-in. profile along one edge and one end.

I made plenty of sawdust for this story! I tested the six routers by making four different cuts in three types of wood.

# *Features that matter*

**Dust extraction port**

1/4" shank

1/2" shank

## 1/4-in. shanks only
Compact routers accept only 1/4-in. shank bits, which aren't outfitted with large profile cutters. For large-profile cutters with a 1/2-in. shank, you'll need a full-size router.

### PLENTY OF POWER
When it comes to power, compact cordless routers can go toe-to-toe with their corded cousins. I tested each cordless model alongside a corded version and found no difference in power.

## Invest in dust extraction
Dust isn't just messy. It builds up while you're routing dadoes and grooves and causes burning. To avoid this and to make it easier to see what you're doing, get a dust port for your router. Many brands include them in their kits. If yours doesn't, it's smart to buy one (about $15).

**Plunge base**

**Turret depth adjustment**

## Consider a plunge base
Some compact router kits include a plunge base, some brands offer one as an add-on and others aren't compatible with a plunge base at all. A plunge base lets you easily rout in stages for easier cutting and a better finish. Plunge bases provide a two-handled grip for better control and an adjustable turret, which lets you adjust the plunge depth without readjusting the final depth.

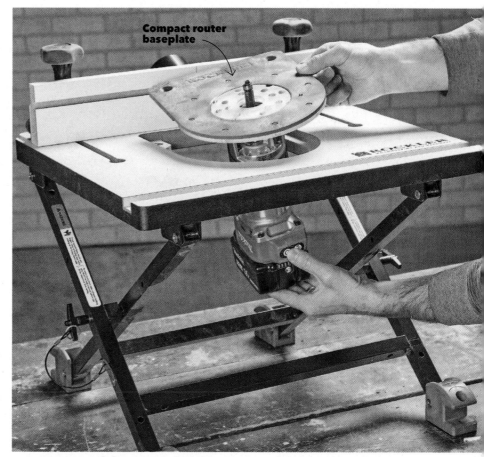

Compact router baseplate

## A router table *is* an option

A router table makes any router much more versatile. Most tables are made for full-size routers, but baseplates are available to accommodate compact routers. They're a worthwhile investment.

## Why does variable speed matter?

Large-profile bits should be run at a lower rpm than small-profile bits. This applies whether the bit has a 1/4-in. shank or a 1/2-in. shank. If the bit is "jumping" or burning your material, slow it down a little.

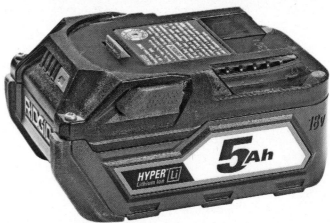

## No need for a bigger battery

During my testing of these routers, I tried 5AH batteries and 2AH batteries to see if there was a power difference. There was no discernible difference. And the 2AH battery gave the router better balance—there was less of that top-heavy feeling. For this reason alone, if you have the option, go with a smaller battery.

# *The routers*

These routers have very similar features: adjustable bases, variable speed dials and the ability to make micro adjustments. But each one has something that separates it from the rest. I paid close attention to the ease of bit adjustment, safety features, accessories and the general feel while cutting.

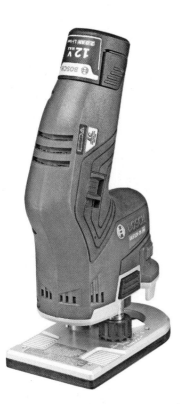

EDITORS' CHOICE BEST OVERALL

## BOSCH 12V (GKF12V)
### $149 (TOOL ONLY)

This model is the only 12V tool on this list, but it has the power to do what the 18V tools can do. It didn't struggle with any of the cuts I made with it. One thing I really like is that the bit is offset to one side, which lets you get more of the tool on the work surface. The height adjustment is very quick and easy.

### PROS
- The tool is very lightweight and compact.
- Depth adjustments are fast with a quick-release button and fine adjustment screw.
- The spindle is offset, providing lots of room for the base to rest on a flat surface.

### CONS
- The base isn't removable.
- The tool isn't compatible with a plunge base.
- The unique grip design takes some getting used to.

## DEWALT (DCW600B)
### $200 (TOOL ONLY)

The DeWalt is the biggest of the bunch, and in a class of compact routers, that's not necessarily a plus. Of the six routers, it has the easiest screw collar height adjustment, and it's very accurate for both macro and micro adjustments. The router cuts smoothly, without chatter.

### PROS
- The base is easy to remove, and the spindle lock button has several stops for easy one-tool bit changes.
- It has a large, squared-off baseplate for accurate routing against a fence.
- It has both a soft-start feature and a fast-acting electric brake.
- The two LEDs light the work area nicely.

### CONS
- All accessories sold separately.
- It's the most expensive tool-only router.

## MAKITA (XTR01Z)
### $129 (TOOL ONLY)

The Makita is the smallest router I tested, but it has a solid feel and a sturdy, mostly aluminum body. Its heft helps with the balance, and it made the smoothest cuts of the group. The rack-and-pinion height adjustment is unique to the Makita and great for rough height changes, but fine adjustments were harder to dial in.

### PROS
- It has a soft-start motor.
- The power switch safety eliminates unintended power-ups.
- As a kit, it's an incredible value: charger, plunge base, edge guide, two batteries, all in a nice tool case for about $350.

### CONS
- Baseplate is small.
- There is no micro adjustment.
- There's no electric brake.

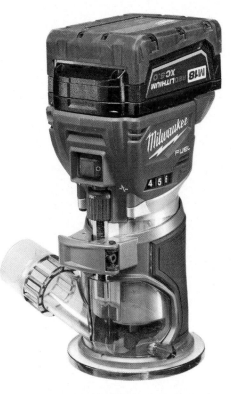

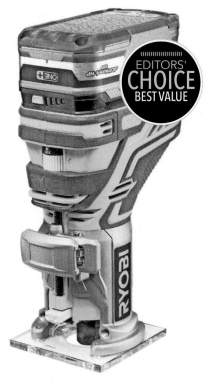

## MILWAUKEE (2723-20)
**$199 (TOOL ONLY)**

The Milwaukee has a comfortable rubberized grip for a solid, controlled feel. The 5AH battery gives a top-heavy feel, but the larger baseplate helps steady it on the work surface. The quick-release button lets you easily remove the base for bit changes. During my first cut, the base shifted slightly, but I tightened the latch and it didn't happen again.

### PROS
- The micro-adjustment knob moved the base smoother than others with a similar design.
- It includes a removable dust extraction port and two baseplates.
- Bit changes are simple and fast.

### CONS
- Out of the box, the latch needed tightening to keep the base from slipping.

## RIDGID (R860443)
**$129 (TOOL-ONLY KIT)**

The Ridgid has features similar to those found in other routers and includes extras like an edge guide and a soft case. The body is plastic, and the base doesn't have a rubberized grip, but it's narrower and still easy to hold. This model chattered a bit on deep cuts but was very smooth on shallow passes.

### PROS
- The tool-only kit includes an edge guide, a dust extraction port and an extra baseplate.
- This router affords the best visibility of the bit from both sides while you're routing.

### CONS
- The switch is awkward to operate.
- I found it difficult to raise the bit against gravity with the micro-adjustment knob. I needed to flip it upside down to make the adjustment.

## RYOBI (P601)
**$70 (TOOL ONLY)**

The Ryobi feels a little top-heavy, especially with the smaller base. On deeper cuts, it chatters quite a bit, but on shallow cuts it performs well. It has high-end features, such as a micro adjustment and a quick-release lever. A plunge base isn't available for this router. The Ryobi cuts really well for light-duty, shallow work.

### PROS
- The quick-adjust is integrated in the same mechanism as the latch that secures the base.
- Micro adjustment is smooth.
- The value is hard to beat.

### CONS
- The grip zone isn't where I would grip the tool while in use.
- The heavy battery and small baseplate make the tool feel unbalanced.
- The base is a little fussy to remove for bit changes.

---

## THE BOTTOM LINE: STICK WITH THE BATTERY SYSTEM YOU HAVE

After testing these routers, I definitely have preferences. But, honestly, there isn't a big difference between my least favorite and my favorite. They're all good tools that I'd be happy to have in my shop. My advice? If you've already invested in a battery platform, get the cordless router of the same brand. The benefit of having extra batteries outweighs any other advantages.

# GET THE RIGHT
# GLUE

## Stick to my advice and you can't go wrong

BY JAY CORK

**MEET THE EXPERT**
Jay Cork, an associate editor at *Family Handyman*, was 11 the first time he glued his fingers together with superglue.

've used just about every type of glue on the market today. Still, if I were to go strictly by the info on the packaging, even I might be a little confused in the glue aisle at my local home center. They all have strengths and weaknesses. Knowing how and when to use each type will make you a better DIYer.

**Olivewood**

**Purple heart**

**Cocobolo**

**Padauk**

## Polyurethane glue for oily woods ▶

The oil in woods such as olivewood, purple heart, cocobolo and padauk can cause standard wood glues to fail. That's why I've always used polyurethane glue with these hardwoods; it penetrates deep into the wood grain and creates an extraordinarily strong bond. To ensure a good result, I thoroughly clean the surface of the wood with acetone before glue-up.

**Clean the surfaces first**

## Best glue for a busted shoe

E6000 craft glue ($5 for 2 oz.) is one of my favorite adhesives. It's useful for many repairs, but I like it especially for fixing shoes. It bonds extremely well to leather and rubber, remains flexible after it's cured and withstands a wide range of temperature.

1/8" gap

## Epoxy fills gaps ▲

Most glues are meant to bond surfaces that fit tightly together. They don't have much "bridging strength" to bond loose-fitting parts. Epoxies, on the other hand, fill gaps very well without sacrificing strength.

Clean with alcohol before gluing

## My go-to for gluing metal ▲

In my experience, the only adhesive that reliably works on metal is J-B Weld Original Formula. I've had great success with this glue in nonstructural and low-stress applications. If a piece of structural steel broke under stress, however, gluing would probably not be the best fix. J-B Weld is available at home centers and auto parts stores for about $7. Like any other epoxy, it's a two-part system that requires mixing.

A little water goes a long way!

## Make your own slow-setting glue

Slow-setting wood glue like Titebond Extend adds extra working time for your glue-up, but it can be hard to find. Here's how to extend the working time of standard wood glue. Pour the glue into a container, add a little water (about 5% by volume at most) and mix it well. This increases the open time without reducing the strength of the bond.

## DON'T RUIN YOUR MIRROR!

Solvent-based construction adhesive can deteriorate mirror plating and show through on the face of the mirror. Check the label and be sure to choose a product intended for mirrors. Loctite PL 530 ($7) is one choice.

## DON'T LET GLUE FREEZE!

If you left your glue in the garage during the winter, it's probably time to get a new bottle. Many adhesives—wood glue especially—are ruined by just one freeze/thaw cycle. Store them in a heated space during cold months.

## USE ACCELERATOR WITH CA GLUE

Apply CA (cyanoacrylate) glue to one surface, spray accelerator on the other and the glue will bond as soon as the surfaces touch. CA glue can often emit a strong odor when used with accelerator. This can be highly irritating, so work in a well-ventilated area.

## STOP THE RATTLING WITH HOT GLUE

As a cabinetmaker, I used hot glue on the underside of drawer bottoms to keep them from loosening over time. I do the same with old cabinet doors with a loose panel. On the back of the door, I'll put a line of hot glue in the edge where the panel meets the rail and stile.

## LET FOAM CURE BEFORE CLEANUP

Polyurethane glues foam as they cure. It's tempting to clean off the squeeze-out right away, but don't! You'll force it into the grain and never get it out. Instead, wait for the glue to cure completely. When it's cured, it's easy to remove with a putty knife.

## Wood glue is often the best choice for wood ▶

With all the new formulations available, you might think there's something better for wood. But plain old wood glue, also known as aliphatic resin, is still usually the best choice. It is nontoxic, has plenty of working time, provides high bond strength and cleans up with water. When applied to well-fitted joints, the bond is stronger than the wood itself. It's usually yellow, but some versions are brown to match darker wood tones.

**The wood fibers gave way before the glue**

## ◀ For epoxies, longer cure times produce stronger bonds

Quick-cure epoxies are available in 1-, 5- and 15-minute setting times. They're great for quick repairs, but I've found they're not as strong as longer-cure epoxies. Often, that's OK, but when I need a higher-strength bond, I choose a 1-hour epoxy and let it cure for at least 48 hours.

## Instant-grab adhesives let you skip the nails ▶

When nailing or clamping just isn't an option, instant-grab construction adhesives can save the day. I like these glues for attaching a chair rail or crown molding to plaster or brick and for delicate pieces of molding where nails just won't work. DAP and Loctite are two common brand names.

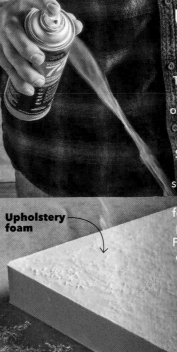

## Use spray adhesive for foam

The easiest way to join two pieces of upholstery foam is to use spray contact adhesive. Some spray adhesives melt foam, so it's important to use a glue that's formulated for this purpose. I like 3M Foam Fast 74 ($30 online). Just spray it on, let it tack up, and join the two pieces.

**Upholstery foam**

## Solvent-based contact cement is best ▶

I prefer using solvent-based contact cement for adhering plastic laminate. Because the fumes are strong and toxic, I have tried low-VOC formulas. The smell is more tolerable, but they lack the instant bond strength I'm used to and I've experienced delamination with them. So I stick with the original and work in a well-ventilated area.

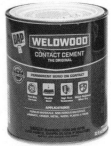

## Use hide glue for antiques ▲

I use hide glue to repair wooden musical instruments and antique furniture because it was most likely used in the original construction. Hide glue is unique in that it rejuvenates any remaining old glue in the joint being repaired. It makes a strong joint that can be taken apart with a little heat or steam. I love traditional granular hide glue, but it's labor intensive and very stinky. Instead, I usually reach for Old Brown Glue ($10 at *woodcraft.com*).

**Traces of old glue**

## Pick the right superglue

CA glue formulations range from watery thin to thick gels. Gels are good in vertical applications where running is a problem, and they are essential with porous materials like ceramics and wood. Those materials soak up thin glues, resulting in a weak bond or no bond at all. Thin CA is the best choice for repairing glass and delicate plastics.

**Gel CA glue doesn't run at all**

**Medium CA glue runs a little**

**Thin CA glue runs a lot**

## Choose waterproof glue for outdoor projects ▲

Epoxies can handle wet conditions, but for bonding wood that is going to be constantly exposed to the elements, I still choose a waterproof wood glue such as Titebond III ($14 for 16 oz.) or Elmer's Wood Glue Max ($10 for 16 oz.). Because of their long open time and water cleanup, I prefer them to a two-part system—like epoxy—that requires mixing.

**Waterproof wood glue is intact after being submerged for two weeks**

**Regular wood glue dissolved**

## Solvent-based glue for plastics ▼

Most glues don't work well on plastics. For polystyrene and ABS plastics, I reach for the old standard: Testors Cement for Plastic Models. You can find it for about $4 at any hobby or crafts store. It contains solvent that "welds" the pieces, creating a strong and lasting bond. There are nontoxic versions of this type of glue, but I've found that they just don't create a bond that's as strong as the original.

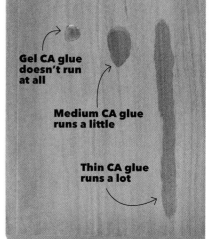

# ESSENTIAL HAND TOOLS

## Sometimes old-fashioned methods are still the best

BY JAY CORK

In this age of power tools, it's easy to ignore old-fashioned hand tools. But you shouldn't. Even if your shop is full of high-end power tools, sometimes a hand tool will get the job done faster, better and neater.

One of our favorite woodworkers, Ralph Truesdell, owns nearly every hand tool there is, and he agreed to tell us about some of his favorites.

RALPH'S FAVORITE PLANE
Jack planes are the most versatile of all bench planes, and the WoodRiver No. 62 Low Angle Jack Plane is Ralph's absolute favorite. The adjustable mouth—the space in front of the blade—can be opened up for a rough cut or closed down for a fine cut.

**MEET THE EXPERT**
Ralph Truesdell is the resident hand tool expert at his local Woodcraft store, where he teaches woodworking classes. He's also a seventh degree tae kwon do master, one of only a handful of people in the world to ever accomplish this.

# Ralph's tool chest

After years of accumulating hand tools, Ralph has quite a collection. Here are some of his favorites.

**SPOKESHAVE**
This tool gets its name from the job it was designed to do: shape spokes for carriage wheels. Many spokeshaves cost well over $100, but Ralph loves this WoodRiver Adjustable Spokeshave ($60).

**CARD SCRAPER**
Cabinet scrapers, also known as "card scrapers," come in various shapes and sizes. A set of three costs about $20 at woodworking stores.

**JAPANESE SAW**
Japanese saws cut on the pull stroke, and their tooth geometry produces very clean cuts in hardwood. Most home centers sell basic Japanese saws, but for higher quality and a wider selection, go to *japanwoodworker.com*.

**DETAIL MITER BOX**
This mini miter box is perfect for cutting small trim. It's available for about $31 at *woodcraft.com*.

**SHOULDER PLANE**
Ralph uses a shoulder plane to make the bottoms of dadoes and rabbets nice and smooth. These specialized planes cost about $150 and up.

**MARKING GAUGE**
This Veritas Dual Marking Gauge & Shaft Clamp can mark two lines at once, which is really handy when you're marking tenons. You can find it for $63 at *leevalley.com*.

**BLOCK PLANE**
This pocket-size block plane is perfect for trimming small areas or the end grain of trim boards. Inexpensive ones are available at home centers for less than $20, but expect to pay closer to $100 for a quality block plane.

## FLUSH-CUTTING SAWS

Most saw teeth stick out to the side a little, but not on these saws. This allows them to trim dowels or through tenons without scratching the wood around the cut. A basic flush-cut saw costs about $15 at home centers.

## BACKSAW

Ralph likes using traditional backsaws for dovetail joinery; their stiff blades allow for precise cuts. Prices vary widely, but many Veritas backsaws cost less than $100. Visit *leevalley.com* to see a great selection.

## CHISEL PLANE

Ralph likes using a chisel plane to clean glue squeeze-out from drawers and boxes. This one costs $90 at *woodcraft.com*.

## CHISELS

Chisels for fine woodworking come in many different shapes and sizes. You can find a good chisel for about $25, but the prices go up from there. Some Japanese chisels might cost you hundreds!

## BENCH PLANES

Common bench planes are 8 in. to more than 20 in. long and are used for roughing, squaring and smoothing lumber. Most home centers and all woodworking stores carry a selection of bench planes.

## BRACE AND BITS

The original cordless drill! The old-fashioned hand brace with the ship auger bit is a formidable boring tool. You can still find basic models online for about $45.

## COPING SAW

This saw acquired its name in the early 20th century when carpenters started using it to cope inside miter joints. However, its lineage can be traced back to the 16th century. Coping saws are still sold in hardware stores everywhere.

# Ralph's essential hand tool tips

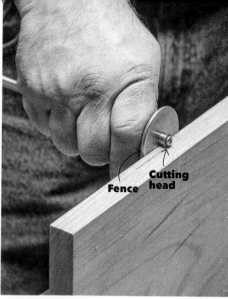

Fence    Cutting head

## MARK WITH PRECISION

A marking gauge, which cuts tiny lines into the wood, is far more precise than a pencil. The fence can be set so you can make the same mark over and over with the same precision. Ralph always uses marking gauges when he's mortising for hinges. When it comes time to "hog out" the wood, his chisel falls perfectly into the line made by the gauge.

Slightly bend the blade when cutting

## A SCRAPER BEATS SANDPAPER

To get wood smoother than sandpaper can, Ralph uses a cabinet scraper. Also known as card scrapers, these simple pieces of steel cut micro-thin shavings of wood. They're great for repairing scratches, final shaping or prepping a surface for finishing. Scraping can be hard work, but the reward comes when you apply the finish; the grain shows much more clearly and vibrantly than it does with sanded wood.

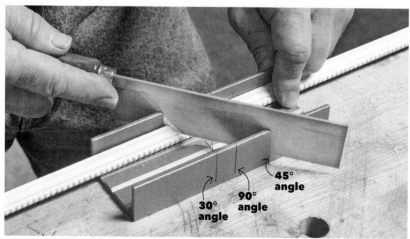

30° angle    90° angle    45° angle

## PERFECT MITERS FOR SMALL STUFF

Ralph uses this small Zona miter box to repair trim details on antiques, cut bracing for acoustic guitars and even install base shoe. Making cuts like these on a powered miter saw not only can be dangerous but also risks destroying delicate, and maybe irreplaceable, pieces of trim.

The gap will close when clamped

## PLANE A PERFECT GLUE JOINT

Making a "spring joint" is easy, and when it comes time for glue-up, you'll only need one clamp! Ralph places two boards back-to-back in a vise and very lightly dishes the edges with a No. 4 bench plane. This creates a slight gap in the middle when he places the two boards together for glue-up. Then one clamp is all he needs to create a perfectly tight glue line.

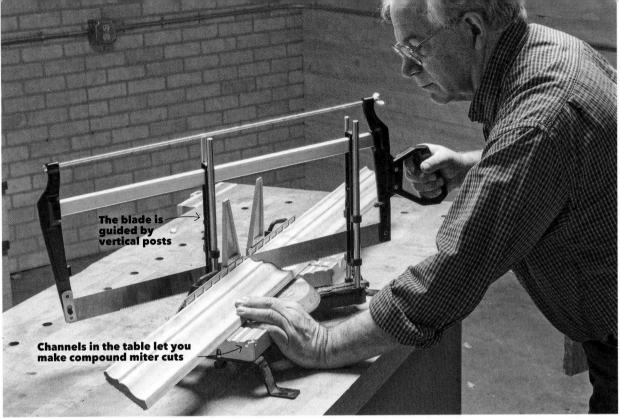

The blade is guided by vertical posts

Channels in the table let you make compound miter cuts

## MAKE SAFE AND ACCURATE CUTS

The Nobex 180 miter saw is a modern version of the old-fashioned bow saw, but it's attached to a precision miter box. It'll cut 2x4s, crown molding or even delicate trim just like a powered miter saw, but it's much safer and doesn't throw dust everywhere. Plus, you certainly don't need earplugs to use it. This saw is a little pricey—about $200 at *leevalley.com*. And Ralph strongly suggests upgrading to the razor-sharp Japanese Ikeda blade ($50).

Angle, or "skew," the stroke

## ANGLE YOUR HAND PLANE

Instead of pushing it straight, Ralph will angle the hand plane just a little. This lowers the angle at which the blade meets the wood, helping it slice through the grain much more easily. Getting into this habit takes a little practice, but the effort is worth it.

family handyman *flashback*

LEVER CAP    IRON
LATERAL ADJUSTING LEVER
CAP
ADJUSTING NUT
FRONT KNOB
HANDLE

### Plain Talk About Wood Planes

#### by PATRICK K. SNOOK

*The wood plane is one of the oldest, most basic tools in your shop, and is today known by a wide variety of models and sizes. Knowing which one to choose for the job—and how to use it—is the key to better work.*

### AS ESSENTIAL AS EVER

**1966** Most DIY tools have improved dramatically over the years. But hand planes, whose origins reach back centuries, have remained very much unchanged. *Family Handyman* may have written more about them back when this photo was taken, but they're still relevant tools today. I believe every DIYer should own at least one. They're extraordinarily satisfying to use, and they just might change the way you think about woodworking projects.

**JAY CORK,** ASSOCIATE EDITOR

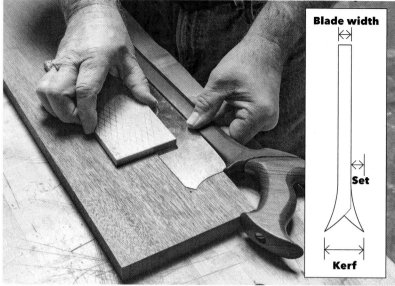

**Always cut downhill**

## SMOOTH CURVES IN SECONDS

Cutting a curve with a band saw or a jigsaw usually leaves a rough edge. Sandpaper is the typical solution but sometimes makes matters worse. Ralph likes to use a spokeshave to get those edges as flat and smooth as glass. The trick is to cut downhill so the blade is always cutting with the grain.

## ALIGN YOUR SAW TEETH

When a saw doesn't want to cut a straight line, the teeth might be to blame. Most saw teeth have a "set," which is how far the teeth stick out on either side of the blade. When the teeth stick out farther on one side than on the other, the blade will drift in that direction. To correct the problem, *very* lightly grind down the protruding teeth with a sharpening stone. One stroke will often be enough.

**Push this way**

**Direction of grain run-out**

## GO WITH THE GRAIN

When you're using hand planes and scrapers, it's important to cut with the grain of the wood. Following the lines of the grain, it's easy to see which direction to push the tool. Tracing the grain with a pencil can help reveal lines in lighter woods. But watch out! Sometimes a board has many directions of grain run-out. When it does, you'll just have to come at it from multiple directions.

## SHARPEN TOOLS THE SIMPLE WAY

The No. 1 reason some people hate hand tools? They've never used one that was properly sharpened. Yes, you can spend a ton on fancy sharpening stones, but you don't need to. With the Veritas Mk.II Honing Guide (about $71 at *leevalley.com*) and wet-or-dry sandpaper from the auto parts store, you can get your tools scary-sharp.

Using spray adhesive, stick wet-or-dry sandpaper to a flat surface like this melamine shelf or a slab of granite. The setup shown goes from 220 to 3,000 grit, plus the yellow honing film ($6 at *woodcraft.com*), but you can get good results using just 220-, 600- and 1,000-grit paper.

**Keep the walls in your entry's "drop zone" looking fresh with this new generation of paints.**

# SCUFF-RESISTANT PAINTS

## BY BILL BERGMANN

Painters and designers agree that flat, matte and eggshell are the best paint sheens for walls. They hide surface imperfections and reflect light evenly. But unlike glossier finishes, they're notorious for showing scuffs and not standing up well to washing.

Newer formulations are changing that. The latest generation of scuff-resistant paints have both the low sheen you want and the scuff resistance and washability of higher-

gloss paint. Behr Ultra Scuff Defense ($33 per gallon) and Sherwin-Williams' Duration ($70) also have a stain-blocking component and antimicrobial mildew resistance, and each is a paint and primer in one. As for washability, Sherwin-Williams offers a guarantee of no color rub-off from washing with mild soap and water.

Minimizing repainting, touch-ups and cleaning is big for pros and homeowners alike. So, if you're

ready to repaint—especially hard-use areas like stairways or mudrooms—consider one of these scuff-resistant paints.

# RETHINK THE WAY YOU BUY PAINT

## Choose your interior paint first, then pick your color

BY JAY CORK

**W**alk into any paint store and you'll immediately see the beautifully lit walls full of color palettes. This an entice you to zero in on a color first. But really, you can get almost any color in almost any paint formulation, so it makes more sense to start by choosing the right paint. For expert advice on selecting paint and primer (and yes, color!), I sat down with Jessica Barr from Behr Paint.

**MEET THE EXPERT**
Jessica Barr is a walking database of paint wisdom. She's also a national trainer and product expert for Behr Paint Company.

## Pay a little more for paint

You can pay $20 or less for a gallon of paint, but Jessica says it's smart to pay at least $50. The reason is simple: More expensive paint contains more expensive ingredients. For the customer, those high-quality ingredients are a good investment that pays off in several ways.

■ **Fewer Coats.** Save time and labor with paint that covers better, often in one coat. With fewer coats, your total paint cost may be less.

■ **Lasting Color.** Higher-quality pigments will resist fading caused by UV exposure.

■ **Greater Durability.** You can repaint less often if you choose a paint that stands up to abuse.

■ **Better Stain Resistance.** Better polymers better resist staining.

## *Priming: When you need to—and when you don't*

Primer has three purposes: to seal a porous surface, to provide a sticky surface for paint adhesion and to block stains. A properly primed surface will make the paint you choose work better and last longer.

### BLOCK WATER STAINS

Water stains on ceilings and walls should always be coated with a stain-blocking primer. Even if you're using a paint-and-primer, water stains will bleed through no matter how many coats you apply.

Water-based primers won't block pet stains or odors. In fact, they can make them worse. Oil-based primers can mask these stains and keep odors sealed.

### HOWEVER, YOU CAN OFTEN SKIP THE PRIMER

It's not just hype. Quality paint-and-primer products are formulated for better adhesion over existing paint and let you skip the primer in most situations. But there are exceptions: The existing paint must be in good condition, and for bare drywall and other porous surfaces, primer is still your best choice. When in doubt, go ahead and prime. As Jessica says, "It's never a crime to prime."

## Establish mood with color

Choosing the right color for a room can sometimes be a challenge. But it's easier if you think about what kind of mood you want to be in when you're in that room. Darker, earthier, subdued tones are calming and restful. Brighter tones tend to lighten the mood and can even make the room seem larger than it is.

## Use a color wheel

A color wheel can help you find attractive color combinations. Complementary colors—those opposite each other on a color wheel—always work well together. Choosing to use the complementary color of your wall paint for style accents and trim will make both colors appear cleaner and brighter than they would paired with noncomplementary colors.

## Buy some samples

Once you've found a color chip you like on a sample card, you might be tempted to call it good and buy all the paint you need. But here's the problem: Those cards are just too small to give you a true read of how that color will look in your room.

Instead, buy a quart of the color you're considering and go paint half a wall. If it's exactly what you were looking for, great! That means you just got a head start on your project. If it's not, try again. That investment in the quart or two of paint just saved you a ton of time, money and effort.

## Look at the color in different lighting

Your perception of color will change depending on the light conditions. After you've applied a sample color, view it in full daylight at different times of the day and at night with just the lamps on. The difference may make you rethink your color choice.

## Don't avoid low-sheen paints

Flat paints have a reputation for staining and marring easily. That's still true for the low-cost ones. But Jessica told us that newer formulations of flat paints are making them more resistant to stains, easier to clean and much more durable.

## Beware of high sheen on bad walls

Choosing a sheen is mostly a matter of personal preference, but there are practical considerations, too. Jessica has a few good rules of thumb: Avoid a glossy sheen on imperfect surfaces; the gloss will highlight imperfections. Lower sheens also have an advantage in high-traffic areas because touch-ups are less visible.

## Choose higher sheens for kitchens and baths

The higher the sheen of the paint, the smoother the finished surface and the easier it is to clean. A higher sheen also makes paint more resistant to moisture damage. That's why Jessica suggests higher sheens in bathrooms and kitchens, where the risk of moisture and stains is higher.

## Buy paint formulated for ceilings

Ceiling paint usually has the lowest sheen available, but it's also typically thicker than wall paint and formulated to be splatter resistant.

**AVOID SHEEN CONFUSION**
The meaning of terms like "flat" and "gloss" is pretty obvious, but in between those extremes, things get confusing. Manufacturers' terms differ a little, but here's a basic range of sheens from dullest to shiniest:

| FLAT | MATTE | EGGSHELL | SATIN | SEMIGLOSS | GLOSS |

**WHAT'S ENAMEL?**
*Enamel* is a confusing term without a clear definition. Generally, it means that a paint is formulated to be smooth and durable, but paints not labeled as enamel can have those same traits. They're sometimes labeled "cabinet and trim" or "door and trim."

## Make leftover paint last

Jessica says that sooner or later, all paints go bad in storage. This is especially true if there's only a quart left in the bottom of a gallon can. But it can be avoided. Leftover paint should be poured into a mason jar and labeled. This will greatly reduce the paint's exposure to oxygen and keep it fresh and ready to use when touch-ups are needed.

## Apply just one coat

Here's what you need to know about "one coat" paints. Behr and other manufacturers offer products that are guaranteed to cover in one coat. Generally, they perform as promised. But be sure to check the label. One-coat coverage is guaranteed only for certain surface conditions and only within a certain color palette. Materials like concrete and unprimed drywall are more porous and are not included in the one-coat guarantee.

## Tips to get the best paint job

■ **AVOID THINNING**
The use of water as a thinning agent is recommended for use only with an airless sprayer and only if absolutely necessary. Paint that is brushed or rolled on should not be thinned. Doing so may weaken the adhesion or cause drips and runs.

■ **AVOID ADDITIVES**
Paint conditioners like Floetrol are used to extend the drying time of a paint, typically to deal with temperamental weather conditions. Be aware that the use of paint additives may void any paint manufacturer warranties. Overuse can also degrade the adhesion, the sheen and even the washability of a paint.

■ **DON'T STORE PAINT IN THE GARAGE**
It's important to protect stored paint from temperature extremes. The paint's composition may degrade if it's been too hot or undergone a freeze/thaw cycle. Jessica says that storing paint at an appropriate, consistent temperature is the only way to make it last.

# Choose the
# BEST ROLLER

**Y**ou can buy a decent paint roller for a couple of bucks, but it's smarter to spend about $6 or $7 and choose one that says "woven" on the label. Here's why:

**1.** Cheap, nonwoven rollers shed tiny fibers and leave ugly lint on the painted surface. A high-quality woven roller will shed few, if any, fibers and will leave the smoothest finish.

> **TIP** *Regardless of the roller, play it safe: Before using, apply tape to the cover and quickly remove tape to pull up any loose fabric fibers.*

**2.** Woven rollers hold and release paint evenly. That means you'll spend less time dipping in the paint tray. A thicker nap holds more paint, but that's a trade-off since a thicker nap also means more stipple/texture.

## BEST ALL-AROUND

A woven 3/8-in. nap is the go-to option for typical drywall applications. It's a good compromise between paint-holding capability and achieving a smooth finish.

**Mark Eichelberger is the director of marketing for Purdy Professional Paint Tools.**

# DIY OR NOT?

## Here's what we did and what we hired out

BY GLENN HANSEN

**T**he projects you do yourself will save you money but cost you time. Think carefully about how much you enjoy the DIY process compared with enjoying your place.

DIY what you can do well, and what you have time to learn. You should not DIY projects requiring expensive equipment you don't own or special skills you don't have, especially where safety is concerned. Here's how we answered the "DIY or not?" question.

## ☑ YES

### FRAMING

Whether you're using hand tools or power tools, screws or nails, framing walls is a DIY project. But we did rely on pros with heavy equipment to position our floor trusses and the large LVL (laminated veneer lumber) spans we used overhead in our *Family Handyman* Getaway.

### WINDOWS

Our Getaway has a lot of windows, some tall and others high. The work required careful planning—from purchase through installation—as well as muscle. We had installed windows before; it's manageable work needing no special tools. And since we took care of the framing, we knew the window openings were right. You can find how-to-install stories at *familyhandyman.com*.

### INSULATION

You can DIY rolls of insulation but not blown-in material. You'll need to understand the different types of insulation, what is going where and why. Also, you'll need to know about R-value and its contributing elements.

### DECK

If you're a regular reader, you know that we know decks. This is a DIY home run for us; it can be for you, too. We dug and poured the deck footings ourselves, built a massive deck and added a cable railing instead of standard posts and balusters.

### BATHROOM

A bathroom project can cover every aspect of DIY, at least indoor DIY. You can do some or all of this yourself. Do you enjoy tile work but not plumbing? You got it. Wanna build a vanity cabinet but not wire in the lighting? No problem. We focused our story (page 38) on the shower with an easy-to-install shower pan and lovely glass doors. You can do it.

### WINDOW TRIM

We finished our windows in a trimless drywall-return style. It's a modern and minimal look that can also save you time and money. You can do it yourself with simple tools.

### KITCHEN ISLAND, CABINETS & COUNTERTOPS

These are great money-saving DIY projects. We used ready-to-assemble (RTA) cabinets and constructed our own kitchen island. We topped it with an affordable and attractive laminate countertop and an undermount sink.

## SHOULD I DIY?

**DO I KNOW HOW TO DIY THIS?** → **YES**

**NO**

**AM I WILLING/ABLE TO LEARN?** → **YES** → **DO I HAVE THE NECESSARY EQUIPMENT/TOOLS?**

**CAN I RENT, BUY OR BORROW THEM?**

**NO** → **YES**

**NO**

**YES**

**DO I HAVE TIME TO DIY THIS?** → **YES** → **CAN I DO IT SAFELY?**

**NO** → **NO**

**NO** → **YES**

**HIRE A PRO**          **DIY IT!**

# [?] YES, IF...

## ROOFING

Most roofing work, especially on a two-story house, is pro-level territory. The roof on our one-story Getaway has a 2/12 pitch, which is relatively flat. If you can do it safely, you can DIY this; we're glad we did. We increased our skills in working with metal roofing, which is perfect material for a wooded retreat. And we saved money.

## SIDING

Installing metal siding requires intermediate to advanced DIY skills, from handling the material to cutting it to its installation and finish. Ask yourself all the DIY questions about costs, tools, time, safety and skills. Lots of ifs here.

## HVAC/WATER HEATER

If you've worked with sheet metal and ducting, you could DIY the HVAC and furnace. But it's a big if. And keep in mind that you'll have to work safely with the energy source, too. Our water heater required basic construction skills to secure it and plumbing know-how to connect it. We let the same pro team do both jobs.

## LIGHTING

We're not talking about wiring your house. This is about lighting design for each room and installing the lights yourself. If you have that skill and want to experiment with lighting, get ready to DIY.

## LANDSCAPING

If you're low on funds at the end of your project, DIY this. Our budget tightened, but we kept three main landscape ideas: DIY, low maintenance and our desire to reuse as many trees and rocks as we could.

# [X] NO

## SITE PREP

You can do some of this work yourself; we did, but not much. We cut down a few trees and then watched Irv, our excavator, pull the stumps and roots. Irv's tool? A 20-ton Caterpillar excavator; a used one costs about $60,000. We installed the silt fence to help with erosion control, but Irv and his Cat dug most of the trench.

## FOUNDATION AND BASEMENT

Digging the foundation and building the basement is not a DIY job, not even close. Digging, shaping, positioning and leveling for the foundation involves a mix of massive power (that Caterpillar) and engineering detail. Hire local pros.

The basement—ours was poured concrete—is another call-a-pro project. A well-built foundation and the basement walls support the entire house and make the rest of the build go smoothly.

## ROLL-UP DOOR

Our goal was to bring the outdoors in with a huge door like the kind you use on your garage (see page 156). We don't recommend the installation of the roll-up door spring as a DIY project. We left much of this work to professionals.

# Great Goofs®

## Laughs and lessons from our readers

## NAILED IT!

For the countertop on a remodeling job, I ordered $800 of prefinished cherry. I was pinning a 3/4-in. cherry strip to the underside of the countertop with 1-1/2-in. brad nails, angling them slightly so they wouldn't break through the piano-grade finish—scary! In the middle of the project, one of my carpenters asked to borrow my gun for a few minutes.

He returned the gun and I finished nailing on the trim. But when I tried to lift the piece up, I realized there was a definite problem—the countertop had been nailed through the drop cloth into the floor. What my knucklehead carpenter failed to tell me was that when he took my gun, he exchanged my nails for ones that were about an inch longer. I had to pay a furniture restorer $200 to fix all the splintered nail holes. I still get mad every time I think about it.

**MARTY HUWALD**

## SAD TO SAY, A TOOL GIVEAWAY

One winter, my wife wanted to borrow my pickup to make the three-hour drive to her mother's house. She loves the four-wheel drive on snowy roads. I told her I wanted to take my power tools and drywall lift out of the truck bed first. But I couldn't get the frozen tailgate open, which also meant I couldn't peel back the tonneau cover to get at the tools. So I left my tools in the truck, and my wife set off on her trip.

Once she was on the road, the sun came out and nudged the temperature above freezing. It turns out I had released the latch but hadn't relatched it. So when everything thawed, the tailgate fell open and my tools slid out the back. My wife never noticed. But somewhere along the 150 miles between our house and my mother-in-law's, there's part of a drywall lift, a screw gun, a reciprocating saw and a few other hand tools.

**BRAD NEJEDLY**

# Index

Visit **familyhandyman.com** *for hundreds of home improvement articles.*

p. 193

p. 199

**p. 240**

**p. 263**

**p.126**

**p. 56**

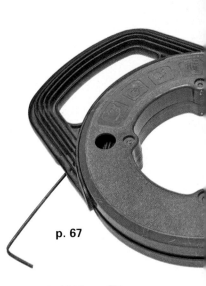

p. 67

p. 242